GOD and the GOALPOSTS

GOD and the GOALPOSTS
the

A Brief History of Sports, Religion, Politics, War, and Art

REVISED EDITION

ORI Z. SOLTES

Bartleby Press
Washington • Baltimore

ISBN 978-0935437-58-4
Library of Congress Control Number: 2020948708

Bartleby Press
P.O. Box 858
Savage, MD 20763
800-953-9929
www.BartlebythePublisher.com

Printed in the United States of America

10 9 8 7 6 5 4 3 2

For Kirk and Mary Beth.
Camp Kundtz is immortal,
like friendship

Contents

Preface to the Revised Edition

*I*magine that there are relatively few authors who don't begin to be haunted by the things that they might have or could have written and did not, once a book is out in the world. Sometimes one who finds himself or herself in that position is lucky, and a cooperative publisher agrees to offer a second edition. So let me begin this preface to the new edition by thanking Jeremy Kay and his intense and committed staff at Bartleby Press for this opportunity—and also to thank Jeremy again for his clear-headed and wide-thinking editorial skills..

There are of course details here and there that one can always consider changing, but in this narrative, that is less the case than two more substantial issues. One is simply that the subject continues to resonate month by month and year by year, so that in the relatively short time since the first edition of this volume there have continued to be interesting cases and discussions that I am happy and eager to add to the refence points in my own discussion.

The second issue—which I had already begun to think about by the time the last few chapters of the first edition were being written—is that there are two important terms and concepts that cannot be excluded from the interweave of "sports, religion, politics, war, and art," especially as one enters into the modern era and moves through the nineteenth and twentieth (to say naught of the twenty-first) centuries: race and gender. While the first edition does bring these categories up, it seems to me that more emphasis is needed—particularly given events in the last decade that have culminated with the MeToo awareness of the past four years and the Black Lives Matter emphases of the past four months.

So it is with these two issues in mind—updating and matrix-expansion—that I have undertaken this revised edition. I have happily benefitted from several years of astute Georgetown students in the *God and the Goalposts* course that I teach—and my friends Kirk and MaryBeth Kundtz, who directly inspired the first edition, remain steadfast, close friends and always remain an inspiration in diverse ways.

Washington, DC
November, 2020

Preface

*J*ust after crossing the goal line, football tucked safely in his arms long enough to score six points for his team, the NFL star—it could be any number of them, from Steve Johnson to Tim Tebow, in any number of times and places—lets the ball go, and then falls on one knee, bows his helmeted head, crosses himself, and utters a short prayer of thanksgiving to God for the divine assistance he credits with helping him earn that touchdown. Elsewhere, Philadelphia Phillies baseball player Ryan Howard, who just doubled, driving in the two runs that put his team ahead of the opposing team—the New York Mets, in the top of the ninth inning, late in the 2008 season—raises his head toward the heavens as he arrives standing up at second base, gestures with both arms toward the sky and two index fingers pointing upward and silently offers a prayerful tip of his spiritual hat to the God whose assistance, he believes, helped him gain that timely, game-changing hit.

In the midst of the dynamic sweep of the Beijing Olympics, a large newspaper article—not relegated to the sports section, but starting on the front page—accompanied by the image of an athlete being baptized by his coach, offers the headline, "Coach, God and Archery Are a Package Deal." The story discusses how the American archery coach has "doubled" as "a sponsor in the baptism of this archer and three others resident" at the U.S. archery training camp, where athletes and their coaches live full-time in the weeks leading up to the Olympic Games—and how the coach finds it "more of a challenge for him when members of the team d[o] not share his beliefs."

These three instances of the penetration of religion into sports particularly caught my eye toward the end of the summer of 2008 because they came across my mental path within barely a week of each other. So closely timed, the two actions and the one article seemed so strongly to suggest a significant surge in that penetration. I say "particularly caught my eye," because any one of these by itself would hardly have merited notice. This is perhaps because those kinds of gestures on the field and maybe even the matter offered for discussion in the archery article have become so common in the last decade and a half. If there is a rise, it began with the mental-spiritual push toward the millennium so evident particularly in the United States, and has persisted as an unrelenting continuation even after the millennial goal-line has long been crossed.

If anything, the sports-religion relationship seems to keep expanding along with the news coverage. A four-year-long tussle regarding whether or not Coach Marcus Borden might bow his head and join his East Brunswick (New Jersey) football team when—presumably unsolicited by him to do so—they drop to one knee and pray as a team before their games or after their night-before-game dinners, reached its conclusion (so far), on Monday, March 2, 2009. On that day the Supreme Court refused to hear the coach's appeal of a school district ban on employees joining student-led prayers that has been in place since 2005.[1]

Conversely, when in a crucial professional football game— aren't they *all* crucial?—aforementioned Buffalo receiver Steve Johnson *dropped* a pass in the end zone that, had he caught it, would have brought the Bills victory over the Pittsburgh Steelers on a November 28, 2010 game, he tweeted in frustration. Not to you and me and his fans, although we were obviously expected to be read-

ing the tweet, but to God. Johnson wrote: "I PRAISE YOU 24/7!!!!!! AND
THIS HOW YOU DO ME!!!!!" In other words, not only is God supposed
by the tweeter to be involved in his sports career, but apparently is
expected to be part of the expanding realm of social media.

The question is: was there truly a notable surge in the connection between religion and sports even as long as fifteen or twenty
years ago? (Borden, for example, had been joining in his players'
prayers perhaps as far back as 1983, when he began coaching at
the school). Could it be parallel to the rise in the overt intersection
of religion and politics, in the United States, anyway—although
one can chart *that* surge from at least as far back as 1976 and Jimmy
Carter's successful presidential bid—as the old century and millennium rushed toward the new?[2] Or was it just that one's consciousness—or at least *my* consciousness—of the relationship between religion and sports was raised through a combination of
other factors, including everything from politics to media focus?
If there has been a surge, is it unique in history, or merely part of
an ongoing ebb and flow?

My awareness raised and my interest piqued, and thinking
back over history and across human geography, I began to wonder
about how long the process of religion and sports interface has been
operative. The more I researched this, the more I became aware of a
long and interesting connection. I also began to think about how diversely angled that relationship has been. What follows is a concise
yet somewhat detailed and wide-ranging historical and geographical account of that complicated saga—and its implications for the
ongoing game (this is the *ultimate* sport!) of trying to understand
what we humans are as a species. Sports is just one among many
areas where religion and its concerns have played a role, and the
interpenetration of sports and religion is as old and far-flung as
sports and as continuous and manifold as religion.

The five contemporary references with which I began this
preface offer three different modes of sport-religion connection:
three pertaining to players and their very public expression of per-

sonal faith; two with two different ways in which a coach expresses his faith in the presence of and in conjunction with his team. But all of these are somewhat different from how we might consider the depiction in classical literature of the Greek and Roman gods on the playing field. In turn, the discussion of biblical athletes offers its own distinct religious connotation: the stories of Samson or David are religious in part simply because they *are* biblical.

Still different is the question of how Islam views sports, or of how successful Jews have been in the Olympics. And how do both Jews and Muslims manage to maintain aspects of their forms of faith when the athletic competitions in which they are involved don't leave much space for that? What is the attitude of Judaism or Islam or Christianity to sports and physical accomplishment in general? The discussion of Native American sports as offering origins associated with religion and religious ritual is still another angle of focus.

Moreover, in all of these parts of the overall narrative, the matter of sports and religion keeps intersecting—from different angles—the issues of sports and warfare, sports and politics, religion and politics, religion and warfare. And all of these kaleidoscopic combinations intertwine varied aspects of the arts, particularly the literary and visual arts, which offer some of the most important evidence for these various intersections across history. So, one engages this subject as a rich interweave of topics that fall somewhere between God and the goal posts, shifting continuously and, hopefully, engaging the reader.[3]

I wish to acknowledge my good friend, Dr. Kirk Kundtz, who inspired me to pursue this subject in the course of a long conversation about a number of issues and ideas—while his sons watched my younger sons, and I could really relax without worrying about what they were up to next—in which the subject of sports and its conjunction with religion came up. And then the idea of war and politics and art as they intersect sports and religion. He suggested that I write a book. Well I have, Kirk. Any other ideas?

I also thank Stephen Stears for reviewing my discussion of Maya sports. He might still disagree with some of my comments, but if there are errors in my thinking they are mine alone.

Finally, I'm grateful for the extraordinary editing skill of my publisher, Jeremy Kay. From syntax and style to matters of substance Jeremy has been singularly responsible for improving the narrative that I have tried to lay out. He has been a knowledgeable friend and not just an editor or a publisher, playing a triple role in making this book possible.

Notes

1 This was reported in a small article in the *New York Times* sports section of Tuesday, March 3, 2009.

2 One could of course argue that religion entered American politics when John F. Kennedy, a Catholic, ran for president in 1960 (and won) or when Al Smith (also a Catholic) ran for that office and lost in 1928, since in both cases the candidates' religion was a significant issue in those races. Or one could argue that religion was already an issue in American politics when Thomas Jefferson, a Deist, ran for president in 1802 and was accused by his opponent of being a non-Christian and anti-Christian—in which case my point is even more valid: that what seems to be a relatively recent phenomenon, perhaps due to exponentially increased media coverage availability, is not recent at all. But see Randall Balmer's *God in the White House: A History* regarding the revitalization of Evangelical Christians as a political force during Carter's first run for the presidency (in his favor) and during his run for reelection (against him) and ever since.

3 A brief note on my transliterations of Greek and Latin (Roman) names: I admit to being a bit inconsistent. Where the Latinized form of a Greek name is very common and, I suppose, likely to be familiar to my readers (e.g., Achilles), I use it in that form; where the name is sufficiently unfamiliar I tend to be more purist and use the English "version" that most effectively conveys the sounds of the Greek name and the letters that make it up (e.g., Hippolytos, rather than Hippolytus). Sometimes, context will effect an apparent inconsistency: thus for instance, if the context is the Greeks, I write "Herakles," but if it is a Roman context, I write "Hercules."

INTRODUCTION
Religion, Art, Politics, War, and Sports

R eligion is as old as human thought, or at least as ancient as
can be *traced* by means of texts and, before texts, by objects
that evidence human creativity, ingenuity, and ideas. The
province and purpose of religion, across time and space, has been
to wrestle with divinity, whether it's *really* out there or is only an
idea that is somehow embedded within the human psyche.

Even before recorded history, humans have believed in some
transcendent "Other"—whether conceived in singular or dual or
endlessly multifarious terms—that has created us and therefore has
the power to destroy us. As that Other is assumed to have the capacity, on the grandest of scales, to create or destroy, help or harm,
further or hinder, bless or curse, so the goal of religion has always
been to push divinity toward blessing us with its positive side rather than cursing us with its negative side. The objective is survival—
whether in the here and now, or, according to some religious traditions, in the hereafter.[1]

The Other that religion has always addressed is a realm fraught
with paradox and contradiction: it does not abide by the same tem-
poral or spatial or situational constraints that limit our own understanding. Its divine aspect has been variously understood across
time and space by diverse human cultures and civilizations. For

the Mesopotamians, Egyptians, and the Greeks and Romans in antiquity, it was defined as a multiplicity of gods and goddess that
were perceived to possess human or animal or combined human
and animal forms, and to be actively engaged in human affairs. Judaism and Islam have defined it as a single God without gender
and rigorously devoid of any sort of physical form.

Christianity shares the monotheistic view of Judaism and Islam, but its concept offers a paradoxical God that is simultaneously
singular and threefold—a triune God—one aspect of which is not
only physical but a specific human being, Jesus of Nazareth. God
is all-powerful and all-good, and yet there is evil in the world, and
part of its agency is a being, very active in Christian conception,
somewhat less so in Muslim conception and still less in Jewish
conception, that first appears in the Book of Job as The Opposer/
Questioner: the *Satan*. These paradoxes—of a being both fully human and fully divine; or all-powerful and all-good yet opposed by
a being that is evil incarnate—has various echoes in other traditions. Zoroastrianism offers an all-powerful being called "the un-
created Creator," Ahura Mazda, who nonetheless allows evil into
the world in the form of an opposing, yet inferior entity, Ahriman.
Ahura Mazda calls upon humans to make a choice: they can either
support him or Ahriman. In the confrontation between these two
forces that occurs at the end of time as we know it, not only will
Ahriman and his acolytes be defeated, they will be drawn over to
the side of Ahura Mazda.[2]

Hinduism offers an endless array of divine beings, like the ancient Greeks and others, but some Hindus give precedence to Shiva,
and others to Vishnu, while others to Brahman or to Devi. Followers of Vishnu regard Krishna as the eighth among the nine avatars
(or manifestations) of Vishnu in our world. On the other hand, followers of Krishna regard him as the consummate godhead. Each
group understands that its devotees arrive directly to God; they
believe that members of other groups also arrive to God but less
directly. The text of the *Baghavad Gita* is the absolute revealed (*shru-*

ti—literally, "heard" in Sanskrit) text to devotees of Krishna. It is, however, embedded in the epic poem, *Mahabharata*, and therefore is simply part of a manmade (*smrti*—literally, "remembered") text to devotees of Shiva, Brahman, Vishnu or Devi. Ultimately, all such individuated god-names and god-concepts are understood by all to be subsumed into one god of pure Being.

And so on. These often very complicated ideas—straightforward and clear to the devotee, confusing to the outsider—include the shared belief that divinity has enormously greater powers than humans and that, unlike us, divinities are immortal. Yet we humans conceive of ourselves as different from all the other mortal species contrived by divinity in that we wonder and worry about what immortality might be—and whether there are ways in which we can achieve it. For example, are such "mortal beings" as Achilles and Moses immortal (or at least possessed of what the Greeks called *kleos aphthiton*: "undying glory") if we are still talking and writing about their life and death thousands of years later?

Among the differences between the god-concepts that the Greeks possessed and that of the Abrahamic religions is that, in spite of their great power, the Greek gods do not possess *limitless* power, whereas the God of Judaism, Christianity, and Islam is limitless in capability. Greek gods cannot, for example, ultimately determine the moment when mortals—even their favorites—will die: this is determined by fate. Thus, as explored in the *Iliad* XVI: 431-90, even the greatest of the gods, Zeus, cannot save the life of Sarpedon, his son by a mortal woman, who had come to fight as an ally of the Trojans in the great war against the Achaeans. Zeus *could* save Sarpedon, as Hera points out to him, because he is the greatest of the gods, but he *cannot*, because to do so would be to abrogate fate and with it, potentially and unpredictably, the very order (*kosmos*) of the universe. But the Abrahamic God combines the qualities of both distant and disconnected fate and the engaged and involved gods of the Greeks and Romans.

This all means that the question of how we are to understand the concept of human will within this context is also complicated. That question preoccupies human literature across a panoply of religious traditions. More fundamentally, the range of religion customs asserts of its God/gods that It/they communicate to us something about what It is/they are, and accordingly, about what we are supposed to be, through diverse revelations. Thus, the foundation upon which nearly every religious culture is built—the primary instrument through which it tries to understand, to explore, and explain the consummate Other, Divinity—is the revealed text.

Revelation is itself problematic and complicated, however. It is communicated through prophets who, assuming that they get it right, are not around forever. In some cases, they are believed to have written it down themselves; more often, the actual written presentations of the revelation appear after their deaths. Did Moses write all or only part of the Torah? Why are there four canonical versions of the Gospels, and how long after the death of Jesus were they written down? The words of God through Muhammad that comprise the Qur'an were written down 32 or 33 years after the Prophet's death—and so on.

So, every religion tradition sooner or later moves from revealed texts to texts of interpretation. The ideas that evolve into these various traditions are shaped by both kinds of literature. In fact, if we consider traditions such as Judaism and Christianity, we realize that even the notion of what constitutes their respective revealed texts—their "Bibles"—is a result of interpretation. For reasons beyond this discussion, Jews believe that by 444 BCE, Israelite-Judaean contact with God that is mediated by prophetic voices like those of Jeremiah and Isaiah ended; but for Christians, such voices continue for hundreds of years beyond that point. So books like Maccabees or the Gospel According to Mark cannot be part of the Bible for Jews—at least because they pertain to events well after 444BCE—but certainly can for Christians.

In fact, this issue will apply not only to what will separate Judaism from Christianity nearly two millennia ago, but to the separations within Christianity that distinguish Catholicism and Orthodox Christianity from Protestantism (the latter not embracing the intertestamental texts, including Maccabees, that both Orthodox and Catholic Christians do) and that distinguish all of these from Ethiopian Christianity, for example, which embraces the Book of Enoch as canonical where none of the other Christian denominations do.

The extensive interpretive process is, in the end, necessary because the primary conduit to God, revealed words, is often not so easily intelligible. If the Sixth Commandment in Exodus 20 and Deuteronomy 5 demands of us that we do not murder, what exactly separates *murder* from the generic concept of *killing*? Where do acts of killing in self-defense or the killing of animals for food or the swatting of mosquitoes on my arm fit into what and how God commands us to be?

Perhaps, in part, because of the complications of revelation and interpretation, the instruments and associations of religion have always been multiple, and not limited to words. By the time spoken language was in operation, humans were devising prayers, hymns, and myths to address and describe divinity, alone and in its interaction with humans. But even thousands of years before such words were available—or at least before we have any survivable, written record of them—our species was already devising visual aids to evoke religious meaning, whether in the decoration of the most basic of tombs or in the creation of both primitive and symbolically sophisticated art.

We can see this, for example, in one of the earliest works of sculpture available to us through paleontology and archaeology: a small figure—less than five inches high—commonly referred to as the "Venus of Willendorf" [fig 1].[3] The last word of its "name" refers to the site in modern Lower Austria where it was found a century ago. The first word refers to the obviousness with which the small figurine represents the abstract concept of "fertility" (and as such, offers an association with the Roman goddess Venus as a goddess of fertility). She is a bulbous undulation of breasts, belly, enlarged umbilicus, with a carefully articulated pubic area. Her arms are mere stripes extended across, and thereby further empha-sizing, her breasts, and her faceless head is adorned with a series of rows of "hair" that look like the rows of a well-plowed field. Moreover, there are seven of these concentric circle rows, an impor-tant number when it comes to interactions between humans and divinity.[4] We might infer that the number of concentric rows is not accidental, but is instead an early expression of that human-divine engagement.

This anonymous figure is indeed fraught with symbolic ele-ments that visually concretize the abstract notion of fertility, an es-sential element of human survival. If we humans are not fertile, our race or, in a more limited context, our community, dies out. If our fields are not productive or our cattle and flocks are not procreative, we are also in danger of perishing.

Such a work of sculpture articulates the concern for survival in which the Other is deemed to play the ultimate role, and it provides an array of indirect visual "reminders" to that Other about what we require in order to survive: fertility. This is even more the case when we realize that the figurine ends up buried, away from our

Figure 1. Venus of Willendorf

reality—away from our everyday, above-earth realm. For that sub-terrestrial, other reality is the analogue of *all* aspects of Otherness, including, most importantly, divinity.

So while prayer and poetry have been servants of religion, visual arts have been as well, from sculpture to painting to architecture—as have other art forms like music and dance. Words, as a human instrument, are most useful in addressing, describing, and seeking to understand the human realm and the world in which humans habitually function. Divinity operates in an altogether different realm, and is perhaps not ideally addressed by words. The movement of dance and the wordless sound of music may serve just as well as or even better than *words* in engaging divinity, just as visual art may.

If the realm of religion is that of human-divine interaction, the realm of human-human interaction is the dominion of politics—in the Aristotelian sense of that word. Aristotle once observed that humans are different from other animals in that we habitually dwell in a *polis*—a city-state, a community.[5] The word "politics" is derived from the Greek adjective *politike*, which refers to that *polis*-centered human inclination. But despite differences in focus, religion and politics have been interwoven for as long as we can trace and understand human behavior.

From the pharaoh who rules as a god to the 18th-century king who claims to rule by Divine Right, the engagement of politics and religion and their respective concerns have also been intertwined with visual (and other forms of) art. To offer just one example of this: there is a splendid diorite statue of the early Egyptian pharaoh, Khafra (otherwise known as Khefren), which shows him seated, ramrod straight, absolutely frontal and symmetrical with respect to his perfect torso and face, and with his stylized hair and beard in absolutely precise order; there's not a hint of the physiological irregularities that ordinary mortals exhibit, from forehead to chin. It's a pose that suggests not only perfection, but an *eternal* and *unchanging* perfection [fig 2]. Moreover, perched behind his neck,

Figure 2. Pharaoh Khafra (detail)

with its outspread wings covering part of his shoulders is a bird—a
hawk falcon, symbol of the god Horus.[6]

The image contains a distinct message: it asserts the connection between the pharaoh and the god. In reminding viewers
that their ruler bears the imprimatur of the god (and at certain
phases of Egyptian history will be understood to be the very embodiment, the *incarnation*, of the god), it implicitly warns them
against any actions that would contradict his will, since to defy
him would be to fall out of favor with the gods whose favor he
preeminently possesses and/or directly represents. The ability
of the pharaoh to rule without resistance from his constituents
is enormously enhanced by the reference to religious sensibility
expressed in visual terms.

Among the traditional proofs of the divinity or at least divine
imprimatur of a pharaoh or shah or king or other political leader
is his skill in war and in the hunt. We can see the articulation of
this principle in many images across history. For instance, on the
wooden coffin cover of the boy-pharaoh, Tutankhamun—he came
to the throne at age nine and was dead by age nineteen—there is
a splendid image of his resounding success against the enemies
of Egypt [fig 3].[7] We see the pharaoh towering over everyone else
(this visual expansion of the key figure in a composition is called
"significance perspective") as, behind and beside him, Egyptian
soldiers are organized in nice, neat, ordered lines, while before

him the enemy, in the process of being scattered, is represented in chaotic, helter-skelter disarray.

The idea that his success is divinely sanctioned and assisted is reinforced by the hieroglyphic labeling and description that are part of the image. This representation is what we have to draw upon for an account of his battle accomplishments—except that to-day, at least, we might well doubt the veracity of the account. A pharaoh who was already dead before he ended his teenage years is not likely to have spent much time excelling in battle, or even participating in it. But the point is that the presentation of his larger than life, divinely approved—religion-based—success in war was offered in order to affirm his political stature.

Analogous to this are images such as one in carved relief depicting the Assyrian monarch, Assurnassirpal II, engaged in a heroic and successful battle with powerful lions (whose blood he would drink after his annual victory, to assert and reassert his lion-like power); or the seventh-century, silver-gilt bowl relief of the Sassanian monarch, Khosrau I, boldly astride a galloping, surging steed amidst a field of wild animals, scattering before the might of his weaponry [fig 4].[8] In each case, such triumphant depictions of

Figure 3. Tutankhamun defeats the Syrians (detail)

Figure 4. Sassanian Shah Khosrau

staged events illustrate the king's calm yet fierce ability to protect the community from ferocious beasts. That the monarch is imbued with a divine connection is also clear—in the case of Khosrau, his soaring helmet is festooned with wings and the symbols of the sun and the moon to reinforce the impression of his divine connection as surely as the representation of the hawk falcon of Horus underscores that idea for the pharaoh.

In these works and countless others, the assertion of the ruler's political predominance is conceptually enhanced by references to his divine connection. That connection is articulated very distinctly to a constituency that, though largely illiterate, would clearly understand the meaning of visual images. Art offered an obvious and unequivocal statement of the ruler's position.

The notion that a ruler must hunt is tied not only to the belief that he can protect the community from all kinds of wild, uncontrollable forces—thus vicious animals are analogues of the wild, uncontrollable, and sometimes negatively disposed gods—but also to the perception that he must stay in battle-shape even when there are no battles, in order to be prepared should a *human* enemy appear on the scene. The royal hunt, as a form of battle, also evolves as something desirable in its own right because it is challenging and thus entertaining: it became a form of *sport*—a pastime that others would eventually engage in, and not just the ruler. Furthermore, many of the skills needed for both battle and the hunt—strength, speed, agility, hand-eye coordination with respect to handling one's weapons or horse or chariot—could be, and came to be, appreciated in their own right.

Let us consider one more of these, for which we have two forms of testimony: a work of art and a later Greek mytho-religious tradition. First is a wall painting from the palace complex of Knossos on the northern coast of the island of Crete.[9] I am thinking of the "bull-jumping" image popularly called "The Toreador Fresco" [fig 5]. It depicts three slender figures jumping over a powerful, virile bull. The first is jumping up, the second has grabbed the bull's horns, and the third has landed on the other side. It has been argued that here and elsewhere in the wall-paintings at Knossos, the darker figures are male and the lighter-skinned ones are female.

One might connect this image to the later Greek story of Theseus, Minos, the fearsome minotaur, and the Cretan labyrinth. According to the tale, in brief: the Cretans under Minos had hegemony (during the Middle Bronze Age, ca 2000-1600 BCE) over the Aegean and demanded the periodic delivery of a certain number of daugh-

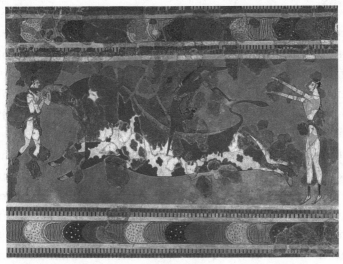

Figure 5. Minoan so-called "Toreador Fresco"

ters and sons belonging to the mainland kingdoms—Athens, Tiryns, Mycenae, and the like—who were fed into an elaborate maze at the center of which dwelt a fierce creature, half-man and half-bull, who would devour them all. The creature was the offspring of Pasiphae, wife of Minos, and a beautiful white bull that Minos had failed to offer in sacrifice to Poseidon; as punishment for this offense, Poseidon caused the king's wife to become infatuated with the bull. When the daughter of Minos, Ariadne, falls in love with Theseus, son of Aegeus, the king of Athens, she helps him survive the perils of the maze by giving him both a sword and a ball of string: with the first he slays the minotaur and with the second he is able to find his way back out—and then sets sail for Athens with Ariadne.[10]

If we connect such stories to the architecture and décor of Knossos, we might conclude that the large, open space at Knossos was used for a dangerous puberty ritual: bull-jumping such as is depicted in that wall painting. The long history of the bull across the Eastern Mediterranean and Middle Eastern cultures as a symbol of fertility and the prevalence of bull-horns as decorative elements at Knossos would permit this suggestion—for which I have no hard proof but am theorizing based on an extensive connecting of dots. The inherent peril of the ritual would explain the need to call upon the noble youths of other kingdoms to serve as surrogates for Minoan noble youth. One might suppose that far more of these surrogates perished than survived, but by contact with them— particularly as they lay bleeding, on the border between life and death—Minoan youth would cross the threshold into adulthood, safe and sound.

There is perhaps more. The Knossos complex was a complicated maze; one can imagine mainland young boys and girls quite terrified as, after their sea-journey, they were led through the maze to the central chamber where, perhaps, Minos himself sat, enthroned, wearing the mask of a bull's head, with fearsome horns, on his own head. He would be remembered many generations later as the Minos-*tauros*: the "Minos-Bull." The other very common decorative symbol found throughout Knossos, its edges upturned like the horns of a bull, is the double ax—*labyros*, in Greek. The *-inthos* suffix means "place of" (as, for example, in *Corinthos*)—so Knossos was "the place of the double-ax," which became synonymous with a maze: a labyrinth.

One further thought and unprovable theory: the ritual of bull-games—whether in its most intense form, bull-jumping, or in more moderate forms—may have been transmitted over time all the way across the Mediterranean, perhaps by those great transmitters of culture and commerce in the Late Bronze Age (ca 1600-1200 BCE), the Phoenicians (as the Greeks would later call them). If this was the case, the religious underpinnings of the Spanish bullfight, with its emphasis on important ritual aspects, may have originated in the bull-games of the Minoans as a particularized mode of the intersection among sports, religion, politics, and art.

War is missing from this picture, thanks to the Minoan thalassocracy. But the destruction of the minotaur by Theseus may be seen as a symbol of the eventual victory of the mainlanders over the Cretans, and the new dominance by the so-called Mykenaeans, who in the last generation of their own greatness would attack and destroy Troy. Their kingdoms would also find themselves subject to invasion and destruction around that time—for who was protecting them while the Trojan War dragged on for a decade? Many never returned from battle, while others, like Odysseus, spent another decade getting home. Eventually, on the ashes of these Late Bronze Age cultures, Greece would arise with the artistic, literary, and other achievements by which we identify its glorious culture.

Eventually, the birth of the Olympics in Greece, in 776 BCE, would represent (among other things) the transference of diverse skills from the battlefield or the hunting ground to the playing field. He who is strongest and swiftest, most agile and most competitive—who can run fastest or jump highest or farthest, or wrestle or box best, or drive his chariot most swiftly around a particular stretch of territory, or throw his spear or shoot his arrow farthest

and/or with greatest accuracy—would not only be valued as a soldier but admired simply as an athlete.

It should not be surprising, then, that a preeminent athlete
would come to be regarded by his fan-constituents as imbued with
divinely imposed powers analogous to those attributed to a ruler,
a priest, a prophet, or a contemporary or far-off hero. The accomplishments of an outstanding athlete came to be regarded as most
similar to those of a celebrated hero or ruler. Like them, he might be
expected to be preeminent on the battlefield where victory would
be associated with a combination of innate skills (presumed to be
gifts from gods or simply his fate) and divine imprimatur. As such,
sports emerge as intertwined with religion, just as politics does. Like
religion and politics, aspects of sports find themselves woven into
the fabric of visual art as it moves across history and geography.

For instance, in the evolution of the full-sized standing male
figure within the Greek world from the seventh through the fifth
centuries BCE, we may recognize a shifting sense of the way in
which the relationship among human and divine physical form,
athletic success, and divine imprimatur were visually articulated.
It has been commonly argued that the early figure of the *kouros*—
the idealized young man in his physical prime—is a stylized representation of the god Apollo *as* an idealized youth [fig 6].[11] We can
easily recognize the influence of Egyptian art in the depiction of the
god: every element is frontal, torso and face both offer perfect sym-
metry, hair is stylized as a perfectly ordered covering for the head,
and though the figure steps slightly and slowly forward, it is still
very much held within the eternalizing, ordered, regularized stone.

By the fifth century, however, the Greeks had become more
interested in the dynamic relationship between stasis and action, in
the problem of how to capture a moment of stillness between an-
tiphonal actions—a moment of shifting weight. Their artists wanted to convey the idea in stone or metal of a living, breathing being that is never inert, even when not moving.[12] This idea replaced
the Egyptian and Archaic Greek tradition of depicting a perfect

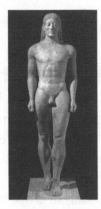

Figure 6. Anavysos Kouros

being in an eternal and unchanging stance. But even the image of Polykleitos' *Doryphoros*, the "Spear-bearer" (which we can only see in Roman copies, for the Greek original no longer exists), while it does not adhere to the stiff, eternalizing *kouros* mode—becoming something more dynamic and thus non-eternal in its shifting of weight and its counterbalances between straight and bent limbs, and tensed and relaxed limbs—still connects its idealized subject to divinity [fig 7].[13]

For this perfectly formed athlete in his prime—some in antiquity asserted that it was a portrait of Achilles, legendary Achaean hero of the Trojan war—can easily be understood to be god-graced

Figure 7. Polyklitos: Doryphoros

in his perfection, in the ease with which he strides casually forward, gracefully adjusting his weight and his limbs as he moves through the world. If the *kouros* represented a god who was like a man, the *Doryphoros* represented a man—specifically, an athlete—who was like a god. One can easily enough imagine that the adulation lavished on such an athlete vied with the reverential admiration usually reserved for a sovereign or, albeit somewhat differently, for a prophet or priest—and that it could even compete with the expressions of worship directed to the gods themselves.

One can also understand how stories might grow and be passed from generation to generation regarding the dangers of being so godlike: that the gods themselves might so *love* such a figure that he would be taken to be among them before he had passed his prime—the message being that those whom the gods love for their perfection and their prowess die young. Or conversely, stories with the opposite moral lesson might be transmitted. The gods might become *jealous* of such godlike figures and out of hatred effect their destruction before a "normative" time of death—since such figures are, after all, *not* gods when all is said and done, and are thus subject to death.

This sense, expressed both verbally and visually—of heroes and great warrior-athletes as godlike or uniquely blessed by the gods but distinctly human, with a mortality that might be specifically effected by the gods for better or worse reasons—has a long history in what becomes the Western tradition.

In arguably the earliest Western epic, the Mesopotamian Gilgamesh confronts us as a splendidly godlike hero—so much so that the goddess Ishtar seeks his hand in marriage. But he himself recognizes that, as a human, he will ultimately encounter disaster with such a match: when he ages, she will inevitably abandon him as she has abandoned or unhappily transformed previous mortal lovers and husbands—as Gilgamesh himself points out in rejecting her proposal.

His refusal begets Ishtar's wrath and so—to make a long story short—she creates a wild beast-man, Enkidu, to take Gilgamesh down. But the plan backfires. In the aftermath of a titanic wrestling-match—think early TV wrestling matches in the late 1950s and early 1960s with Bruno Sammartino taking on Bobo Brazil; or later 1980s version of "Wrestlemania" epics pitting Hulk Hogan against Andre the Giant—they instead become bosom-buddies, engaging together in an array of great adventures.

In early Mesopotamian art, we see a figure that is arguably Gilgamesh on the soundboard of a harp dating from ca 2700 BCE and found in the tomb of one Queen Pu'abi. The hero is depicted as the "master of beasts," occupying the center of the space in a frontal position and holding in both his outstretched hands a wild animal (each of which possesses a human face) [fig 8].[14] The image not only symbolizes his complete control of the wild animals but defines him as a bringer of order to his part of the world.

He is shown to be accomplishing, on a limited level, what the gods have done on the most sweeping level: imposing order over chaos. In the first place, his ability to do so, of course, is a function of the divine connection that he possesses as a hero-athlete in the first place. But we are reminded that those ties are double-edged, inherently neutral but potentially both positive and negative, like the gods themselves, who can—and do—both create and destroy on the greatest or smallest of scales.

Gilgamesh has been able to foil the vengeful plans that the goddess Ishtar has for him, but she is not to be so easily defeated: she sends a fatal illness to Enkidu, which brings Gilgamesh to great grief. Undeterred, the hero undertakes the greatest of his adventures—alone this time—to *Dilmun*, the Garden of Paradise and Immortality, and there finds the immortal Xiusudra/Utnapishtim,[15] the Mesopotamian Noah, who, together with his wife, has been placed there by the gods in the aftermath of the great flood. Xiusudra/Utnapishtim directs Gilgamesh to a body of water that contains the flower of immortality in its depths.

The hero dives deep and plucks it, hoping to journey back to the ailing Enkidu to feed it to him. But exhausted from his ef-

Figure 8. Harp of Queen Pu'abi:
Gilgamesh as Master of Beasts (detail)

forts, Gilgamesh falls asleep, at which point a serpent slithers by and devours the flower. The serpent promptly sloughs off its old skin and is reborn, rejuvenated: immortal. Gilgamesh must return home to the city of Uruk empty-handed but for the knowledge he has gained: that all humans, however heroic, are ultimately mortal; that even he, Gilgamesh, is fated to die eventually, for eternal life is reserved only for the gods.

The stories in the Greek tradition express this sense of heroic mortality that also contains a certain tragic element embedded within it—perhaps because the culture's heroes are deemed either to have an immortal parent or to be the subject of such powerful divine imprimatur that death seems a particularly unhappy paradox in their cases.[16] For example, the mortal hero Herakles, son of a human mother but fathered by Zeus himself, is on the one hand the preeminent hero-athlete in the Greek tradition, renowned, among other things, for the twelve labors—the tasks by which he helps to bring civilization to the chaotic world of the early Hellenes.

Ironically, his labors actually derive from a punishment that results from the goddess Hera's animosity against him.[17] Her un-abated hostility[18] will in the end lead to Herakles's demise, albe-it one in which he will rise up from his funeral pyre to reside on Olympus among the gods and goddesses. The process of his down-fall is also intimately tied to King Eurystheos, the task-master in Herakles' Twelve Labors, who revels in having such a hero-athlete in his service.

Achilles is understood by the Greek tradition to have been born into a later period. In his case, his father is human and his mother a sea-goddess. Hero-Athlete Achilles far excels any of his contemporaries in strength, speed, and agility, whether competing on the field of play or participating in the Trojan War as a soldier. However, he is doomed, as he and everyone else knows, to perish on the battlefield, trading the immortality of "undying glory" for an early mortality.

Part of what drives both Achilles's success and the poignan-cy of his story is the conflict with Agamemnon, chief among the Achaean chieftains, which sets the *Iliad* in motion. The fact of Achil-les's prowess butts up against the fact of Agamemnon's position of political authority, just as it does against the intervention of the gods — in particular, the goddess Athena, who, at Hera's insistence, descends swiftly from Olympus to stay Achilles's hand when he is about to draw his sword against Agamemnon in the midst of their argument. As is so often the case, politics and religion are linked to the fate of the hero-athlete.

A more benign message is found in the story of Kleobis and Biton. Their mother, Kydippe, is a priestess of the goddess, Hera, and is due to attend a festival honoring the goddess nearly nine miles from her home. The oxen that are expected to draw her in a cart to the temple fail to arrive on schedule, so her two athletic sons harness themselves to the vehicle instead. The citizens of the town of Argos are amazed and moved, and Kydippe is so pleased that she prays to Hera to honor her marvelous sons with the greatest

gift that a goddess can bestow on a mortal. Hera responds and Kydippe's sons, exhausted from their efforts, fall asleep on the temple
steps and never wake up again; the goddess's gift is for them to die
in the prime of their youth. They will never grow old and thus, they
will always be remembered as athletic, pious, and youthful.

In each of these three anecdotes, either the athletic prowess or the
reward for the pious exercise of athletic skill is connected to divinity.
Not only are sports and religion entangled in some fundamental way,
they are also bound up with the issue of politics across the history and
geography of human experience. Like the diverse forms of religion
and the assorted exhibition of sporting events, the ways in which the
two are joined and intertwined with politics and war, is intricate.

Notes

1. For a fuller discussion of how this Other is[was?] conceptualized and
originally articulated — "divinity" or "the sacred" prove to be too limited as both
concepts and terms — see the introduction to Soltes, *Our Sacred Signs: How Judaism,
Christianity and Islam Draw from the Same Sources* (New York: Westview Press, 2005)
or, somewhat more detailed, to Soltes: *Jewish, Christian and Muslim Mysticism:
Searching for Oneness* (Lanham, MD: Rowman and Littlefield, 2008).

2. This, as opposed to being destroyed, as happens to the Satan and his
followers in Christianity, at the end of the Book of Revelation.

3. This work, most recently dated to between 24,000 and 22,000 BCE, is found
in the Natural History Museum in Vienna.

4. See below, chapter one, 29 and fn 7.

5. See *Politics* I:1253a.

6. This particular version of this image of the Fourth Dynasty ruler (ca 1520
BCE) was found in Giza and now resides in the Cairo Museum.

7 This work, dating from ca 1350 BCE, is found in the Cairo Museum.

8. This work, dating from the seventh century CE, is found in the *Cabinet des
Medailles*, Paris. There are, however, dozens of variations on this theme involving
a variety of different shahs from the fourth through the seventh centuries.

9. A fascinating book, *The Secret of Crete*, (Souvenir Press, 1975), by the
German geologist Hans Georg Wunderlich, argues very convincingly that the
palace complex was not used by the living; rather, it was an elaborately conceived

city of the dead: a necropolis. For the purposes of our discussion, this does not matter, since the ritual that I am discussing could pertain to crossing the boundary between life and death, rather than between childhood and adulthood: all boundaries are analogues of each other in religious sensibility. (See the two books referenced above in fn 1.)

10. There are many other threads in this tapestry of a story—from Daedalos and Ikaros to Ariadne and Dionysos to why the Aegean Sea is so-named—but they would carry us too far afield.

11. Many examples of these will be found in the National Museum in Athens and in other museums around the world, from the Metropolitan Museum of Art in New York City to the Louvre in Paris and the British Museum in London.

12. Most obviously, a stationary human or animal is breathing, its lungs expanding and contracting; its heart is beating and blood is coursing through its arteries, veins, and capillaries; the instruments of sense are in action; and so on.

13. This work is found in the National Archaeological Museum in Naples. The original by Polykleitos would have dated from about 440 BCE; this Roman copy probably dates from the first century CE.

14. This work is found in the University of Pennsylvania Art Museum.

15. The Sumerian version of the epic gives the Sumerian "Xiusudra" as the name; the Akkadian version gives the Akkadian "Utnapishtim" as the name.

16. And indeed, as larger, more successful, more powerful, more speedy, more beautiful, more clever versions of the rest of us who yearn for immortality, they offer to us an ironic and tragic quality because they have so much further to fall in arriving down to the pit of mortality.

17. In a nutshell, Herakles is driven mad by Hera and, mistaking his wife, Megara, and their children for his enemies, he slays them all. Apollodoros asserts that it is in part to atone for this that he enters the service of king Eurystheos for 12 years, and it is Eurystheos who appoints the twelve tasks that Herakles is obliged to perform. The Euripidean version has the hero go mad and slay his wife and children *after* he completes those tasks. Not incidental to our topic, the Greek word that is typically rendered in English as "labors" is *athloi*, (singular: *athlos*), a term that usually refers to an event or contest, in which an athlete (which word comes, of course, from the same Greek root) engages, and that yields some prize, known as an *athlon*.

18. Her hostility is a function of her anger against Zeus, who betrays her by seducing the mortal woman, Alkmene, who becomes Herakles's mother. There is nothing that Hera can do to punish Zeus for this or any of his sexual betrayals, so instead her anger generally redirects itself to the mortal women whom her husband seduces or to the offspring resulting from these dalliances.

CHAPTER ONE
Sports, Athletic Heroes, and God in the Shaping of Israelite History

*J*ews, Christians, and Muslims traditionally understand their respective faiths to offer the same starting point: Abraham. In turn, Abraham fathered two sons, Isaac and Ishmael. For Jews and Christians, Isaac is the "primary" son, who carried forth the covenantal relationship with God. For Muslims, the "primary" son is Ishmael, whose line not only furthers the covenantal relationship between God and Abraham but also continues in a direct path all the way to the prophet Muhammad—the Seal of the Prophets—some 25 centuries later.

The Isaacian line, as Jews and Christians understand it, is explored in the Book of Genesis; the Ishmaelian line is explored in the Qur'an and subsequent Muslim religious literature.[1] Isaac is represented as having two sons, the twins Esau and Jacob—born in that order, with Jacob said to have been hanging on to his brother's heel as the two exited the womb. Whereas Esau moves swiftly off the stage of religious history, Jacob moves to the center. Indeed, having enraged Esau due to the matter of the first-born birthright blessing from their father (Gen. 27), Jacob flees for his life,[2] not returning home for 20 years. From here, the text focuses on *his* story in the course of that exile, not the story of his parents and brother.

n his parents' house to that of his mother's
 of the children of the east" (Gen. 29:1). There,
ds have placed a heavy stone over the watering
jacob sees Rachel, he is so smitten with her that he is
essly roll the massive stone away from the well mouth
nel's flocks can be watered. This act of physical prowess,
ggests a change from the rather unimposing man he has
red to be while still in his parents' house, is the prelude to
b's success on both the spiritual and the material levels. Over
.1e course of 20 years, he becomes wealthy both in terms of his
family, with his dozen sons and with regard to his many flocks of
cattle, sheep and goats; he conceives a desire to go home—in part,
no doubt, to show off his success.

On the eve before making the final approach to the encamp-
ment of his elderly parents, Isaac and Rebecca, and the brother
whose current feelings for him he cannot yet discern after their
20-year estrangement, Jacob separates himself from his wives, children, servants, and herds. Hoping that, should Esau still harbor
murderous intentions, they will be directed to him alone, he spends
the night across the river from everyone and everything of emotional or material consequence to him. In the long, restless night
that follows he is said to wrestle with God—the God of his father
Isaac and grandfather Abraham with whom he had made his own
covenantal pact in the aftermath of his first night away from home
20 years earlier, and who now appears to him, somehow, in the
form of a man.

Or perhaps it is an angel with whom he strives all night long,
or perhaps it is his dreams, and beneath them, his conscience, with
which he wrestles. All we know is that in this account, we witness
the first substantial wrestling match in Abrahamic history and
myth—Abrahamic history and religion. The end point of this titanic match is multiply repercussive. Firstly, Jacob has the upper hand
as dawn is about to arrive, and his opponent, whatever it is, cannot
remain into the sunrise. But Jacob will only let him go in exchange

for a blessing, which becomes a transformation of his name—from Jacob to Israel. The first name is based on the Hebrew root word for "heel," and is based on the aforementioned idea that, when Jacob exited his mother's womb he was clinging to the heel of his twin. The new name means "one who has striven with God." From a heel-grabber to one who has and continues to have such an intimate relationship with God represents quite a change!

The second repercussion is that Jacob's dozen sons and their families—and subsequently, their many descendants—will be known as Children of Israel: Israelites. So, those descendants will regard themselves as inheritors of a blood line of covenantal connection to God, for better and for worse.

The third repercussion is that, when some 18 centuries later, there is a spiritual schism among the descendants of Jacob-Israel, two contending forms of faith will result as a consequence: Judaism and Christianity. One of the eventual defining distinctions between Judaism and Christianity—each initially seeing itself as the legitimate heir to the generations of evolving covenantal relationship with the God of Israel—was a gastronomic one. Certain kinds of food were perceived by Jews then (as they are for Jewish traditionalists now) as objectionable to God.

The prohibited foods include(d) the loin, because Jacob-Israel is said in the text of Genesis 32:26 to have strained his thigh—his loin—toward the end of that extraordinary night-long wrestling match. So, traditional Jews across the planet do not eat sirloin steak, for example—unless the sciatic nerve is removed—but that's complicated. Moreover, as far afield as Kai Feng Fu, along the Yellow River in China, where Jews settled by the 11th century at the height of the success of the Northern Sung dynasty, they came most commonly to be referred to as *T'iao chin-chiao*: "the sect that plucks out the sinews." This referred to the custom of eliminating the loin artery as an alternative to not consuming the meat at all.

In short, then, this first major patriarchal sporting event was and remains intimately interwoven with religion in yielding not only one of the primary terms of religious, God-directed identity for both Jews and Christians[3] but in establishing for traditional Jews a practical observance in its most everyday aspect. The primary purpose of the dietary restrictions was to connect Jewish thinking even in the most daily, unsacred of contexts to God and God's expectations for a covenantal people.

Jacob and his sons, daughter and daughters-in-law end up dwelling in Egypt. Jacob's favorite son, Joseph, had been sold by his jealous brothers to traders who in turn sold him into bondage in Egypt, but he emerges through a series of trials, tribulations and challenges, as Prime Minister of Egypt, organizing its food supplies, among other things. His family arrives during a time of famine in Canaan, he is ultimately reconciled with his brothers and are invited to settle there—but thereafter their descendants are enslaved for many generations, according to the tradition begun in Exodus 1. There will eventually emerge a man of the Israelite people, of the tribe of Levi—Moses—who will lead the Israelites out of Egypt and back to Canaan. But Moses arrives at the point of being designated by God as the one to accomplish that task through a concatenation of actions that, while motivated by his compassion for others, are centered in the here and now on acts of physical prowess.

Thus, "when Moses was grown up, ...he went out unto his brethren, and looked on their burdens; and he saw an Egyptian smiting a Hebrew, one of his brethren. And he looked this way and that way, and when he saw that there was no man, he smote the Egyptian, and hid him in the sand" (Ex 2:11-12). One might presume that his speed and strength, combined with his Achilles-like passion, got the better of him, if the beating he administered left the Egyptian taskmaster dead. But in any case, as the word gets out that he has killed a man, he has to flee Egypt, for "when the pharaoh heard this thing, he sought to slay Moses. But Moses fled... and stayed in the land of Midian; and he sat down by a well" (v 15). There, the seven daughters of Jethro, the priest of Midian, come to water their flocks, but the Midianite shepherds drive them away.

Somewhat reminiscent of his ancestor, Jacob, Moses stands up to the shepherds and single-handedly drives *them* off so that the shepherdesses might get water for their father's flocks.

The consequence of this act of Rambo-like athleticism on the part of the prophet-hero is threefold. In the first place, Moses is hosted by Jethro and rewarded by being given Tzipporah, Jethro's daughter, as a wife. In the second place, Moses becomes a shepherd, keeping the flocks of his father-in-law—while meanwhile, back in Egypt, one pharaoh dies and another ascends the throne, and the suffering of the Israelites becomes worse. And so, in the third place, while tending his father-in-law's flocks out "in the farthest extremity of the wilderness (Ex 3:1)" Moses encounters the Burning Bush, and with it, the new direction for his life: to go back to Egypt, convince the new, young pharaoh to permit the Israelites to leave Egypt, convince the Israelites that they will be better off leaving Egypt than staying there, and eventually to lead them back to the edge of the Promised Land.

Moses was chosen, to be sure, because he had demonstrated his skill at tending and leading a far-flung flock and showed compassion for the downtrodden. But one might also note the small but important connection between these moments that illustrated his athletic prowess in his youth (against the Egyptian taskmaster and against the Midianite shepherds) and the turns of events that led to his preeminence as a man of God in his maturity. He became the prophet of prophets in the Jewish tradition; the ultimate prophet within the Christian tradition until the arrival into history of Jesus as more than a prophet; and the consummate prophet in Islam until the arrival into history of Muhammad as the final prophet.

The Hebrew Bible does not leave the issue of athletic prowess behind as an aspect of demonstrating the connection between God and God's chosen mouthpieces to humankind as its narrative carries beyond Moses and the Torah into the books of historiography and prophecy that follow. Moses is succeeded as the leader of the Israelites by Joshua, who is followed by a series known as the Judges—this being a term that refers to individuals who both adjudicated disputes, dealing with issues within the Israelite community, and also defended it against dangerous outsiders, most often, however, in a localized and temporary manner.[4]

Most noteworthy among these dangerous non-Israelites were the Philistines, who may have arrived onto the southwest coast of Canaan, aka, Syro-Palestine—to the specific area now known as Gaza—not long after the Israelites themselves had returned from Egypt.[5]

Among the Judges most renowned for dealing with the Philistines was Samson—from his tearing a lion apart with his bare hands, posing a riddle about this to the Philistines and being betrayed by his wife, an unnamed woman from Timnah (14:5-17); to his slaying a thousand Philistines with the jawbone of an ass (Judges 15:15-17); to his passionate relationship with Delilah, who betrays him to the Philistines with regard to his strength (16:4-24); to his suicide-destruction of countless numbers of them and their house of feasting (16:25-30).

The most noteworthy feature of Samson (besides his interest in women who betray him), is his prodigious strength and capacity as a warrior against both men and wild animals. That athleticism is directly connected to his relationship with God. From our first meeting with him, one verse after his birth and growing up are reported, we are told that "the spirit of the Lord began to move him" (Judges 13:25). The above-mentioned riddle, by which the Philistine woman betrays his trust, and which pertains, in part, to his having slain a lion with his bare hands on his way into Timnah, presents a remarkable deed that is made possible because "the spirit of the Lord came mightily upon him" (14:6). When he is bound with new ropes and given over to the Philistines after he commits some mischief in their fields—for which they slay his Timnite wife and father-in-law and Samson, in turn, slays many of them (16:3-8)—once more "the spirit of the Lord came mightily upon him"

(16:14) and he bursts the ropes and slays a thousand of them with that aforementioned jawbone.

Most famously, of course, Samson's personal covenantal relationship with God as a Nazirite entails the obligation for him not to cut his hair. Thus, when he reveals this secret to Delilah: that "if I be shaven, then my strength will go from me, and I shall become weak, and be like any other man" (16:17), he sets himself up for disaster. It is the revelation of this secret that finally affords Delilah the opportunity to betray her mighty, foolish lover to the Philistines—she "had the seven locks of his head shaven off" (16:19) so that he loses his strength, and is captured and blinded by his enemies, for "the Lord was departed from him" (16:20).

One notes the pattern of his hair, specifically described as seven locks—evoking that important number, symbol of perfection and completion, with its long history of significance in the matter of human-divine relations both within and outside the Bible.[6] From the completion of the divinely enacted creation cycle so that God "rested" (in Hebrew: *shavvat*) on the seventh day (Gen. 2:2-3) to the commandment from Sinai delivered by Moses (Exodus 20:8-11) to emulate the divine act of resting by enacted a seventh-day Sabbath (in Hebrew: *Shabbat*), "sevenness" is intimately interwoven with the Israelite understanding of its own covenantal peoplehood. The importance of the number is reinforced again and again. One example is the divine prescription of a priestly-enacted sin offering that Moses details, beginning with the slaying of a bullock and the sprinkling of its blood by the priest "seven times before the Lord, in front of the veil of the sanctuary" (Lev. 4:6). Thus, the "sevenness" of Samson's hair underscores its purpose as an instrument of priest-like, prophet-like connection to God.

One also notes that Samson's hair immediately begins to grow back while he is grinding grain in the prison-house—a development that the Philistines fail to observe. When he is brought out of prison to be mocked by his feasting enemies some time later (with his hair well on its way toward proper Nazirite splendor), he can legitimately call upon the Lord to "strengthen me, I pray thee, only this once, O God" (16:28), and is strengthened sufficiently to crumble the house of feasting as if he himself is an earthquake.

There is, then, a direct correlation between Samson's athletic skills and a specific form of God's favor that rests upon him. Generations later, after a succession of Judges but a lack of unity, the Israelites beg Samuel, the primary spiritual leader of the scattered community, to impose a conventional leader, a king, upon them (I Samuel 8). Samuel's first divinely guided choice is Saul, who very much looks the part of a king: "from his shoulders and upward he was higher than any of the people" (9:2). So Samuel anoints Saul as king (10:1).[8] But the lesson being shaped in these chapters of the biblical text is that the unique God of Israel, Who has marked out a covenant with a unique people, does not operate according to human conventions. Saul has some successes and, in the end, greater failures—inevitably tied to his failures of faith, in himself as king and in the God Who directed Its priest-prophet, Samuel, to select him as king. Those failures culminate with the loss of Saul's own life and that of his son, Jonathan, on Mount Gilboa in an epic final battle against the Philistines.

By then, God has long designated a successor from another house, the youngest son in the family of Jesse—like the patriarchs and like Moses, a keeper of flocks—concerning whom God warns Samuel: "look not on his countenance, nor on the height of his stature... for it is not as man sees, for man looks on the outward appearance, but the Lord looks on the heart" (16:7). That youngest son is David, whom Samuel anoints "in the midst of his brethren; and the spirit of the Lord came mightily upon David from that day forward" (16:13). It is the might of that spirit that enables David to play the harp so sweetly—sweetly enough to drive the madness out of King Saul's mind, for stretches of time, at least—and to go forth boldly against the gigantic Philistine warrior, Goliath, with the confidence that "the Lord that delivered me out of the paw of the lion and out of the paw of the bear [while he was tending his father's flocks], ...will deliver me out of the hand of this Philistine" (17:37).

As the child faces the giant, he reiterates his conviction that Goliath might "come to me with a sword, and with a spear, and with a javelin; [but] I come to you in the name of the Lord of hosts, the God of the armies of Israel, whom you have taunted. This day will the Lord deliver you into my hand" (17:45-6). So, David himself recognizes how fully his athletic success—his skill with the sling shot, the trueness of his aim, and the power of his throw to bring a giant down—will be a divinely ordained success. The future king of Israel, the ultimate king of Israel, begins his ascent to that political post—the Israelites were already chanting that "Saul has slain his thousands, [but] David his ten thousands" (18:7)—with a dramatic athletic victory in which he is partnered by God, so that spirit and not body is the determining factor.

From an Abrahamic perspective the direct relationship between athletic skill and support by the One God is no surprise. Even to the end of the Hebrew Bible, in the Book of Esther, where, given the opportunity merely to arm and defend themselves against their enemies and would-be destroyers, the Judaeans prevail mightily, and "no man could withstand them; for the fear of them was fallen upon all the peoples" (Esther 9:2), one might infer a divine hand intervening on behalf of the covenantal people.[9] But how does one understand the framing of that sort of relationship in the context of *many* gods and their varied adherents, cults—and disagreements? To that question we turn in the chapter that follows.

Notes

1. I am following the Isaacian line in this chapter and will pick up the Ishmaelian line in chapters 7 and 8.

2. The older son—in his case, Esau—would have been entitled to the primary paternal blessing that includes a unique relationship with God (for reasons beyond this discussion), but Jacob, with the help of the twins' mother, Rebecca, ends up maneuvering to get the blessing. This is far from the only time in the Hebrew Bible when the younger son gains primacy. Shortly after Jacob's flight, Esau takes to wife Mahalat, the daughter of Ishmael, thus incidentally forging a further ethnic

relationship between the two generations of brothers upon whom Genesis does not primarily focus in its narrative (Gen. 28:9).

3. One must keep in mind, of course, that, in the sibling rivalry between Judaism and Christianity regarding which group possesses the real inside track with regard to God's affections, it became common fairly early in Christian expression—and remains so in many Christian circles to this day—to refer to Christians in a supercessionist mode as *verus Israel*: "[the] true Israel," as distinguished from the now-passed-over, no *longer true* Israel of the Jews. Needless to say, Jews see themselves as the continuous true Israel.

4. By this last clause I mean that, whereas the entire tribal confederation of Israel is led by Moses and Joshua, after Joshua's death the confederation yields increasingly to fragmentation, each tribe having received a given portion of territory by Joshua before his death (See Joshua 13-19), and typically a Judge seemed connected to one or more but not all of the tribes.

5. The Philistines (in Hebrew: *P'leeshteem*) may well have been the so-called "Sea Peoples" to whom the Egyptians refer, arriving onto their coast in the very Late Bronze Age. The Egyptians claim to have successfully pushed them further along—presumably toward Gaza. The references to a newly arrived group called variously *Peleshet, Peletu,* and *Keretu* (linguistically cognate terms, the explanation of which carries beyond this narrative) by the Tyrians, northern neighbors of the Israelites through the period of the Judges and Kings David and Solomon; and the bemoaning by the Tyrians that they interfered with the Tyrian (aka Phoenician) trade routes; and the warm alliance between Tyre and Israel that resulted after David defeated the Philistines (whatever the specific historical reality of the Goliath figure may have been)—all of this suggests that the Philistines and the *Peleshet-Peletu-Keretu* and the Sea Peoples might be one and the same, and that they arrived from Crete (hence: *Keretu*) with the Late Bonze Age collapse of the Minoan/Mykenaean culture on that island.

6. Where hair in particular is concerned, we have hypothesized regarding the importance of this number all the way back to the Venus of Willendorf. (See above, Introduction, 5-7).

7. In turn, the Hebrew Biblical narrative and the Israelite mytho-historical tradition draw from an idea that can ultimately be traced back at least to the Sumerians and the Egyptians—although the configuration of the Venus of Willendorf's hair, to repeat, suggests that the idea is much older. The point of "sevenness" as offering a connection to divinity is in any case not difficult to deduce. As one continuously observes the heavens, one may note that, "within" the sphere sprinkled with countless stars that move in a constant spatial relationship to each other—later known as the "sphere of fixed stars"—and different from the occasional celestial visitors one might also see, such as one-time momentary

visitors (meteors) and periodic longer-lasting visitors (comets), there are seven heavenly beings that move with a reliable and recognizable periodicity across the heavens by night or day. These are the sun, the moon and the five planets that we see with the naked eye. All seven of these were referred to in antiquity as "wanderers" across the heavens—the word "planet" derives from the Greek verb *planeo*, meaning "to wander"—and were assumed to be associated with divinities governing various aspects of what transpires on heaven and earth. Not surprisingly, then, each of the seven wanderers was called by the name of a god, as most still are today, albeit by way of Latin (Roman) names: Mercury, Venus, Mars, Jupiter, Saturn, together with Luna/Diana (the Moon) and Sol/Apollo (the Sun). These seven names are the culmination, then, of a long tradition of sevenness as a sacred number, associated with completion and perfection. This is reflected in the Babylonian calendar, which is structured according to a seven-day week; it is echoed in the Egyptian notion of the soul as having seven aspects, each with its own name and "job" to do, and flourishes in the biblical tradition that includes Samson and his hair.

8. The Hebrew term translated by the verbal past participle "anointed" is *mashiah*. The Greek translation of *mashiah* is *christos*. These two terms are eventually anglicized as "messiah" and "christ" respectively.

9. In fact—this is why I use the phrase "to the end of the Hebrew Bible"— this was the last book to be accepted into the canon due to a rabbinic reluctance to embrace it as divinely inspired, in large part because the name of God never explicitly appears in it. One must, in this case, infer God's role!

Chapter Two
From War Games to Funerary Games in Epic Greek Poetry: Warrior-Athletes in the *Iliad*

*T*he epic poem, the *Iliad*, is a magnificent tale that encompasses a central piece of the world of Greek gods and humans. It delineates a mere ten or eleven days in the last year of a ten-year-long war which is, in turn, part of a longer narrative that begins with the falling in love of a goddess—the sea-nymph, Thetis—and a human, Peleus. The intermingling of these two inherently opposite elements—one that is immortal, eternal, unchanging, and the other that is mortal, transient, mutable— must yield simultaneously glorious and disastrous consequences as the Greek tradition understands reality. Thus, on the one hand, at the wedding feast on Olympus between Thetis and Peleus, the gods fail to invite the goddess Eris—the personification of strife— to the celebration of love. But has there ever been a wedding ceremony at which strife of one sort or another fails to put in an appearance?

In brief: Eris arrives uninvited and unexpectedly, and drops a piece of fruit onto the banquet table, attached to which is a small note, "to the fairest"—and three goddesses reach for it, each asserting that she is the proper recipient of the fruit. Not daring—for all his great power—to judge among Hera, Athena, and Aphrodite,

Zeus, king of gods, decides that the question as to who of the three is the fairest ought to be answered by the shepherd-prince Alexandros (Paris is what the Romans later call him). It happens that Alexandros/Paris is out on Mount Ida tending the royal flocks of Troy; he's being kept as far away from the city as possible, because prior to his birth it had been prophesied that he would bring ruin upon the city.

Disaster arrives in the form of the three goddesses—and to make a long story short, Alexandros chooses Aphrodite as the "fairest" one, thus turning her into an ally and making Hera and Athena enemies, not only of the prince but of his home city. He chooses Aphrodite because the bribe she offers appeals to him most fully: that she will help him win the most beautiful woman in the world. Unfortunately, that woman, Helen, is married to Menelaus of Sparta, which means that she must be spirited away by Alexandros (with help, of course, from Aphrodite).

Many Achaeans had sought Helen's hand in marriage. At that time, Helen's father was concerned that the large group of her suitors would end up killing each other (and perhaps him) over his preternaturally beautiful daughter, so (with the help of Odysseus) he managed to get them all to agree to two things: that they would respect her choice of a husband; and that, should anyone ever interfere and manage to spirit her away from her husband, they would all organize themselves together to get her back for him.[1]

Sometime after Helen chooses Menelaus, Alexandros comes along and spirits her away. If this sequence of events is, thanks to Eris, one culmination of the love and marriage of Peleus and Thetis, the other, of course, is that they produce a son: Achilles, who, with divine blood flowing through his veins, grows up to be big and strong, fast and agile—the consummate athlete-warrior. Chronological order involving the gods is often different from the human-understood norm. As a youth of marriageable age, Achilles was among the suitors for Helen's hand, but Helen's abduction should have happened not long after the wedding of Peleus and Thetis on Olympus, and thus before or, at most, shortly after Achilles was born.

No matter. The important thing is that, after the disappearance of his wife, Menelaus goes knocking on the door of his big brother Agamemnon, king of Mykenae, and reminds him of the suitors' pledge. Agamemnon sends out the word and the Achaean warriors gather their ships to sail to Troy to bring Helen back. Only Achilles does not join the expedition, for he knows the prophecy regarding *him*: that if he ventures to Troy he will acquit himself spectacularly as a warrior, gaining undying glory (*kleos aphthiton*), but he will be killed before the city is taken and Helen is rescued. He chooses to avoid that fate and to settle instead for a long, obscure life on his father's farm.

Put another way: Achilles is on the one hand uniquely blessed by the divine side of his parentage. He possesses divine favor or grace—the Greek word is *kharis*, from which we derive the English word "charismatic." So we might say of Achilles that he is charismatic in a manner analogous to the way in which the Egyptian pharaoh Khafra (see introduction, p. 7-8) is charismatic and depicted to indicate this in a diorite statue. Khafra possesses the *kharis* (favor) of the god Horus, who rests in a literal, concretized visual manner on his shoulders in the form of a hawk falcon with outspread wings.

But on the other hand, the blessing of *kharis* that makes Achilles such a splendid soldier-athlete also curses him, endowing him with the foreknowledge of the consequences of specific choices with which he will be confronted. If he chooses unwisely, Achilles knows his life may be very brief. He is all-too-aware that if he pledges to fight at Troy, it will be the beginning of a slippery slope of choices that will *guarantee* that his life will be brief, even if the same choices also lead him, by seeming paradox, to a form of immortality: the undying glory of his name.

In the end, arguments by Odysseus convince Achilles that he really has *no* choice. So, the war is on, Achilles becomes a rather unwilling part of it—and the *Iliad* brings us right into the middle of things. The poem offers us an argument between Achilles and Agamemnon, at the outset, wherein the great warrior, insulted by the main Achaean commander (for reasons beyond this discussion), chooses to sit out the battle for a time. He asks his divine mother to call upon Zeus to cause the Trojans to prevail during this period. Achilles wants the Achaeans to recognize how important he is to them and how lost they are without him. This is a football team stripped of its star quarterback, a basketball team bereft of its most prolific scorer, a baseball team whose best hitter is sitting in the dug-out while they are being drubbed by the opposing team— because the player has been publicly insulted by the coach.

So we recognize that divine intervention can be part not only of the success of a star warrior-athlete like Achilles but also of the *prevention* of success—in this case, the Achaeans suffer at the hands of the opposition (the Trojans). The second thing that we note is that, as the Achilles-less battle proceeds, a number of other soldiers get involved, starring in mini-Achilles-like roles, serving, as it were, as appetizers to the main course to which readers are treated only when Achilles finally returns to the fray.

In all of these engagements, we further observe that gods and goddesses are constantly getting directly involved. Thus, in *Iliad*, V. 711ff, when Hera notices that the battle is not going well for the Achaeans—as Hektor and the Trojans are being assisted by Ares— she calls upon Athena, "daughter of Zeus of the aegis... all about which Terror hangs like a garland... and took up a spear... [while] Hera laid the lash swiftly on the horses [of her chariot]..." and with Zeus's permission, they enter the battle.

On the one hand, these engagements reflect indirect divine intervention in the matter of the heroes' lineages and therefore their inherent potential for success and failure against each other. Thus, for instance, In V.628ff, one of the Achaean warriors, Tlepolemos, comes up against Sarpedon, a Lykian chieftain fighting on the side of the Trojans. We are immediately informed that the father of

Tlepolemos is none other than Herakles—making the former a heroic warrior whose father was a semi-divine hero. But Sarpedon
is the son of Zeus, making him a semi-divine hero whose father is
a god. It is inevitable, therefore, that in their confrontation Sarpedon will triumph, striking Tlepolemos "in the middle of the throat"
whereas Sarpedon receives a painful wound in the left thigh, but
Zeus makes certain that it is not fatal.

On the other hand, key heroes battle as much with gods and
goddesses as with men, even prevailing over the divinities under
certain conditions. Hera shouts, "likening herself to high-hearted,
bronze-voiced Stentor" (V.785), in order to encourage the Achaeans, while Athena heads directly for the Achaean hero Diomedes,
and strengthens his tired and wounded limbs with her inspiring
words and takes over as his charioteer, steering and protecting him
as he fights directly with Ares. The goddess guides Diomedes's
spear, and "driving it deep in the fair flesh [of Ares] wrenched the
spear out again. Then Ares the brazen bellowed with a sound as
great as nine thousand men make, or ten thousand..."

We might also note that, however badly wounded gods or
goddesses may be, their recoveries come speedily: the injured Ares
flies up "with the clouds into the wide heaven," shows Zeus his
wound and complains about Athena's egging on of Diomedes—
and is then swiftly healed by Paieon (V.900), just as Aphrodite, who
had also been wounded by Diomedes, is quickly restored to health.
If the fundamental distinction between gods and even the greatest
of heroes is the mortality of the latter, we also observe how divine
intervention can help heal the wounds of the gods and, up to a
point, rescue warriors from the battle who might otherwise perish.
Thus, not only is the semi-divine hero Sarpedon merely wounded
(thanks to Zeus's watchful care) in the same series of exchanges in
which the hero Diomedes stands out, but more central figures are
rescued by their divine patrons, *provided that fate allows it*.[2]

Alexandros is bested on the battlefield by Menelaus to within
an inch of his life—who "balanced the spear far-shadowed, and

threw it and struck the shield of Priam's son on its perfect circle. All the way through the glittering shield went the heavy spearhead and smashed its way through the intricately worked corselet... Drawing his sword with the silver nails, the son of Atreus heaving backward struck at the horn of his [Alexandros's] helmet... and flashing forward laid hold of the horse-haired helmet and spun him about, and dragged him away toward the strong-greaved Achaians" (III.355-70). But his life is saved, as Aphrodite intervenes and breaks the chin strap by which the Trojan prince is being dragged and strangled, and "caught up Paris easily, since she was divine, and wrapped him in a thick mist" (III.380-1) and wafted him away from danger, plunking him down safely into his own "perfumed bedchamber"—hastening to bring Helen in to tend him, up in the lofty citadel of Troy. For had Alexandros perished at this point, Helen would presumably have been returned to Menelaus, the war would have been over, the fate of others (such as Sarpedon and Hektor and Achilles) would have been altered—and the great poem would have ended after only three books.

So, too, the Trojan hero Aeneas, wounded, is rescued from the mortal danger most particularly posed by an inspired Diomedes. Aeneas is aided first by Aphrodite—she moves, obviously, with divine speed, between saving Alexandros and saving Aeneas! However, she, too, is wounded by Diomedes. Next, (as the goddess flies up to Olympus to be healed), "though he [Diomedes] saw how Apollo himself held his hands over him [Aeneas],... three times, furious to cut him [Aeneas] down he [Diomedes] drove forward, and three times Apollo battered aside the bright shield... Apollo caught Aeneas now away from the onslaught, and set him down in the sacred keep of Pergamos where was built his [Apollo's] own temple..." (V.432-46). This outcome ultimately reflects the fact that Aeneas is fated to survive the debacle that will ultimately engulf Troy and to lead a band of Trojan survivors away.[3]

But all of these salvational moments are part of a series of build-ups to the ultimate battle within the *Iliad*—that between Achilles and Hektor—and its aftermath. Each of these duels highlights the *aristeia*—"nobility [in battle skill]"—of great heroes, like Diomedes and Menelaus, who are still less than these two preeminent figures. The gods are involved and intertwined with events, and intervene with the failures and successes of all of these figures as the reader moves breathlessly forward toward the culminating confrontation.

There are three primary stages that lead to it. The first stage arrives in Book IX, when Agamemnon sends an embassy of three prominent Achaeans—Odysseus, of course, but also Ajax, arguably the most important Achaean fighter aside from Achilles, and the elderly and verbose Phoinix—to offer to Achilles an array of gifts to induce him to return to the fight. Among these, Agamemnon includes one of his own daughters to wed[4] along with the beautiful maiden Briseis,[5] whom he swears never to have touched while she was in his possession. Achilles is not able to step out of his anger at Agamemnon and come to terms with his leader. One might say that his anger is ultimately directed toward the gods and the fates: in his speech to the three ambassadors, he underscores the fact that he will in any case perish if he returns to battle so that all these gifts will be meaningless to him. Neither the chance to display his prowess nor concern for his fellow Achaeans can dissuade him from continuing his vacation from the battle.

The second stage occurs when Achilles's dearest of companions, Patroklos, who is concerned for the welfare of the Achaeans, tries to convince his friend to return to the fray; when Patroklos is unable to do so, he pleads with Achilles to lend him his armor. This drama brief between best friends is preceded by a number of instances of *aristeia* by other warriors. For example, in Book XV, we see Hektor warring with Ajax, as if he is a surrogate for Achilles, who will eventually battle Hektor. The endpoint of this long build-up of heroic, athletic battling is that Patroklos weeps to Achilles as he recounts what is happening to their friends, and he begs him to at least "'give me your armor to wear on my shoulders into the fighting; so perhaps the Trojans might think I am you, and give

way from their attack...' ...So he spoke supplicating in his great innocence; this was his own death and evil destruction that he was
entreating." (XVI: 40-1, 46-7).

For as much as Patroklos has been "soft" compared with
Achilles' "hardness" up to this point, he is somehow transformed
by the armor he then dons. And as much as Achilles begs him not
to go too far—not only lest he get hurt, but lest his success cause
the Achaeans to forget about their need for Achilles, and his own
honor be diminished—Patroklos cannot resist. Suddenly, it seems
to him that he can *be* Achilles—until in the confrontation with Hektor he meets more than his own match. The illusion dissipates, but
it comes too late, and Patroklos is killed. Indeed, after Patroklos
and the Achaeans had killed Sarpedon, son of Zeus, he had raced
forward three times among the Trojans and mowed them down,
"as for the fourth time he swept in... there, Patroklos, the end of
your life was shown forth, since Phoibos [Apollo] came against
you there in the strong encounter..." (XVI: 786-8). Hektor strips the
gleaming armor—Achilles's armor—from Patroklos's body and
dons it himself.

This will lead to the third stage of bringing Achilles back into
battle, a stage that, in fact, has two components. The first is the intense grief that envelops the hero when word reaches him that Patroklos has been killed. This is followed by the transformation of
his anger: no longer directed at Agamemnon, but against Hektor—
and no doubt against himself, since his refusal to reenter the battle
when Agamemnon begged him to do so is ultimately the reason
Patroklos fought in his place—and died.

As in the question of who is responsible for the war itself—
gods or men or the fates that reside beyond both—so one might
ask of Patroklos's demise: is it due to fate? Or the gods (specifically
Apollo)? Or Hektor, who dealt the death blow? Or Achilles, whose
pride is too unrelenting to give in to the three ambassadors and
to Patroklos, who entreated him to go back into battle in his own
armor? Or Patroklos himself, whose overweening pride (*hubris*)

causes him to go too far in armor that is not his, forgetting who he is and, more to the point, who and what he is not?

In any case, Patroklos, the Enkidu to Achilles's Gilgamesh is dead—and there is nothing that Achilles can do to act on his redirected anger, since he no longer possesses his armor. Once again, though, he can and does turn to his divine mother for help, and she, in turn, entreats the smith-god, Hephaistos, to manufacture new armor for her son (XVIII: 70-616). The famous shield that is elaborately described by the poet is extensively carved by the god to offer a kind of microcosm of the world, with the river of Ocean (*Okeanos*) depicted flowing around the edge of the human realm and scenes in the center that suggest the human tension between love and strife of which the entire Trojan War cycle is a larger microcosm

The consequence of the new armor is that in the poem's final confrontation between Hektor and Achilles, Hektor's destiny is sealed. That is, aside from the matter of fate and whatever assumptions one might make regarding the comparative skills of the two warriors, it is virtually inevitable that a warrior wearing divinely wrought armor will triumph over one wearing man-made armor. One might note that, among the many ironies that anchor this text, is the image that this confrontation yields to us—of two Achilles, one in the old armor and one in the new, battling each other. That image brings with it an underscoring of how Achilles's furor is in the process of transformation, since the anger at Hektor, which must also be anger against himself, is reflected in the fact that every time he faces his enemy, and casts his spear or a huge boulder at him, he is seeing himself before his eyes.

The final battle between the two champions appears to offer a final vision of the intertwining of human and divine elements in the matter of physical conflict—the semi-divine hero-athlete against the outstanding but merely human hero-athlete, the one in divinely wrought armor versus the other in man-made armor. But sandwiched between the making of Achilles's armor and that battle are several "events," which further delay the suspense of that confrontation.

First is Achilles's official renouncing of his wrath against Agamemnon, his acceptance of all the gifts that had been promised him by his leader back in Book IX—from tripods to women (including Agamemnon's daughter) to shiploads of loot to entire conquered cities—and his trying on the new armor. The culmination of this chunk of narrative comes when one of Achilles's immortal horses, Xanthos, is gifted for a moment with the power of human speech by "the goddess of the white arms, Hera." The loyal horse promises to keep his charioteer safe—this time—for "yet the day of your death is near, but it is not we who are to blame, but a great god and powerful destiny" (XIX: 409-10).

The second "event" is what we may see as the "curtain calls" of the gods as the poem pushes toward its final dramatic act. Book XX offers, quite literally, a roll call of deities who now swoop down from Olympus for the final battle before Achilles enters onto the stage: Hera, Pallas Athena, Poseidon, Hermes, Hephaistos—fighting on the side of the Achaeans—and Ares, Phoibos Apollo, Artemis, Aphrodite, Leto and Xanthos on the side of the Trojans (XX. 31-40). The fate of Aeneas is articulated: that he will survive the war, as "lord over the Trojans, and his sons' sons, and those who are born of their seed hereafter" (XX. 307-8).

The third moment presents Achilles's first extraordinary actions on the battlefield, when, god-like in his power and presumption, he battles the powerful river that flows by Troy, the Xanthos, in Book XXI.[6] He even pursues Apollo, until the god, at the outset of Book XXII, warns him not to go too far in testing his mortal speed and strength against that of an immortal.

It is in this book that Achilles and Hektor finally face off. Here, too, gods are not only involved indirectly—by way of the Hephaistean arms and armor of Achilles and the inherent advantage that they offer him, to go along with the benefits of having one parent who is divine—but by throwing themselves into the engagement.

Apollo initially protects Hektor from being run down by Achilles—three times, but the scales of Zeus are finally balanced toward Hektor's death day, so on the fourth occasion "Phoibos Apollo forsook him" (XXII.202-214). Athena stands beside Achilles and encourages him (214-23) and intervenes to deceive Hektor by assuming the form of his brother, Deiphobos, encouraging the hero to "stand fast against [Achilles] and beat him back from us" (225-46). And when Achilles casts his magnificent spear but Hektor is able to dodge it, so that it "flew over his shoulder and stuck in the ground, ...Pallas Athena snatched it out and gave it back to Achilles, unseen by Hektor..." (274-7).

Hektor is killed, and a furious Achilles drags his foe's body—attaching it by the heels to his chariot—around and around the doomed city. There are two additional "events" necessary to carry the epic to a satisfying conclusion. The *second* of these will be arrived at in the last book of the poem. It offers the final resolution of Achilles's fury, his return to the best among human customs: he gives back Hektor's body to the latter's suppliant father, Priam, who is assisted by Hermes—for Achilles pictures his own father back home, fated to lose the son who, in the ordinary course of events would have protected him in his old age and would have outlived his father. He decrees a cease-fire so that an appropriate funeral may be celebrated for his fallen, noble enemy, and that funeral takes place as Book XXIV comes to a close.

The poem ends on a distinctly melancholy note, recognizing that what ultimately marks these heroes as men and not as divinities is the brevity of their lives and the absoluteness and inevitability of their deaths. Death indeed seems to have the last word. Well, in the obvious sense it does, but on a subtler level of which the Greek audience in particular would have been very conscious, it does not—and not only because for generations, right up to this day, as we read and talk and write about Hektor and Achilles and all the others, they outlive death. But because the very brevity of their time on the planet when compared with the never-ending time and youth available to the gods makes them in some crucial way more noble than the gods themselves—so it may be said the heroic human nobility and its poignant underpinnings really have the final word.

In any case, it is a double last word. For the *first* of the two key events following Hektor's death, in Book XXIII, is dominated by the celebration of funeral games for Patroklos over which Achilles presides. This penultimate passage in the narrative, in which each of the key Achaean warriors participates—in effect, taking a "curtain call," like the gods in Book XX, as the drama comes to its end—in fact, shows the beginning of the process of the softening and humanizing (in the positive sense of those words) of Achilles that will culminate in the last book. It also underscores the relationship between war and sports, and between warrior heroes and athletic heroes—which is why I have chosen to refer to it last—and thus points us forward, specifically regarding the role of the gods in these areas, which will be depicted in history and art history in the millennia to follow.

At the outset, we are reminded of Achilles's bitter treatment of Hektor's body—which is protected from post-mortem damage by Aphrodite, who "drove the dogs back from him day and night, and anointed him with rosy immortal oil, so Achilles, when he dragged him about, might not tear him" (XXIII.185-7). The games are celebrated by the Achaeans to give solace to Patroklos's soul, and thus, to allow the funeral pyre to ignite. Achilles presides over the competitions, his transformation clearly beginning. He sits out of the chariot race, which, he reminds the others—warriors whom we have seen in action: Eumelos, Diomedes, Menelaus, Antilochos, and Meriones—he would easily win, since he possesses immortal horses.

The gods are once again involved: Apollo, still angry at Diomedes for his attacks on gods back in Book V, strikes the whip from Diomedes's hand when he might otherwise have overtaken Eumelos (XXIII.382-7). "Yet Athena did not fail to see the foul play of

Apollo on Tydeus's son [i.e., Diomedes]. She sped in speed to the shepherd of the people [i.e., again, Diomedes] and gave him back his whip, and inspired strength into his horses. Then in her wrath she went on after the son of Admetos [i.e., Eumelos] and she, a goddess, smashed his chariot yoke, and his horses ran on either side of the way, the pole dragged, and Eumelos himself was sent spinning out beside the wheel of the chariot..." (388-94).

As the race goes on, there are further issues and complications—and arguments flare up among those watching the race. Ajax and Oileos begin to quarrel, and things would have gotten out of hand "had not Achilles himself risen up and spoken between them" (490-1): Achilles becomes the peacemaker, furthering his transformation. He also adjudicates the matter of who actually has won the race, offering a second prize to Eumelos, who, in spite of his divinely occasioned accident and therefore last-place finish, is regarded by the son of Peleus as actually the best among the charioteers. But that upsets Antilochos (who would thereby lose the second-place prize), who argues that "[Eumelos] should have prayed to the immortal gods. That is why he came in last of all in the running" (546-7).

Other events follow after the chariot race, with other heroes, other divine interventions, other arguments, and other instances of Achilles rising again and again to the occasion as a peacemaker. For our purposes, the significance of all of this is two-fold. First, that there is a direct correlation between those who perform heroically on the battlefield and those who perform majestically on the playing field, so that the divinely aided success in the first context is often echoed in the second context. Similarly, the important correlation between these two modes of physical prowess has implications for the relationship between sports and religion as well.

This is not merely metaphorical, but literal. For warrior-athletes recognize the divine intervention that is repeated both on the battlefield and on the playing field. As they pray to the gods for success against their enemies in war battles, so might they be expected to pray to the gods for success against their opponents in athletic competitions. If they earn prizes on the running field or chariot-course it is not only due to their inherent skills and the dictates of destiny but in part because they have properly prayed to the gods and the gods have hearkened to those prayers—and thus they owe thanks to the gods—just as they do if they succeed in killing enemies and surviving on the battlefield.

Furthermore, one might say that two sides of the same religious spirit shape Achilles's conduct as the *sacerdos*—the priestly intermediator between gods and men—presiding over the games. Thus, on the one hand, he sacrifices Trojan prisoners to his friend's spirit, throwing them onto the pyre that he has built for Patroklos. This act is also, in a fundamental sense, the culminating manifestation of his rage against the Trojans as killers of his friend, a kind of epilogue to his destruction of Hektor and his dragging of the latter's dead body around and around the doomed city. The sacrifices reveal both a positive and a negative aspect of Achilles. On the other hand, in his presiding over the games devoted to Patroklos's soul, and in consistently playing the role of a peacemaker between angry contestants, he shows the way he is transforming his wrath in a new direction. It is a change that he will complete in the last book of the poem, when Priam, the father of Hektor, comes calling on Achilles to beg for his son's body back and for time to celebrate Hektor's funeral.

Notes

1. Please note that, consistent with my policy of selective consistency/inconsistency, I am using the less familiar Greek version of the name of Alexandros/Paris, the Greek-based spelling of Hektor and Patroklos (a few pages hence) and the less common, Greek-based, spelling for less familiar names, like Mykenae, Lykian, and Tlepolemos (also a few pages hence) but for other familiar names—Peleus, Achilleus/Achilles, Menelaos/Menelaus, Odysseios/Odysseus, Mount Olympos/Olympus—I am opting for the more common transliterations, even if at times these are, strictly speaking, more inaccurate, usually being Latin-based.

2. There is considerable irony here, for Sarpedon will perish later on in *spite* of his divine father's desire to save him, because at that point his fate—that he will die in the course of the war, at the hand of Patroklos—will override the wishes of even the king of the gods (XVI.431-90).

3. In a separate, Roman thread of tradition Aeneas will be seen in the end to have brought those survivors to Italy. (See below, 53ff).

4. Once again, there's irony: a separate thread in the Trojan war tapestry maintains that just before the beginning of the war, Agamemnon deceived his wife, Clytemnestra, and his daughter, Iphigenia—when he suggested that the latter be sent down to Aulis to be married to Achilles when, in fact, he knew she was needed as a sacrifice to Artemis so that the ships might sail. So, now he offers Achilles a choice from among his *surviving* daughters. This is aside from the irony, which Achilles himself recognizes, that, at some time after returning to battle and before Troy is taken, he is fated to perish, before he has a chance to be married to *anybody*.

5. It is Agamemnon's confiscation of Briseis as an "honor-prize" from Achilles that leads to their argument and to Achilles's decision to sit out the battle at the beginning of the poem.

6. Yes, the river bears the same name as does Achilles's temporarily speaking horse!

Chapter Three
The Epic Continuum: From Odysseus to Aeneas

We may observe how the issue of the relationship between both battlefield and playing-field success and the gods follows the Greek epic cycle forward. Odysseus (whose difficulties stem from Poseidon's hostility towards him) finally makes it home, aided by Athena, after ten additional years of wandering. That help includes but is not limited to imbuing him with the aura of an immortal when he first meets the Phaeacian princess, Nausikaa (*Odyssey*, Book VI), whose father's crew actually carries him home at last; to helping him overcome the man-into-beast-transforming magic of the goddess Circe (Book X); to convincing the goddess Calypso that it is time to let him go home after their seven-year dalliance (Book V); and to disguising him as an old beggar when he gets home so that he may devise a plan with his son Telemakhos to reclaim his home from the greedy suitors who have been besetting it for years (Book XIII).

Divine intervention on behalf of Odysseus culminates in the endgame of the *Odyssey*. Having slain all of the suitors and their handmaiden allies, Odysseus and Telemakhos and their loyal servants take refuge out at the country farm of Odysseus's father, Laertes. The families of the suitors organize themselves for revenge.

But Odysseus and his men prepare themselves — "Odysseus who with his followers made four, together with the six sons of Dolios; and with them Dolios [a loyal retainer — the gardener — of Laertes and Odysseus] and Laertes who also put on their armor (XXIV: 497-8) — to fend off the attack. "But now came their way the daughter of Zeus, Athena, likening herself in appearance and voice to Mentor [and old friend of Odysseus, who had been left in charge of Telemakhos' upbringing when Odysseus went off to Troy]" (502-3). She stood next to Laertes and instructed him to "make your prayer to the gray-eyed girl [i.e., Athena] and to Zeus her father, then quickly balance your far-shadowing spear, and throw it" (518-19).

With the breath of Athena within him and making a prayer to Athena, Laertes — an old man, but in his youth a warrior of quality — sends his spear flying and strikes Eupeithes in the side of his helmet, killing him (520-5). Inspired by this successful attack, Odysseus and Telemakhos begin to cut furiously through the front ranks of the warriors confronting them, and would have killed them all, according to the poet, if Athena had not cried out in a loud voice for them to stop. In their guts, the warriors recognize that this is a divinity and not merely Mentor speaking now, for thus "the green fear took hold of them, and in their terror they let fall from their hands their weapons" (533-4) and start to flee — and Odysseus begins to pursue them.

But now Zeus himself intervenes, casting a thunderbolt before Athena, who then warns Odysseus against further killing, lest he anger Zeus. "So spoke Athena, and with happy heart he obeyed her. And pledges for the days to come, sworn by both sides, were settled by Pallas Athena, daughter of Zeus of the aegis, who had likened herself in appearance and voice to Mentor" (545-8).

So the epic ends not only with a final act of divine intervention that aids Odysseus's cause, but with a resolution of the conflict between the two human groups mediated by the gods.

This sort of support, intervention and mediation is evident in the Latin-language poem that recounts the adventures of the

Roman hero, Aeneas. The epic—the *Aeneid*—that recounts his exploits combines adventures echoing those of the far-wandering Odysseus with battle exploits modeled largely on those of Achilles. As often in Latin literature, particularly poetry, (as well as in Roman art and architecture), we may find clear Greek antecedents, sometimes merely translated into Latin and sometimes more complexly transformed to accord with Roman rather than Greek values (for example the Roman emphasis on community versus the Greek emphasis on individuality).

This is certainly true of the character and dramatic role of Aeneas. We last encountered him as a Trojan warrior in the *Iliad*, in which in his final appearance he was saved by divine intervention to become the future leader of the survivors of the debacle. But in the *Aeneid*, penned by the Roman poet, Virgil (70-19 BCE), we first find him leading that band of refugees far from Troy: their ships land on the coast of North Africa—specifically, near the city of Carthage—and, while there, he recites to the Carthaginian queen, Dido, his adventures between Troy and Carthage. We follow him from Carthage to Italy, (toward which site he is impelled by the gods and Fate, in obligation to his community and in spite of his individual desire to remain with Dido), where the descendants of his descendants—specifically, Romulus, by tradition, some 430 years after the destruction of Troy—will eventually found the city of Rome.

As with the Greeks, the Romans in their epic poetry combine an interest in in literary composition with a distinct religious sensibility. Aeneas's support comes not from Athena, like Odysseus, or the sea goddess, Thetis, like Achilles, but from his mother, Aphrodite—or rather, Venus, as the Romans call her. Aside from being the hero's mother, we recall from the *Iliad* that she is a pro-Trojan Olympian (not surprising, given the fact that the Trojan prince Paris/Alexandros had chosen her over Athena and Hera in that fateful beauty contest). Aeneas's divine nemesis is not Poseidon—who, on the contrary, is a largely pro-Trojan god, although he was forced to be a key instrument in the destruction of Troy when, as we learn in Book II of the *Aeneid*, fate decrees that that city should fall.[1] Aeneas's divine nemesis is Hera (Juno, in Roman terms), who hates him as the son of the goddess who bested her in the contest judged by Aeneas's fellow Trojan.

Aeneas's story has echoes of Odysseus's tale: Virgil tells of his wanderings, which lead early in his narrative to a love affair with the Carthaginian queen, Dido—ending disastrously for her. That affair is facilitated, in large part, by Venus, not only in how she helps manipulate Dido's emotions, most particularly by substituting her own son, Eros/Cupid, for Aeneas's son, Ascanius, during the feast on the evening when the queen and hero meet and talk for the first time. But more broadly, she convinces Juno to be part of the process of bringing the two together, fooling her fellow goddess into believing that the result will be a "win-win" outcome for both of the humans whom they patronize. In the end, it benefits Aeneas—and leads to Dido's suicide. From the backward-looking Virgilian Roman viewpoint, this will have consequences in the series of Punic Wars fought between Rome and Carthage nearly a millennium after the time of Aeneas and before the time of Virgil—so Virgil's poetry, the politics of the Augustan world and the wars of Rome's coming to dominate the Western Mediterranean are all connected to Aeneas.

He sails, then from Carthage, finally, to Italy. As a community-minded leader, exhibiting Roman virtues, rather than as a self-focused, individual-minded leader, like both Achilles and Odysseus, he pulls himself away from the pleasure he finds in Dido's company (Books II-IV), leaves Carthage as the gods remind him he must, and arrives at his destination with his band of refugees largely intact. There, among other *Iliad*-reminiscent moments, Aeneas meets up with his mother, Venus, who provides him, in Book VIII, with a new set of armor—made by Vulcan (the Roman equivalent of Hephaestos) and thus all but invincible—thereby encouraging him to be fearless in his soon-to-come encounter with Turnus, the local star athlete and leader of those who oppose the settlement of the Trojan refugees on Italian soil.

Meanwhile, Anchises—the father whom Aeneas originally carried on his shoulders out of the burning city of Troy; the hero's piety extends from gods to humans, from his father to his young son—had died along the way between Troy and Carthage. Aeneas encounters him, too, between Carthage and Italy, in the Underworld.[2] We once again recall Odysseus. In his visit to the edge of reality, following Circe's directions he had fashioned an opening between our world and the Underworld, (in *Odyssey* XI), and had learned about the condition of deprivation associated with being dead (from the mouth of the dead Achilles) and ultimately about his own future (from the mouth of the dead blind seer, Teiresias). By parallel and contrast, Aeneas, in his journey *through* the Underworld, (in *Aeneid* VI) ultimately learns about the future history of the Trojan band that he has been leading forward: the communal mytho-history of Rome, right up to the time of Virgil. In other words, he is presented with a vision of his future (and then some) by his own *father*, Anchises—the last figure tied to his past.

Key cultural differences between Roman and Greek ideology emerge, in particular from Books VI and VIII. Where the Greek hero Odysseus's informant about *himself* is Teiresias, the Roman hero Aeneas's informant about the *communal* future is his father. Whereas the newly fashioned shield of Achilles (in *Iliad* XVIII) offers images that are at once generic commentaries on the intertwining of love and strife in human and divine reality and may be seen, in part, as offering snapshots of the events of the Trojan War story, the newly fashioned shield of Aeneas offers a summary of mytho-history as it extends from the story of the she-wolf suckling Romulus and Remus to the firming up of the Augustan *Imperium*.

Aeneas, of course, cannot *recognize* any of what he sees in the Underworld or on his new shield, since what his father shows him and what the smith-god has depicted pertains to people and events in the future, but in both cases he recognizes that the imagery spells out fame and glory for himself and his descendants—beginning with the first moment he himself will put the new shield, sword,

and other armor into action. And even with his inability to understand the meaning of all the details inscribed on the shield by Vulcan and shown him in the Underworld by Anchises, if Aeneas is
half as smart as he is pious, he must understand that he is a small
part of a much larger narrative being worked out by fate. He is, in
fact, constantly reminded that the story is not all about himself.

The odd culmination of the arrival in Italy that fills most of the
last half of the poem—marked by warfare against certain of the locals
and in particular Turnus. All of this echoes but is distinct from the *Iliadic* battle epic—and turns Aeneas momentarily in a "Greek" (rather
than "Roman") direction: destructive rather than constructive, self-focused rather than community-focused. His final battle encounter with
Turnus recalls one of Achilles's final battles with a Trojan, Lycaon, after his battle against the Xanthos River and shortly before his battle
with Hektor—and perhaps the battle with Hektor itself.

More specifically, one might say that Aeneas falls between the
two aspects of Achilles—the *warrior* Achilles (who, in his furious
anger, refuses any mercy to Lycaon in *Iliad* XXI.34-135 and who still
curses at Hektor after he has already slain him, with both words
and actions, in *Iliad* XXII.364-404) and the *peacemaker* Achilles (who,
assuaged both by his role as patron and adjudicator in the funeral
games for Patroklos and by thoughts of his own father, gives up
the body of Hektor for proper burial to Hektor's divinely-assisted
father in Book XXIV). Aeneas's final act in the epic named for him
has elements of both—but it is ultimately the first Achilles whom
he emulates as he slays Turnus in spite of the latter's request for
clemency and Aeneas's own usual inclination to be merciful.

The final scene of the *Aeneid* is a disturbing one, particularly
given Aeneas's overall persona as the preeminent Roman hero,
who ordinarily does and is always expected to exhibit the trait—*pietas* (piety)—that trails him as an epithet. Whereas the Greek heroes
Achilles and Odysseus are respectively called "swift-footed" and
"swift-witted" (among others), Aeneas is called "pious": *pius*. And
the Roman understanding of *pietas* is that one offers proper rever-

ence not only to the gods, but to one's parents and ancestors, one's contemporaries—be they friend or foe—and one's children and descendants. But the poem ends abruptly: Turnus pleas for mercy to an Aeneas who might have been expected, given his *pietas*, to have yielded to a suppliant. But the Trojan-Roman hero, suddenly enraged by the sight of the girdle stripped from his young friend, Pallas, across Turnus's shoulder, doesn't heed the latter's request; instead he runs him through with his sword.[3]

Thus, instead of offering a final vision of the hero at his moral best, the last lines of the epic offer Turnus's angry soul fleeing *indignans* to the Underworld, leaving behind no appeasement, no assuagement, no resolution. There is no absolute way to explain this stunning gaffe by the poet. Of course, Virgil is said to have written his poem in a prose form originally, and slowly, at the rate of two lines per day, committed it to poetic form, and as he lay dying from fever he had requested that what he considered to be an unfinished work be destroyed. But the tone of the ending is not likely to be a consequence of the alleged unfinished state of the poetry. I would propose a theory—it is and can be no more than a theory—for the disturbing ending. It would tie in to another Virgilian "gaffe," at the end of Book VI and to Virgil's own religion and politics.

My theory's starting point is both the poet's and his hero's sense of how individuals on the stage of life can be—and ultimately *must be*—part of larger dramas articulated not only by the gods but by the fates that transcend even the gods in power. Events (related to the forces of nature, the gods, and his own sense of obligation) that seem to push Aeneas along through the first five books of the poem arrive at a kind of denouement by way of his journey through the Underworld in Book VI, where, as we have noted, he sees the articulation of a grand future for his family/community line. And that articulation is presented along the lines of a Pythagorean cycle of existence as a pattern of birth, death, and rebirth, and of a certain continuity.

For Virgil was known to be drawn to Orphism as a religious

preference, and the Orphics, like the Pythagoreans, had a strong belief in the transmigration and reincarnation of souls.[4] Augustus, who asserted that he was the savior of the Republic, even as he completed its destruction and became the founder (the first Emperor) of the Empire, and who was also Virgil's patron—who fortunately for us, disregarded his favorite poet's request to destroy the "unfinished" *Aeneid*—is easily recognized as Aeneas reborn, allegorically. But why only allegorically? To an Orphic such as Virgil, that notion could certainly be entertained literally.

In this case, one might understand that it is not Aeneas, but an *eidolon* (a kind of double) of Aeneas who returns from the Underworld through the ivory gate of false dreams, rather than the horn gate of true dreams.[5] Thus, the falseness is not a reference to the visions vouchsafed to the hero, but to the hero himself—a "false" version of himself returns to our world. This explains all of the aggressive, un-Aeneas-like conduct of the second half of the epic, culminating with the death-blow that he administers to Turnus and the tone with which he administers it. It also accounts for the language of those last lines in Virgil's poem, in which Aeneas's sword arm seems to be separated from himself.[6]

The Virgilian Orphic ideology connects the mystery of Aeneas's exit from the *Underworld* to the mystery of Aeneas's exit from the *poem* by way of a merciless act that sends Turnus to the Underworld. It also connects these mysteries to the arrival of Augustus onto the stage of history as Rome's "savior" and as Virgil's patron. For to that patron—Virgil's primary audience and "pupil" of a proper *pius* ideology—the soul of the true Aeneas is presented as having waited more than a thousand years to be reincarnated *as* Augustus, implicitly being reminded to be ever *pius*. This, in turn, also connects our detour (nearly as long as Aeneas's own detour!) directly to our focus on the relationship between religion and politics—and between religion and sports.

As we have seen, in *Iliad* XXIII, Achilles sponsors funeral games in honor of his dead friend, Patroklos, and in *Aeneid* V,

Aeneas sponsors such games to honor the deceased father who will guide him through the Underworld in *Aeneid* VI. And in those latter games, among the echoes of the *Iliadic* games—celebrated on the heels of Aeneas's departure from Carthage, with the smoke from Dido's pyre, (he does not yet know that it is from her pyre, he won't realize it until he encounters her in the Underworld) rising behind him—are sacrifices, albeit of animals, not of Trojan prisoners (and in both cases the offerings are to the spirit of the departed and not, per se, to the gods).

The gods are specifically addressed, however, in the first competitive event, which is a race among four ships (as opposed to five chariots in the *Iliad*). One commander, Cloanthus, promises to the "gods of the seas, whose waters I skim, whose empire lifts me up, ...gladly... a snow-white bullock at altars on this shore, and wine for the ocean, and the entrails flung to the flood." And indeed, "under the waves the Nereids heard him... [and] boosted him on his way" (235-42), making his victory possible.

The second event is a footrace, and even more than in the boat race, we recognize the inherently contemporary Roman inspiration for Virgil's delineation of the contestants. For they come from a variety of places in and around Sicily, as opposed to all being Trojans. Once more, then, the diverse ethnic makeup of the empire of the future is anticipated by the poet. The would-be winner, Nisus, slips on blood that he doesn't notice, from the sacrificed bullocks, and his buddy Euryalus wins as Nisus manages to trip up Salius; the argument of "foul!" (which recalls similar accusations in the *Iliad*'s games) comes forth, but Aeneas adjudicates easily enough through his own generosity, just as Achilles had back on the Trojan plain. The boxing match results in Entellus offering the prize he has won, a bullock, as a sacrifice to the gods. The arrow-shooting competition ends with the local elderly king Acestes shooting an arrow that miraculously catches flame as it soars through the clouds—and so Aeneas loads him with presents, declaring that the "the king of heaven" has willed this miracle.

We observe, by way of Book XXIII of the *Iliad* and the funeral games for Patroklos, as well as the funeral games for Anchises in Book V of the *Aeneid,* how various sporting events bear a distinct relationship to battle events. The protagonists in some events—the chariot race, for instance, or the racing of ships—may be seen to do for sport what on the battlefield they must do to kill and not be killed: hurry, feint, outmaneuver, and ultimately outstrip their competitors. The athlete's success in footraces can have parallel consequences on the battlefield, whether he is fleeing from or pursuing an enemy on foot (think of Hektor being chased by Achilles). Even events that might not seem to have such an obvious, direct battlefield corollary—boxing, perhaps—are inherently related to the latter in terms of general speed, strength, and accuracy skills; competition with others; governance by divinities who are recognized and exercised through prayers and offerings; and intervention by gods and goddesses who have the power to help affect the outcome.

It is this last feature that is of primary concern to our narrative: the invocation of the gods whether through sacrifice or prayer, or the reference to the gods as potentially involved and/or responsible for competitive outcomes. Most overtly, the intervention by gods in the *Iliad*'s chariot race is echoed by the intervention of Nereids in the *Aeneid*'s boat race. On the other hand, the importance of athletic competitions as stand-ins for military confrontations offers a particular emphasis in the *Aeneid* beyond what we find in the *Iliad*. For after the archery contest, Aeneas quietly sends for his young son and the other boys, who, to honor the spirit of Anchises, present themselves in arms. In three groups they parade before the crowd, then "wheeled, made mock charge, with lances at the ready... in a mimic battle, mimic retreat, and mimic peace... in flight and sport" (580-93). So in the context of, and as a culmination of the athletic competitions, the youth, still too young to fight but already training for the battlefield, enact a mock-battle, which echoes sporting events that are themselves mock-battles of sorts.

Meanwhile, the ever-angry goddess, Juno, prepares mischief, by sending the goddess Iris, in disguise, to stir up the Trojan women to burn the ships that they will need to carry them further than the coast of Sicily to their ultimate goal: Latium. It is only Aeneas' powerful prayer to Jupiter, king of gods, who responds with a sudden cloudburst, "with darkness and black tempest streaming, and thunder rumbling over plain and hillock, the whole sky pouring rain" that saves most of the fleet from destruction (685-99). They will sail on, Aeneas will encounter his father in the Underworld, and arrive into Latium and eventually fight the deathly battle with Turnus that will carry the epic to its uncomfortable conclusion.

The most renowned visual image of the Emperor Augustus—Virgil's patron and, according to my interpretation, intended to be understood as a reincarnation, as it were, of the *true* Aeneas, and not of the one who killed Turnus—is a sculpture that represents him both as divinely connected (accompanied by the dolphin and cupid that are symbols of the goddess Venus) and as a heroic warrior, attired in his uniform [fig 9]. The statue, at the Empress Livia's villa at Prima Porta, is formally modeled on the Greek classical image of the heroic athlete, Polyklitos's *Doryphoros*, which some have believed was intended to be understood as a "portrait" of Achilles. Subsequent Roman emperors sometimes

Figure 9. Augustus of Prima Porta

had themselves portrayed as Herakles, with his Nemean Lion's pet "cape" and club—and sometimes these emperors participated in the athletic competitions in the arena, which contests we shall discuss subsequently. From Achilles and the *Doryphoros* to Aeneas and the *Augustus of Prima Porta* and from Herakles to competition in the Roman Arena, the relationship among sports, war, religion, politics, and art moves from one end of antiquity to the other.

Notes

1. For he sends an enormous pair of serpents up out of the sea to destroy his devotee, Laokoon, and the latter's sons, when the priest insists to the Trojans that they not take the now-famous wooden horse left behind by the Achaeans into the citadel. Catastrophe follows from the wooden horse stratagem in short course.

2. The Underworld is, for both the Greeks and Romans, the place to which the dead go—or at least their disembodied souls, or their shades, shaped like their living bodies but without any physical substance. There are different parts of the Underworld (sometimes called "Hades," which is also the Greek version of the name of the God who presides over the Underworld), although this is nowhere articulated in a consistent theological manner: Elysium, where the truly blessed end up; Erebos, where most everybody else goes; and Tartarus, where the souls of the truly bac people are placed.

3. The girdle had been given to Pallas by Aeneas as a gift, but Pallas had been killed in battle by Turnus, who stripped the girdle form his victim. This transpired while Aeneas was still away tending to other matters. We recognize the parallels yet differences between this succession of events and those in the *Iliad*. Pallas, Turnus, and Aeneas obviously all play roles analogous to but not identical with those of Patroklos, Hektor, and Achilles in the *Iliad*. Most obviously, too, the reason for Aeneas's absence at the time of Pallas's death is very different from the reason for Achilles's absence at the time of Patroklos's death, and the confrontation between Turnus and Aeneas derives from issues that are fundamentally different from those driving the confrontation between Hektor and Achilles—except for this moment of enraged death-dealing.

4. Regarding Virgil's connection to Orphism, see the classic commentary by Eduard Norden, *P. Vergilius Maro, Aeneis, Buch VI* (Leipzig, G. Teubner, 1903) and much more recently, the article by J.N. Brenner, "The Golden Bough: Orphic, Eleusinian, and Hellenistic-Jewish Sources of Virgil's Underworld in *Aeneid* VI," in *Kernos* 22 (2009), 183-208.

5. An *eidolon* is an image, but the nuance of the term in this sort of context is as something insubstantial, rather than full-fleshed and three-dimensional. Thus it is an image of Aeneas, a kind of insubstantial double, that returns through the gate.

6. Thus, Aeneas cries ("in wrath"): "Pallas, Pallas exacts his vengeance, and the blow is Pallas, making sacrifice" — as if it is not Aeneas himself at all who is completing the destruction of Turnus with such heated, Achilles-like passion. And Turnus "went with a moan indignant (*indignans*) to the shadows," ending the epic on a troubling, unresolved, unhappy, un-*pius* note.

CHAPTER FOUR
From Lyric to Tragic to Comic: Pindar's Heroic Athletes and Their Poetic Successors

*L*et us step back to the Greeks once again, before continuing forward. As Greek history and poetry moved further away from the era of heroes and the cultural convention of focusing all of literature on them, epic poetry yielded pride of place to lyric poetry, which sought to trumpet the victories of athletes in various competitions.[1]

Such competitions emerged every two or four years at various sites across Greece—Corinth, Delphi, Nemea and above all, Olympia. They represented a continuation of the idea of athletic games as a surrogate for war, just as the training and preparation for them also served as a form of training and preparation for battle.

The competitions also offered a self-conscious means of limiting warfare among the Hellenic *poleis*—of siphoning off some of the energized testosterone that helped contribute to the fight and redirecting it to nonfatal confrontations that involved diverse peoples from diverse places. Thereby, they also provided another context in which to encounter each other that fell between peaceful commerce and cultural exchange on the one hand and martial confrontations on the other. Finally, as in the case of war and in the case of the games associated with the heroic era of Achilles and Odysseus, the

Olympic and other games took place under the patronage of, and with consistent reference to, the gods.

Thus, both the Olympic and Nemean games were celebrated in honor of Zeus—tradition had it that Herakles instituted the Nemean games in his father's honor after his (Herakles's) defeat of the Nemean lion—while the Pythian games at Delphi were celebrated in honor of Apollo, and the Isthmian games at Corinth were in honor of Poseidon. These were all Panhellenic games: Hellenes (and only Hellenes)[2] from throughout Greece and anywhere among the Greek colonies were invited to participate. In order to afford athletes the opportunity to compete in all of them, the various competitions took place at different times. The Olympics took place every four years, as did the Pythian games, in the third year following the Olympics. Both the Nemean and Isthmian games took place every two years—the year before and the year after the Olympics— but in different months.

The use of the Olympics as a reference point for the timing of the other competitions was no doubt a result of their having been the first to be organized. The written record shows the Olympics as having begun in 776 BCE, but the tradition may well have preceded that date by a considerable amount of time. Conversely, although the Nemean games, for instance, later ascribe their beginnings to Herakles, (who would have lived in an age well before even the events associated with the Trojan War), it seems almost certain that they were begun, together with the Pythian and Isthmian games, around 600 BCE—in other words, around the time when the various Greek *poleis* were beginning to clarify their distinctive administrative forms.

The prizes for victory in each of the games were more symbolic than substantial: a wreath of wild olive in the Olympic games, a wreath of bay laurel in the Pythian games, a wreath of wild parsley in the Nemean games, and a wreath of wild parsley or pine in the Isthmian games. Hence, the idea that the athletes who participated did so out of love of honor (this is, of course, what the word "amateur" means: "one who loves"), not for lucre. Then again, a successful athlete might expect that the native city to which he had brought honor with his victory might reward him—by gifting him and feting him for a long time.

If traditions ascribe the founding of such competitions to the early heroic period, we also recognize most of the sports in which athletes engaged as having a literary "precedent" in the funeral games for Patroklos in Book XXIII of the *Iliad*. Thus, chariot races and footraces, and boxing and wrestling matches dominated the scene.

There are two issues of note to recall with regard to the *Iliadic* "models" that we have already considered. First is the matter of the general religious underpinnings of those models. They were, after all, *funeral* games, designed to celebrate the memory of, and in a directly articulated sense, to appease the soul of, the deceased, helping his or her journey to the Underworld.

The second religious element is the actual and imagined presence of the gods during the various *Iliadic* competitions. Just as the games offer echoes of the battles that the reader has witnessed through the previous books of the poem; and just as each of the competitors may be seen to be taking a kind of curtain call after his performance on the battle stage; so the intervention of the gods, witnessed again and again during the fight scenes, is echoed by evocations of the gods and goddesses and occasional divine appearances during these athletic events.

Thus, the epic poetic tradition of ancient Greece offers the interweaving of two issues toward the outset of Western literature and thought: the relationship between *heroic-warrior identity* and *champion-athletic ability*; and the relationship between both of these images and *divine interest, presence,* and *intervention*. But then, the next question is twofold. How are both of these subjects visible in the athletic competitions being enacted at different Greek sites over the centuries that follow, and how are they reflected in the lyric poetry designed to commemorate—to immortalize—those fully human (as opposed to human/divine) competitions?

We can answer these questions and see a further connection between the historical activity of the athletic competitions of ancient Greece and some of its most stirring literature by considering some of the lyric poetry that emerges in the wake of the golden age of Greek epic poetry.

Most of the lyric poets speak in their own voices of their own experiences, hopes, desires, needs, successes, and failures. But one in particular, Pindar, included, among his many works, poems dedicated to—and commissioned and paid for by—winners of athletic competitions of the sort we would recognize from the funeral games described in Book XXIII of the *Iliad*.[3] Such competitions emerged from literature to history at Olympia, Delphi, Corinth, and Nemea in the eighth and seventh centuries BCE.

Pindar was born some time between 526 and 518 BCE and died some time after 446, perhaps as late as 438 BCE. He was prolific, his works ultimately organized into 17 books of diverse genres, four of which—the victory odes celebrating various individuals' athletic successes—survive in near-completeness, together with many fragments of other types of poems. Most often, the victor whose success is being sung by Pindar is compared by the poet to some mythological hero, and his success ascribed explicitly or implicitly to one or more of the gods.

For one instance, the very first Olympian ode, dedicated to Hieron of Syracuse, who hosted Pindar when he arrived on an extended visit to Sicily in 476—invokes the story of Tantalus and Pelops and their family line. At first glance, this seems an odd choice, since the standard understanding of that story is that it carries disaster from one generation to the next, beginning with the attempt by Tantalus to fool the gods by serving them a meal that featured his son, Pelops, in a stew. But Pindar tells us in the midst of his second stanza that "I shall speak against what earlier poets assert of you," opining rather that Poseidon snatched Pelops away from the banquet, "his mind wild with desire, and on golden horses carried you to the high halls of Zeus." But some jealous neighbor spread the rumor, when Pelops disappeared, that "you had been cut limb from limb and…at the final course [they] divided and ate your flesh."

Pindar then follows the story of Pelops, re-angling his narrative toward the hero. With the help and support of both Poseidon and Aphrodite, Pelops manages to do what 13 wannabes before him could not do (and so lost their lives trying): defeat the father of Hippodemeia in a chariot race, and thereby win her hand in marriage. And there, of course, the connection shifts suddenly into place: Hieron in his chariot victory is likened to Pelops in his; both have skills in this event that suggest divine support. Thus, the athlete is likened to a mythological figure whose father, Tantalus, had been known as the best human friend of the gods and who was himself a favorite of the gods—who dined with them on Olympus and in his own home, as opposed to having wrecked his relationship with them through an act of cruel gastronomic tomfoolery.

The third Olympian ode is dedicated to Pindar's other primary host-patron in Sicily, Theron of Akragas, victorious in the chariot races of 466. It begins with the words "I shall honor glorious Akragas and please the Dioskuroi…," reminding us that divinities can be as pleased by poetic prowess as by athletic prowess—and in this case both enterprises will go hand-in-hand. As Pindar moves past the description of the honors placed on Theron's brow in the form of a wreath, he recalls how "long ago, Amphytrion's son carried the silver olive tree from the shadowy springs of the Danube, to be the handsomest symbol of the Olympian games," convincing the "Hyperboreans, people of Apollo" to give him a sprig "for Zeus's garden."

The mythical hero—Herakles, son of Zeus by the mortal queen Alcmene but raised by her husband Amphytrion as his own son—journeyed far afield to complete the vegetation of the area around Olympia. He is welcomed in Arkadia by Artemis, after which he goes on a "mission to bring back the gold-horned doe that Taygeta one day wrote down to be sacrificed as a fee to Artemis Orthosia. Chasing the doe, he saw the distant land behind the cold north wind..." — racing with the sort of speed, in other words, that would be replicated in a different context by Theron in his chariot. And Theron might be further implicitly likened to Herakles who "at Olympus charged those future stars to guide the wonderful games where men's courage and chariot-speed are tested.[4] My heart impels me to say that glory has come to Theron and the children of Emmenos as a gift from the horsemen Dioskuroi."[5] The charioteer is thus both likened to a mythological hero — Herakles — and associated in his victory with those virtual sons of Zeus, known as superb horsemen and boxers, who favor particular charioteers and poets alike.

The fourth Pythian Ode — to choose just one of these — is dedicated to Arkesilas of Cyrene, winner in the chariot race in 462 BCE. In its first lines, the Muses are called upon to sing forth on behalf of the victor, who is likened in his songworthiness to "the children of Leto [Apollo and Artemis]." That prelude completes itself with reference to Medea's alleged words to Jason and the Argonauts, with whom she sailed after they had claimed the Golden Fleece of Colchis with her help. Her words — or rather, those placed in her mouth by the poet — foretell the victory, 17 generations later, of Arkesilas, as they recount a story of heroic human success favored by the gods, led by none other than Zeus himself, and also speak of Apollo's establishment of his Pythian shrine at Delphi.

A good deal of extended mythological meandering arrives at the genealogical point of connecting Arkesilas to the story, thus explaining why "it was Apollo and Pytho who granted him glory in the chariot race..." (l. 66). This statement then becomes a take-off point for further expansion of the story, centering around the mythological hero, Jason, and his gathering of all the god-and-goddess-sprung heroes who arrive to partake in the great adventure, the journey to Colchis, for which "Hera it was who kindled in those demigods the all-persuasive desire for the ship Argo, that none should be left behind..." (ll. 184-5).

Pindar proceeds to tell the story of the capture of the fleece, reminding Arkesilas of how it was that Apollo "caused your race to bring prosperity to the plain of Libya by the honors granted by the gods" (ll. 259-60). The poet then veers off to evoke the later part of the story of Oedipus—exiled from his city—and to refer to Atlas (still holding up the heavens) as the poem arrives at its last words directed to Arkesilas. This same victor and the same victory are also celebrated in Pindar's Fifth Pythian ode, in which Arkesilas is reminded not to forget to give glory to the gods, acknowledging their support in his triumph (ll. 22ff)—and so on.

Such complicated and long-winded odes contrast interestingly with the first surviving one that Pindar ever wrote, the so-called tenth Pythian, dedicated to the victory of Hippokleas of Thessaly in the boys' double footrace in 498 BCE. It was written when the poet was himself barely out of his boyhood and begins by invoking Herakles as the ancestor of the victor. The ode moves swiftly to opine that Apollo must have had a hand in the victor's success, for "the beginning and the end both grow sweet when a god urges on a man's work. No doubt he accomplished this with the help of your counsels"—thus, surely punning on and connecting Hippokleas's athletic triumph to his own success as a poet, whose obvious divine patron would be Apollo, master of Mount Parnassus, home of the muses.

The poet moves on to intertwine references to the successes of Perseus with the athletic triumphs of Hippokleas's father with Ares at *his* back, in order to suggest a lineage of victors that would esteem the current footrace victory as merely the latest in a line stretching back to the age of heroes. Even in this relatively simple ode, the self-conscious agglomeration of allusions and references, of reflections and self-reflections, are summarized when—almost in passing—he notes in lines 53-4 that "the choicest hymn of praise flits from theme to theme, like a bee" and, in retrospect, we can see how over time Pindar would epitomize that conviction with ever-longer and more complex poems. He interweaves *politics* with *sports* in the praise of Hippokleas as an *athlete*, and he concludes by building further on this theme. Pindar ties the idea of familial line as formula for victory to the success of *cities* that are governed *from* father to son, as in the case of Thessaly, the city of Hippokleas.

That theme—of associating the success of cities with the athletic accomplishments of the noble families who govern them—will be carried forward to what is believed by some[6] to be the last extant victory poem written by Pindar. That ode is the eighth Pythian, dedicated to and written for Aristomenes of Aegina, who was victorious in 446 BCE in the wrestling competition. The poet asserts that what "makes cities great"—"kindly peace, daughter of justice"—accrues to them from due recognition and honor of the sort accorded "to Aristomenes for his Pythian victory." For that honor is *shared* between athlete and city—in this case a city, which "from the beginning is her fame perfect, for she is sung of as the nurse of heroes foremost in many games and in violent battles; and in her mortal men she is also preeminent" (ll. 24-7).

It is in this context—the wrestling champion as a reflection of a glorious *polis*—that the victor is addressed as a link in a chain of athletic heroes that includes his own uncles and his entire clan. The poet addresses the victor's father, wishing a continuation of successes to the family, but, as so often is the case, he also notes that "such things lie not with men; it is gods who order them, who set up one and put down another so that the latter is bound beneath the hands of his adversary" (ll. 76-8). The reader is thus reminded that both success and failure in these athletic competitions must be laid at the feet of the gods, at least in part—and it is the question of *how large a part* that makes the entire issue so intriguing.

Indeed, this ode offers what is arguably Pindar's most affecting observation: that the quality of human achievement is slender within the vastness of time and space and yet it can glow if the gods permit it: "Things of a day—what are we, and what are we not? Man is but a dream of shadows. Yet nonetheless, when a glory from the gods has shined upon them, a clear light abides upon men, and a serene life" (ll. 95-7).

The poet's last words in the ode are directed to Aegina, the nymph who is the divine protector of the island *polis* (city-state; community) of that name: the athlete and his *polis* are interchangeable as victors, and victories for both men and cities are dependent upon the good will of the gods, both greater and lesser.

Thus, the Pindarian sort of lyric poetry, which anticipates tragic theater by combining in its recitation individual with choral voices, turns the association between the gods and athletic success in a contemporary direction. Pindar relegates the mythological references that, in Greek epic poetry, are simply and straightforwardly part of the drama being described, to a conceptual, contextual background for the success in the sporting event that is the main subject. Whereas gods and humans are interactive in the epic tradition (and the relationship between warrior and athlete becomes explicit only with the side-stories of funeral games), the lyric poet uses the divine-heroic relationship, in war or otherwise, to glorify sports accomplishments. The latter is presented as echoing the former, as it were. Pindar also often links the praise of the athlete with that of the city-state—the *polis*—that he represents.

We are reminded in all of this that the association of religion and politics is not only a constant of history, and is often related to the arts—as in the image of the Egyptian Pharaoh Khafra with the wings of the falcon hawk Horus spread over his shoulders, as discussed earlier[7]—but that religion and politics can also be interwoven in particular ways at particular times and places with sports. In other words, it is not *only* religion and sports that we find: the invocation of and references to the gods by athletes. City-states whose overall reputations were tied in part to the successes of their athletes, prided themselves on the success of their native-born stars. The *poleis* were often more than willing to accord particular foreigners citizenship, (to say nothing of substantial material rewards—we might call these incentive and bonus packages), if these stars were willing to re-create themselves as foreign-born "native sons."

We are reminded of this aspect of ancient Greece's sports

world—albeit more specifically of the high value accorded by *po-leis* to the success of their athletes than of their willingness to pur-chase that success from outside the *polis* limits—by Socrates in the last part of his *Apology*. As rendered by Plato, Socrates responds to his Athenian jurors when asked what treatment he deserves—af-ter having been found guilty of impiety ("bringing false gods into the city") and of corrupting the youth—by saying that, as a public benefactor to the city, he should be rewarded handsomely. "Noth-ing could be more appropriate for such a person than free mainte-nance at the State's expense. *He deserves it much more than any victor in the races at Olympia, whether he wins with a single horse or a pair or a team of four...*" (36d8-10; emphasis added).

This small fragment within Socrates's long speech offers an ironic twist because the accusation to which he so boldly responds pertains to the matter of religion. Socrates is a scapegoat for the Athenians' frustration over having lost the Peloponnesian Wars when victory had seemed inevitable to them at the outset; they con-clude that they must have displeased the gods—or that a key citi-zen among them must have done so. Socrates is viewed by many of them as that citizen.

But the irony is that not only is he, as far as one can deduce from our sources,[8] a pious devotee of the gods, but that his compul-sion to raise the issues he spent a lifetime raising—which annoyed enough people and, in particular, a handful of powerful political figures who became his enemies—was a consequence (as he ex-plains earlier in the *Apology*) of his sense of divine pressure *upon him* to raise those issues.[9] He considers his activity of issue-raising and question-asking, of pressing moral questions directly and im-plicitly on his fellow-citizens, to have been an important service to the city he loves—and compares it favorably to the sort of outstand-ing *athletic* service to cities that, according to poets like Pindar, is made possible by divine interest and intervention. So the connec-tion among sports, religion, and politics is asserted here from a dif-ferent angle than we have thus far considered.

Occasionally, other lyric poets follow the Pindarean lead—as, for example, his younger contemporary, Bacchylides who, like Pindar, arrived on an extended visit to Sicily in 476 BCE. Very little of Bacchylides's work survived from antiquity until the year 1896—by pleasant coincidence, the beginning year of the modern Olympics—when an extensive papyrus find in Egypt yielded 20 hitherto unknown works, making his known repertoire second only to Pindar in quantity of preserved poetry.

In one of Bacchylides's charming shorter odes, he lauds Idas, who wins Marpessa—a wife, not a race, but written about as if the victory had been achieved in an athletic competition. Idas's feat—of winning his wife when competing for her favor with the god Apollo—is accomplished because "Poseidon the sea lord gave him a chariot and horses equal to the wind." This enables Idas to win the daughter of Evenus, who is "the son of [another god,] Ares of the gold shield." So gods are involved on all sides in this race trumpeted by the poet.

And as Greek poetry moves from its lyric form toward the shaping of tragic theater, subject matter shifts, too—first, back to religion and mythology (rather than connecting religion and mythology to contemporary contexts/events). Greek tragedy typically shapes its stories as combinations of destiny, divinity, and heroic human beings. So, Aeschylus and Sophocles wrestle with the layered ironies attached to a human condition in which free will and predetermination—the irresistible outcomes of fate, the intervention of the gods, and the notion of real choice—contend.

But then, with Euripides, questions begin to be raised with regard to the manner in which we imagine these three elements to be interconnected. It is only in Euripidean drama, and then only rarely, that one encounters the presence of sports as opposed to heroic adventure and warfare. One thinks specifically of *Hippolytos*, a play named for an athlete—a charioteer—by that name, who is the son of the hero, Theseus, and a devotee of the goddess, Artemis, patron goddess of athletes.

The story of Hippolytos, however, is the tale of his failure to honor the goddess Aphrodite as a consequence of his unwavering focus on Artemis, of the reckless invocation of the gods (specifically, Poseidon) by Theseus, and of how the combination of these human shortfalls leads to the destruction of Hippolytos (and also of his step-mother, Phaedra). If there is a relationship between sports and divinity in this context, it is that the athlete's devotion to a particular goddess cannot save him—*she* cannot save him—when he eschews a second goddess, who takes her revenge by desiring his destruction.Euripides's intention is to be an iconoclast—a "breaker of images"—with respect to how his contemporaries view the gods. How powerful and beneficent *are* they if they cannot protect their own devotees from the wrath of other gods (and goddesses)?

In the next generation, the principle of iconoclasm will take a further step in the hands of the comic playwright, Aristophanes. For him, most obviously in his play, *Frogs*, the gods are made fun of, along with other tragic playwrights. In *Frogs*, the consummate athlete-hero, Herakles—who among his renowned accomplishments, visited the Underworld, and even rescued Theseus (the same Theseus, cousin of Herakles, who also appears in *Hippolytos*)—is made fun of, as is the god Dionysius (two for the price of one!). Aristophanes shows a sissified Dionysius attempting to disguise himself as Herakles in order to go down to the Underworld.

The purpose of the journey is to bring back up to life a tragic poet, because after the deaths of Aeschylus, Sophocles, and Euripides, there is no decent original tragic theater being produced in Athens. The penultimate episode in the narrative is the *agon*[10]—the competition between Euripides and Aeschylus that mockingly imitates athletic competition—to determine who is greater and should thus be brought back to the world of the living.[11] The victory goes to Aeschylus, but not before both playwrights, and Euripides in particular, endure what for an astute Athenian audience would have been a solid ribbing.

One might say that Aristophanes's work combines several aspects of religion as it relates to sports. Theater is understood to be performed under the patronage of the gods—specifically Apollo and Dionysius—so within his play, in mocking Dionysius, the playwright is mocking the very patron of the play being performed. That mockery encompasses both gods and the ultimate athlete, Herakles, son of the ultimate Greek god, Zeus, as well as other playwrights who craft their dramas under divine patronage. This is certainly an oblique way of presenting a connection between religion and sports, but it may be seen as part of this subject as a broad issue. Like many broad issues, "religion and sports" offers somewhat kaleidoscopically shifting aspects that invite varied angles of approach as one follows it through history.

In fact, one might add yet another twist. The Athenians arrived to hegemony in the Hellenic world in large part because of their leadership in preventing the Achaemenid Persians from swallowing up that world—and made Athens the cultural center toward which tragic and comic poets alike turned to present their work. The symbolic moment for this was the Athenian-led victory against the Persians and their largely mercenary army on the plain of Marathon in 490 BCE. The news of that victory was carried to Athens by a figure who acquired iconic status (a kind of divinely ordained *kleos aphthiton*) for his act: Pheidippides, who ran the entire distance, without stopping, delivered his news and collapsed dead, in a manner reminiscent of Kleobis and Biton.[12]

Both that status and the consequent inclusion of a race that emulates the distance from Marathon to Athens within the Olympic games would take more than two millennia to crystallize, however. The event was included in the first modern Olympics, in 1896, but the distance of 26 miles, 385 yards, was not standardized until 1921. By then the god-connected aura associated with Pheidippides's moment had passed as the Olympian gods had long been replaced by other divine concepts, and religion, sports, war, and politics continued forward.

Notes

1. Epic and lyric poetry are distinguished from each other in several ways. The most obvious are that, whereas epic Greek poetry is chanted without instrumental accompaniment and follows a strict rhythmic pattern of dactylic hexameter—each line is comprised of six "feet" and each foot is either made of three syllabic beats providing a long-short-short or long-long pattern—lyric poetry is accompanied by a lyre (hence the name, "lyric"), and it offers a range of different metrical patterns.

2. There were occasional exceptions to this, most noteworthy among them the Roman Emperor Nero, who was naturally not denied the right to compete when he asked—i.e., demanded—to do so.

3. Some of Pindar's poems focusing on athletic victories may have been offered as a guest's gifts to generous hosts who had been the victors he praises in his verses.

4. This alludes to the tradition referred to above (66) that Herakles instituted the Olympian games in honor of his father, Zeus.

5. They were the offspring of Leda and Zeus in his guise as a swan—or more precisely: Castor was the son of Zeus, and his fraternal twin, Pollux, was the son of Leda's human husband. But the two arrived together into the heavens—at the request of Castor, when his mortal brother met his human fate—where they preside as the constellation Gemini.

6. There are those who have argued that it must have been written soon after the Hellenic victory over the Persians at Salamis. If this is so, then since the battle took place in 479 BCE, this ode would have been written well before the end of Pindar's writing career—in fact, nearer to its midpoint.

7. See Introduction, 7-8.

8. These are Plato and Xenophon.

9. I am referring to Sokrates's discussion of the "divine voice" that he often heard and that guided him—and which stopped speaking to him after he was condemned to die, thus making it clear to him that his divinely ordained "work" was complete and he was free to die. See *Apology* 31c-d.

10. This is the Greek term from which the English word "agony" is derived, referring to the struggle between two athletes (or in this case, two debaters) to gain victory over each other.

11. Sophocles is not part of the competition because he readily acknowledges Aeschylus as the superior playwright, but Euripides continues to insist that his plays are superior, hence the need for an on-the-spot competition.

12. See above, Introduction, 19-20. The account of the run from Marathon to Athens first appears in Plutarch's *Moralia* 347c, in the essay "On the Glory of

Athens" (1st century CE). Plutarch quotes from a lost work by Heraclides Pontikos, in which the runner's name was either Thersippos of Erchios or Eukles. The satirist Lucian of Samosata (ca 125-180 CE) also refers to the story but calls the runner Philippides, not Pheidippides. Not surprisingly, there is some debate about the historical accuracy of this legend. The Greek historian Herodotos, our main source for information on the Greek-Persian wars, mentions Pheidippides—but as the messenger who ran from Athens to Sparta seeking help against the Persians, and then ran back, a distance of over 150 miles each way. In some Herodotos manuscripts, the name of the runner between Athens and Sparta is also given as Philippides. Herodotos makes no mention of a messenger sent from Marathon to Athens, but tells how the main part of the Athenian army, exhausted after having fought and won at Marathon, marched quickly back from the battle to Athens in less than a day, fearing a naval raid on the undefended city by the Persian fleet.

CHAPTER FIVE
Gladiatorial Contests from the Pagan Era to the Early Christian Era

*T*he Olympic, Nemean, Pythian, and Isthmian games continued even as the Greek world was gradually being swallowed up by the Roman *Imperium*. Meanwhile, Rome itself was creating new forms of sports entertainment. It would seem that the relatively benign footraces and wrestling or boxing matches inherited from the Hellenic world got pushed to the background. Chariot races continued—entire teams of charioteers competed with each other, in an atmosphere that was often deadly competitive. And a new form of one-on-one combat—reminiscent of boxing and wrestling competitions but with weapons and an aura of death—began to step to the front of the historical stage: gladiatorial combat.

Such contests may have originated with the Etruscans, or with the Campanians (particularly the Samnites) and Lucanians.[1] Some have argued that the Campanians adapted some of the funeral games—with human sacrifices—of the Greeks that they picked up through commercial and cultural contacts in the eighth century BCE. Regardless, the earliest literary reference to gladiatorial games is found in the first-century BCE Roman writer, Livy (in his *de Urbe Condita* 9.40.17), who suggests that the Campanians reenacted their military victory over the Samnites[2] in games held around 310 BCE.

The first Roman gladiatorial competitions on record apparently took place in Rome itself somewhat later, in 264 BCE, at the outset of the First Punic War. Decimus Junius Brutus Albinus is said to have staged these games in honor of his dead father, Brutus Pera, in which case they were, in effect, funeral games that recalled those found earlier in the *Iliad* and later in the *Aeneid*. And, indeed, the games were treated as an elaborate ritual, termed a *munus*: a duty paid to a dead ancestor to keep his memory alive. We can thus discern a direct connection to religion and its rituals in this new type of competition.

The Brutus-sponsored games were actually a series of matches fought between pairs of slaves chosen from among some 22 prisoners of war. The matches were fought in the area of the cattle market (the *Forum Boarium*). Subsequently, they were followed by similar games, as other aristocratic figures took up the practice of sponsoring them—in lieu of the earlier custom of sacrificing prisoners at and on the graves of warriors (as Achilles was described as doing in the *Iliad*). That earlier custom had apparently been practiced not only at the time of or shortly after the death of some notable individual but over the years that followed, ranging in frequency from every year to every five years.

The popularity of the *new* custom—of games rather than sacrifices—spread during the last centuries of the Republic. They became particularly popular, interestingly enough, in Greece, most of which came under Roman rule by 146 BCE. There is a number of recorded instances of prominent Greeks who died while, in effect, exhorting their survivors-to-be to sponsor games in their memories. So, too, sponsors began to try to outdo one another. Thus, whereas Brutus Pera was commemorated by three competitions sponsored by his sons, 200 years later Julius Caesar promised 320 pairings following the death of his daughter, Julia.[3] Even considering who Julius Caesar was by that time, this obviously represents an enormous growth of interest and ambition. In fact, by then the entire production was being criticized because of its extravagance and the number of those who perished in the fights.[4]

In any case, by the time of Julius Caesar's own death by assassination in 44 BCE, the nature of such games had completely shifted: the athletic competitions presented after his demise were no longer associated, per se, with funerary rituals, but, because of the bad omens perceived by the Roman soothsayers in the aftermath of his murder, games were presented as a means of pleasing the gods and thus of saving the city from divine anger. So, their spiritual purpose intensified, if anything, even if the specifics of religious focus had changed.

Indeed, over time, as Rome could no longer be considered anything but an Empire,[5] a distinction came to be made between games as *munera* (plural of *munus*) offered by private citizens and *ludi*—games organized by public officials, be they senators (or out in the provinces, local governors) or the emperor himself.[6] Such public games were presented 10 or 12 days each year, often coinciding with the celebration of the Saturnalia, the feast associated with the dedication of the Temple to Saturn (Kronos; father of Jupiter/ Zeus).[7] Other kinds of entertainments directly honored the various gods, but not these competitions, so they did not take place as often.

So, too, formal and appropriate venues for both *munera* and *ludi*, but especially public *ludi*, began to be built with increasing, far-flung frequency. The earliest permanent structure for gladiatorial and other related entertainments in Rome itself had been shaped around 30 BCE, toward the outset of Augustus Caesar's rule.[8] Like those that shortly followed, the structure was of wood. The first stone structure was that built around 80-85 CE near the colossal statue of Nero as sun-god. That image, by way simply of its size, lent its name to the stone sports entertainment structure known as the Colosseum ("Temple of the Colossus").

This sort of an arena marked a new architectural and engineering concept introduced by Rome to the world. The Greeks carved theatres—the term comes from a Greek verb, *theao*, meaning "to look at"—out of the mountainside, so that the seating, in a half-moon configuration, faced out toward the stage and its backdrop. The Romans certainly emulated and continued that architectural tradition, but they also moved it in a new direction in order to accommodate the human and animal performances that provided for so many thousands of citizens day-long entertainments that were very different from those of Euripides and Aristophanes or their Roman equivalents. They took the semi-circle out of the hillside, stood it up on its own columns and arches, and doubled it, creating a fully circular—or oval-shaped—structure called an amphitheatre.

The term "amphitheatre" means "both theatre"—the "both" (*"amphi/ambi"*) referring to the fact that there are two theatre-shaped entities facing each other and fused together. It was in such amphitheatres—the Colosseum in Rome is the most famous of these—that combats between animals, between animals and men, and between men, variously armed, took place. And although sand was often scattered across the competition space, mostly to cover the blood between one contest and the next—the word "arena" derives from the Latin term, *harena*, meaning "sand"—those surfaces were rarely the smooth, beach-like areas with which we may be familiar from Hollywood representations.

The entire point of the disposition of the playing field was that it would resemble a natural landscape, with little hills and valleys, trees, bushes, perhaps even bodies of water.[9] On the one hand, such a topographical formula conformed to the overall Roman ethos of reshaping the physical reality of the world under their ordered and organized control.[10] On the other hand, it offered a good deal more drama to the spectator: competitors might not see each other or the animals that awaited them around the next bend, whereas the audience, seated above the fray, could see its elements developing.

The importance of the games is reflected in the finances devoted to them and to the shaping of such details. Aside from entertainment, one can argue that they fostered "Roman" values, most obviously strength/courage (*fortitudo*), training/discipline (*disciplina*), firmness (*constantia*), endurance (*patientia*), as well as love of glory (*amor laudis*), the desire to win (*cupido victoriae*), and above all, contempt of death (*contemptus mortis*). When all is said and done, this fundamentally warrior culture, which lived and died by the might of its sword, used the gladiatorial games as a surrogate means of teaching Romans what their armies learned in battle: *virtus*, for the fights in the amphitheatre effectively demonstrated soldierly values and illustrated military ideas by punishing cowardly gladiators and rewarding courageous ones.[11] Through witnessing the spectacle of men fighting to their deaths, it was presumed that the audience could drink in such values through surrogates.[12]

More to the point, the spectators, however lowly their station in everyday life, would become, for the duration of the athletic competition, godlike. From above, they looked down onto the action, able to anticipate its unfolding even as the competitors below could operate with only the instinct-response of the moment to attack or defend themselves against attack. Moreover, in the aftermath of a well-fought battle between two contestants, when one had wounded or otherwise clearly defeated the other, it could fall to the audience and not only or necessarily to the emperor (assuming that he was present) to determine whether the loser had fought well enough and bravely enough so that his life would be spared rather than forfeited. So the fans of diverse classes and kinds sitting throughout the amphitheatre culminated their godlike experience by ruling over life and death, as gods might.

However, there were apparently times when members of the audience might be taken out of the crowd and thrown into the arena as participants in its dangerous games. According to Suetonius, this happened during the reigns of the emperors Caligula (37-41 CE), Claudius (41-54 CE), and Domitian (81-96 CE); the Roman historiographer, Lucius Cassius Dio (155-235 CE) also describes this happening under Domitian.[13] One might say that a spectator could be like an immortal god at one moment and at the next, painfully and unequivocally returned to a condition of mortality.

Thus religion, the *invocation* of the gods, would be transformed in the gladiatorial context into the religious experience of *feeling* for a moment almost as gods must have felt. And even as the context had evolved from an emphatically god-directed one (funerary rituals) to a largely secular one, specific features still survived that recalled the earlier religious intentions of the competitions.

When a man went down, the amphitheatre resounded with cries of *habet, hoc habet!*—"He's had it!" (literally, "He has it!")—and with cries of *mitte!* ("Let him go!"; literally, "Send forth/away!") or *ugula!* ("Kill [him]!"). A mortally wounded fighter (in other words: already dying) was not killed before the arena audience but was carried from the site to be properly killed away from public view. One fallen, but not yet fatally, would lay down his weapon if he could, and raise his index finger (usually of the left—or in Latin, *sinister*—hand) to ask for mercy from his opponent, the judge, and/or the crowd. If the spectators approved that he be spared, because he had fought gallantly enough, they would signify that approval by turning their thumbs: *police verso*—"with the thumb turned." But the interesting thing is that we have no clear idea of whether *verso*—"turned"—means turned *up* or turned *down*, so in spite of the evolution of the English phrases "thumbs up" and "thumbs down" to signify approval and disapproval respectively, we cannot with any certainty say which direction the Romans were signifying.[14]

Should the audience rule in favor of death for the defeated athlete, a specific ritual mode of execution was followed—underscoring the original religious significance of the entire performance and the need that its elements conform to patterns that would be pleasing and not offensive to the gods. Thus, with one knee on the earth, the loser would grasp the thigh of the victor, who held the helmet or head of his opponent and then—depending upon the weapon that he was using—either plunged his sword into the latter's neck or slit his throat.

After the combat death of such a competitor, two figures dressed as Charon (who ferries the dead across the River Styx to the Underworld) and Mercury (messenger god among the Olympians, and the leader of souls—*psychopompos*—into Hades) would march out to the body of the deceased. "Charon" would strike his skull with a heavy mallet and "Mercury" would prod him with a hot poker disguised to look like the god's caduceus as final tests of his dead condition. (Perhaps the mallet blow rendered his death unequivocal). The body was then placed by bearers on the "couch of Libitina" and taken out of the amphitheatre through the funerary gate (the *Porta Libitina*).

However, during these competitions, contestants were already viewed as functionally dead—that is, they were not a part of real Roman society, since most of them were prisoners of war or criminals.[15] But one who fought well enough, either to win a number of times and receive his freedom or, despite losing, to have his life spared, might be seen to have *overcome* death both in the sense of not having his throat slit and in the sense of resuming his place in the community. Thus, the "religious" context of the games was twofold, involving both humans and gods and the living and the dead.

As for the nature of both the public competitions and the athletes, there was a range of types of both—all carefully organized by the *editor*: the planner of the games. The morning's entertainment included both contests between different kinds of animals and the *venationes*: animal hunts, (i.e., humans versus animals) for which the human specialists were called *venatores*. Broadly speaking, *bestiarii* were those who fought against wild beasts in whatever mode, whereas the *venatores* would be considered a subset group of these, specializing in *hunting* them.[16] One can imagine how the landscaping of the arena would have rendered these kinds of entertainments particularly, well, *entertaining*, as the spectators watched things develop that the competitors themselves could not see shaping up.

Tens of thousands of animals, from elephants and hippos to

lions and leopards were imported from all directions to be part of these *venationes*. The first giraffe to "participate" was brought in for the games sponsored by Julius Caesar in his daughter's honor. Eventually, the empire was virtually denuded of many of its *fauna* as a consequence of the taste for such entertainments.[17] The larger meaning of the *venationes* may be said to have been to offer a symbol of the empire's ability, and more broadly of the human ability, to assert order against the inherent chaos of nature. Perhaps, the excruciating volume of slaughter made that symbol all the more emphatic.

During lunchtime, lower-class criminals condemned (*damnati*) to death were executed—this was known as the *humiliores*—but it was considered in poor taste to be entertained by watching these, so typically the upper-crust citizens would take their lunch elsewhere. There were exceptions, of course: the Emperor Claudius was said to have enjoyed staying for this half-time show, for which he was criticized by many. But who could resist the excitement—as it was often played out—of these uniquely-styled executions? One criminal would take on the next until only one was left alive, and that surviving criminal would then be executed or sometimes pardoned.

Contrary to popular belief, early Christians were rarely, if ever, among the *damnati*. They *might* have been, possibly through most of the second, and certainly in the third and early fourth centuries. For during much of that time, Christianity, for reasons beyond this discussion, was considered politically subversive by the imperial authorities. The term for such subversion was *superstitio*; its converse, referring to a form of faith that was regarded as legal, was *religio licita*. Until the Emperor Constantine declared Christianity a *religio licita* with his edict of Milan in 313 CE, not only was that form of faith often at risk, it was subject to periods of active persecution, such as those under the Emperors Septimius Severus (193-211), Maximinus Thrax (235-8), Decius (249-51) and Diocletian (284-305). But there does not seem to be any evidence that citizens found guilty of being Christian, and therefore of being politically subversive, were killed among the *damnati* in the arenas of the empire: crucifixion was a more likely mode of executing them.

There is one noteworthy possible exception. One group of early Christians, the Donatists, may have actively and even eagerly sought death by martyrdom as a means and statement of emulating Jesus's self-sacrifice, of witnessing for their faith in a maximal manner.[18] So emphatically were they regarded by mainstream Christians as heretical that Constantine mounted a brief if unsuccessful persecutory attempt to eradicate them between 319 and 321. Long after Christianity had become the official *religio* of the Empire under Emperor Theodosius, (around the year 381), the scholar and Bishop of Hippo, North Africa, St. Augustine (354-428) was writing treatises—in the early fifth century—criticizing their heretical doctrines and trying to eliminate them.

The Donatists were mainly located in Augustine's backyard, where, in what is today Tunisia, there are well-preserved remains of a Roman amphitheatre in which we might imagine some of them being martyred—under Constantine or still later when the now-Christian state under Emperor Honorius sought to eliminate them in 409. Donatist literature revels in stories of torture and martyrdom. So, some of them *may* have ended up in the arena—most likely in some version of the *venatio* whereby they would have been pursued and destroyed by wild animals. But, by and large, Christians did not end up in the arena and this mythic tradition offers *no* meeting point between sports and religion.

It is possible that earlier, around 65 CE, under Nero—in the aftermath of the fires that swept through Rome in 64 and which, according to Tacitus, were probably set at Nero's instruction but for which he blamed the Christians—that Christians could have been victimized in the *venationes*. But the problem with that supposition is that—see below, 94—at that early date it would have been almost impossible for Nero or any other outsider to distinguish "Christians" from "Jews" within the Judaean community in Rome's Trastevere area. Tacitus wrote from the vantage point of 50 years later (ca 115 CE) and even he was not clear as to what and who "Christians" were, so we can hardly be certain that any of them were devoured in the arena. In any case, that particular arena—the Colosseum—did not yet exist in Rome during Nero's emperorship. It was not built until more than 15 years after the fire, and the wooden amphitheatre that preexisted the fire was destroyed by it, so how could Nero have executed Christians in it after the fire he allegedly accused them of starting?[19]

But—to return to the discussion of the order of events, when there *was* a functional site for them—after the lunchtime *damnati* execution performances, the culminating entertainments of the day would begin. A great procession (*pompa*) moved into and through the amphitheatre: the *editor* was followed by his entourage, which included the smiths, who did an almost ritual checking (*probatio armorum*) to attest to the solid condition of the various weapons. Perhaps, in the games in Rome itself, the emperor, or some honored guest whom he would designate, would perform this act in conjunction with the *editor*. The fighters would end their *pompa* before the imperial podium (or its representative equivalent) and declare *Ave, Imperator, morituri te salutant*! ("Hail, Emperor, those who are about to die salute you!") Or perhaps this only happened occasionally—or even only once, as Suetonius suggests in his narrative of the reign of the Emperor Claudius.[20]

Usually farcical, bloodless preliminary battles might be offered to warm the crowd up, duels between *paegniarii*, who fought with whips and wooden weaponry --clubs and shields. Then, at last, the main events took place. These involved war-like competitions—an average match involved between 10 and 13 pairs (*ordinarii*) of fighters, each bout lasting only 10 to 15 minutes—between individuals rarely armed the same way. Strictly speaking, "gladiators" were those who fought using a *gladius*—a short sword. Other terms referred to combatants armed in other ways. For instance, the aforementioned *paegniarii*. Or the *retarii*, who were typically armed with daggers, tridents, and nets with which to ensnare their opponents. *Thraeces* carried a scimitar (*sica*) and a small square shield (*parmula*), whereas *hoplomachi* carried a small round shield, a lance, and a short straight sword.[21]

Originally, there was a relationship between the type of equipment and the ethnicity of the fighter, since the competitors were prisoners of war and expected to fight with the equipment that was their normal battle gear. Thus the Samnites were a key Campanian tribe with whom the Romans fought (with whom they eventually conquered, of course) in the fourth and third centuries BCE and it was they who provided the model for the early gladiators in terms of weapons, as noted above.[22] Their equipment included not only the *gladius* but a large, oblong shield called a *scutum*, a wide leather belt (a *balteus*), and a fancy helmet (*galea*). Fighters so attired were originally called *Samniti*, before the terminology shifted to focus on the killing weapon in their arsenal of gear. Two other gladiatorial categories, the *Galli* and the just-mentioned *Thraeces* derived their names not from their weaponry but from the conquered ethnic groups well west and east of Italy of which they were part: the Gauls and the Thracians respectively.

Special note was apparently made of lefties, for Roman gravestone descriptions include more than a few references to the deceased having been a left-handed fighter. However, such fighters would still have comprised a clear and distinct minority, and their left-handedness would have been a rarity that would have made them popular with the viewing audience. It would also have given them an advantage with respect to right-handed fighters, since a lefty would have been trained to fight righties but righties would not have been trained to fight lefties. It is also noteworthy that the traditional prejudice against (and fear of) someone exhibiting the oddity of left-handedness—as noted previously, *sinister* is the Latin word for left—seems to have been abandoned in the face of the spectacle fascination occasioned by such fighters.

The very notion of sinisterity ("leftness") as offering either good or bad luck reminds us, too, that gladiators became such a centerpiece of Roman culture that superstitions regarding them abounded—particularly with regard to dying or dead gladiators. Thus, there developed a Roman custom for brides that, rather than the ponytails they had worn as girls, they should part their hair, ideally for the first time with a bent iron spear—particularly one taken from a mortally wounded gladiator. Such a spear was supposed to bring the bride good luck (and presumably enhanced her capacity to bear healthy male children, given the commonly held notion that gladiators were particularly virile). A more extreme superstition was the belief that the warm blood of a gladiator killed in the arena was able to cure epilepsy.[23]

Of course, gladiators themselves were notoriously superstitious. By "superstitious" I mean two things. First, that they worshipped diverse gods and goddesses—not surprisingly, since they came from diverse peoples and ethnic groups with their own religious traditions and affiliations—and that some of their forms of faith might on occasion be viewed as politically subversive by the Roman authorities.[24] They wore amulets inscribed and dedicated to diverse Egyptian, Eastern Mediterranean,[25] and Mesopotamian gods as well as to the Olympians—especially Mars, god of war—and made offerings of honey and wine and oil and meal to them, according to varied prescriptions.

Second, according to common parlance, the word "superstitious" applied to them because they believed in a range of good- and bad-luck talismans and customs that we might view as functionally useless. Myriad curse tablets and various amphitheatre-found inscriptions—prescribing both good and bad luck to this contestant or that—have turned up in the archaeological record. There are ample examples, too, of "magical papyri," which either prescribe or foretell disaster. We have the assertion of a former Sicilian astrologer and soothsayer, Firmicus Maternus, (speaking retrospectively, after he had converted to Christianity), that one could predict doom or success for gladiators before their bouts by reading the stars. So, too, the food that these athletes consumed prior to a competition was sometimes specialized and prescribed by sooth-sayers like Firmicus.

The interesting thing about such customs is that they have survived in one form or another in the athletic competitions of our own era. Thus, the year Gaylord Perry, at age 40, won 21 games and the Cy Young Award while pitching for the San Diego Padres (1978), when he arrived at a record of 20-2, an article about him appeared in the Cleveland *Plain Dealer*[26] in which reference was made to the particulars of a chicken dinner that he would eat the night before he pitched a game, a custom that started as he began winning. It became a ritual for him to eat the identical meal before every game in which he pitched, for good luck. Similarly, (forgive the turn to a personal reference), my best friend in high school would always wear a t-shirt with an inscription that included the letter "A"—this was the first letter of his first name—and he would touch it before every foul shot in our basketball games, for good luck.

There may have been women gladiators, although if so, they were a decidedly small population. An inscription from Pompeii asserts that its author, an *editor*, was the first to bring women in to compete in the arena. So, too, a 1996 archaeological discovery in the Southwark part of London turned up the remains of a woman who was apparently buried with a number of objects suggesting that she was a gladiator. The Emperor Septimius Severus (r. 193-211) is said to have allowed women to fight in the arena initially, but then banned the practice in the year 200.

A number of emperors were themselves said to have fought in the arena. The list includes Caligula, Titus, Hadrian, Lucius Verus, Caracalla, Geta, and Didius Julianus—all of whom may have fought once or often. In addition, another emperor, Commodus, seems to have been a devotee of the action; he is said to have participated often as a *secutor* who fought, as a left-hander, under the "stage-name" Hercules. In any case, he had marble-sculpted portraits made of himself in the guise of Hercules, complete with Nemean Lion skin and club.[27]

Although gladiators may have been well-muscled, they also seem to have been often overweight, cultivating layers of fat to help protect their vital organs from the slicing blows of their opponents. In order for the games to be maximally entertaining, fighters were paired obliquely with regard to their instruments. Thus, it would be less likely for two *gladiatores* to compete against each other than for a *gladiator* to face off against, say, a *retarius*. Different strategies and not only different weaponry would be matched against each other.

Since the majority of gladiatorial fighters was comprised of groups of foreign prisoners who had been captured in war, it is not surprising that, after the suppression of the five-year-long Judaean Revolt against Rome's political power, which culminated with the destruction of the Judaean Temple in Jerusalem in the year 70, there was a surge in the number of Judaean gladiators. We know this because gladiators seem to have been typically very proud of their ethnic origins, and included such designations on their gravestones.

On the other hand, at that time in the religious history of Judaeanism—its evolving bifurcation into what we can eventually recognize as Judaism and Christianity was still in process— it is impossible to know whether or not a given Judaean was an adherent to the growing cult of Jesus of Nazareth as the *christos* ("anointed one"). So, languages, (Hebrew, Aramaic, Greek, Latin, Persian, et al), specific vocabulary, and visual symbols were all still being shared across lines of increasingly divergent faith, at least until early in the second century. Thus, just as it is difficult to accept at face value the notion that "Christians" were fed to starving wild beasts in the arena under Nero, it is a challenge to ascertain whether the Judaean captives *cum* gladiators (and other kinds of arena athletes besides gladiators) under Nero's immediate successors were "Jews" as opposed to "Christians."[28]

Nonetheless, by the second century, the distinction between the two groups began to become clearer. So, too, we may also mark the slow shift in the fortunes of Christianity within the empire.

Thus, after a long stretch in which Christianity was often treated as a *superstitio*, culminating with the persecutions under Diocletian — and perhaps individuals found guilty of that "political subversion" were consigned to the gladiatorial ranks (but not to the ranks of the *damnati*) — the Church was accepted as a *religio licita* by Constantine in 313. And by the end of the fourth century, under Theodosius, it became the official religion of the empire.

Thereafter, as the Christian Church was on the ascendant, and the Roman Empire was on a long, slow descent, we may speak of the beginning of the end of antiquity and the advent of the medieval period. Where gladiatorial games are concerned, we might note that the Christian discomfort with their continuation had less to do with the cruelty that one might associate with them than with the notion that — in the symbolic world of the arena — the fighter could be saved not by recourse to divine intervention, but by his own *virtus*: his own manly virtue as an athlete-warrior. In other words, God was perceived to be insufficiently involved.[29]

Moreover, the assessment by the human audience, imperial and otherwise, seated (godlike) in the stands, that the athlete's skill was driven by and derived from his *virtus*, was also considered, in effect, sacrilegious. So the gladiatorial games with their particular associations with religion would go the way of paganism and the Roman Empire. And as Western history moved forward as *Christian* history, moving from antiquity into the Middle Ages, we must ask how the dialogue between sports and religion continues.[30]

Notes

1. These are names of several among the many Italic peoples ultimately incorporated into the *res romana* (the "Roman thing") about which we know less rather than more. The Samnites, for instance, consisted as a group, of four tribes, the Pentri, Carecini, Caudini, and Irpini; they later perhaps included others, such as the Frentani. But they came to occupy part of Campania (south and west of their "homeland" territory) by perhaps the late sixth century BCE, so they might also be referred to as Campanians by the era of Roman domination of the peninsula. And you thought Roman history was simple!

2. Given the previous footnote, Livy was confused. If anything, he should have been referring to the victories of the Samnites against the Romans in 321 and/or 316 BCE! The Samnites were the last group in Italy to hold out against the Romans in the Social War (91-88 BCE) and they were still a sufficient threat thereafter, so that the Roman leader Sulla instituted a significant slaughter of them and a dispersion of the survivors in 82 BCE.

3. The time of her death (46 BCE) coincided nicely with the aftermath of his victories in both Gaul and Egypt, so the extravagance of those games no doubt also celebrated himself. He may also have offered a more limited panoply of games two decades earlier, in 65 BCE, to honor his father who died that year.

4. See Dio XLIII.24

5. As opposed to the long-held self-deluding Roman fiction that the state was still a republic—a *res publica*; "people's thing."

6. Although, to repeat, we must recall that it persisted in considering itself a republic, and retained key formal aspects of republican government—most obviously, a senate, in which institution the emperor was theoretically and officially regarded as no more than *primus inter pares* ("first among equals"), however much the actual emphasis was on *"primus"*—until the collapse of the Western Empire in 476 CE.

7. The festival originally lasted a day, but due, no doubt, to its enormous popularity—with its Mardi Gras atmosphere and custom of reversing social roles, masters acting as slaves and slaves as masters, for instance—it eventually lasted a week by the time of the late Republic.

8. To be more precise: Octavian was the nephew and adopted son of Julius Caesar, who soon after Caesar's death formed a triumvirate with Marc Antony and Crassus; with Crassus's death in 36 BCE the partnership was down to two. Octavian—who by then was calling himself Caesar in order to remind people of his connection to his popular, dead uncle—defeated Antony (and Antony's girlfriend, Cleopatra) at the Battle of Actium in 31 BCE. (The battle was really won by Octavian's best friend, Agrippa). Four years later, in 27 BCE, the senate voted Octavian into his first of 41 consulships and decreed that he be honored with the epithet "Augustus" ("great one"). Thereafter he is known as Augustus Caesar—who would claim to have saved the Republic as he drove the last nails into its coffin.

9. There has been considerable discussion over the last few centuries as to whether or not the arena within the Colosseum itself was ever filled with water in order to allow small-scale sea-battles: *naumachia*. It probably did not, but that discussion falls beyond our scope.

10. Thus, for example, Roman wall painting "eliminates" the walls of interiors, and Roman aqueduct systems bring water over distances across a carefully calibrated and subtly tilted channel elevated on extended arcades or sometimes burrowing through the earth in defiance of the ups and downs and irregularities of the natural landscape

11. *Virtus*, from which we directly derive "virtue" in English, translates Greek *arête*. Interestingly, the Greek term which originally meant a kind of "knack" or "skill" began to acquire an ethical nuance only with Socrates. By contrast, *virtus* is built on the Latin word *"vir,"* meaning "man," Thus *virtus* is "manliness" and manliness is what soldiers in particular, and all Roman (males) in general are expected to exhibit, along with *pietas*.

12. Appropriately enough, this recalls—albeit in a different way, at a different "level," what Aristotle refers to in his *Poetics* as the value of tragic theatre. In seeing a hero/king who, at the outset, seems to have it all—think of Agamemnon or Oedipus, for example—but is brought down by the end of the play, the audience experiences *katharsis* ("purification") of the negative feelings toward its own rulers with which it may have entered the theatre that day. *Katharsis* is achieved because the audience experiences the events that are on stage as a kind of surrogate process.

13. See Suetonius, *The Lives of the Caesars* X, XXIV, XXV; and Dio LIX.10.

14. *Pollux infestus*, meaning "thumb up" was typically used as an insult in Rome—analogous to how in the United States of today one might visually insult someone by pointing one's middle finger up—so it does not seem likely that such a gesture would be used to approve clemency. Juvenal's third *Satire* (34-7) suggests that thumb down signified that the loser was to be spared and thumb up that he should be killed. There is a logic to that supposition, since thumb down could signify "lower your weapon" and thumb up—gesturing toward the throat—could signify both that he be killed and where the coup de grace should be administered. Or perhaps the phrase *police compresso* ("with the thumb pressed in"), which may have referred to raising the fist with the thumb pressed inside it, could have signified clemency whereas the thumb held out and waved in any direction, either up *or* down, might have meant "kill him." There is, in fact, an extant relief carving of a gladiator being spared in which the hand signal depicted represents the thumb laid flat and tightly along the hand—with two fingers extended and two closed.

15. Even to the extent that free citizens chose to become gladiators, as some did, they did so at the price of their position in society as free citizens; the contracts to which they agreed, in effect, reduced them to slaves and/or noncitizen status. Apparently, the swashbuckling, untethered image (or actual life) of the gladiator made it romantically attractive to some.

16. The *venatio* could actually be the reverse of this: hungry wild animals pursuing unarmed humans, the "entertainment factor" being how the humans tried to escape, failed to do so, and were torn apart and devoured.

17. Cicero complains that the Roman enthusiasm for *venationes* is so intense, and consequently the volume of capture and slaughter of animals from Africa so outsized, that the entire African continent is in danger of becoming completely empty of animals. For instance, in his last letter to M. Caelius Rufus of Rome (26 November 51 BCE), sent from Pindenissus, where Cicero had been serving as governor, he responds to repeated requests that he supply panthers for the games by noting there is by now "an extraordinary scarcity of [panthers], and it is said that those panthers that are here complain bitterly that they are the only living creatures in my province against whom any harm is mediated."

18. *Martyros* is the Greek word for "witness."

19. Tacitus might well have been confused by the fact that in that same year, 65 CE, the revolt against Roman power in Judaea broke out; perhaps he conflated the suppression of the Judaean (Jewish) Revolt with the persecution of Judaeans (Christians) who resided within the Judaean (Jewish) community in Rome. Given that the term *iudaeus* in Latin (and *ioudaios* in Greek, *yehoodee* in Hebrew and *yehoodae* in Aramaic) may be rendered as either "Jew/ish" or "Judaean," and given that the early "Jews" and "Christians" were all Judaeans, both ancient pagan writers like Tacitus and modern readers and translators of Tacitus might easily be confused as to who exactly was who at that time.

20. See Suetonius: *The Lives of the Caesars*, Claudius, XXI:1214.

21. There were also *equites*, who entered the arena on horseback; *essedarii*, who fought from war chariots (no doubt introduced by Julius Caesar after he conquered Briton, since the British Celts characteristically fought from chariots); *laquearii*, who used a lance and a rope as a kind of lasso to ensnare their opponents; and *dimachaeri*, who fought using two swords. The range of entertainment modes expanded over time to include groups that fought from a distance, like *velites*, who hurled small spears; and *sagittarii*, who used bows and arrows; and even *andabatae*, who fought effectively blind, since their helmets acted as virtual blindfolds.

22. See 81 and fn 1,2.

23. See Pliny, *Natural History*, Book XXVIII.II.4 for a discussion of this last-named belief.

24. See above, 88-9, and below, 95, 104: Christianity was the most likely faith to be considered politically subversive, at least until the year 313.

25. This included the Judaean God, as we shall see below. 94-5.

26. He had been a Cleveland Indian for several years, winning over 20 games (and the Cy Young Award) in 1972 and again in 1974. Hence, the interest on the part of a Cleveland paper and its readership.

27. Commodus was, of course—glad you asked—portrayed by Joaquin Phoenix in the 2000 movie, *Gladiator*.

28. More to the point, the Latin term *iudaeus* and its equivalent in those other languages in widespread use from Rome to Mesopotamia can be translated into English either as "Jew/Jewish" or as "Judaean," making it virtually impossible for us to determine the precise faith of the individual so-labeled until at least the late first century CE—as previously noted in fn 19. And since, for example, a symbol such as the cross did not become distinctively and unequivocally Christian for another several centuries, the visual images that accompanied the term more often than not do not help us with the distinction.

29. Obviously, too, athletes who still invoked pagan gods were deemed to be not religious but *superstitious*, since they were invoking "false" gods.

30. For excellent, more detailed discussions of the gladiatorial games, see Ludwig. Friedlaender, *Roman Life and Manners*, Vol 2 (New York: Arno Press, 1979); Michael Grant, *Gladiators* (London: Weidenfeld & Nicholson, 1976); and, above all, Keith Hopkins, *Death and Renewal: Studies in Roman History*, Vol 2 (Cambridge: Cambridge University Press, 1983).

CHAPTER SIX
Sports and War in Medieval Christendom: From Jousting to Crusading for God

*T*oward the beginning of this narrative the issue arose as to how sports competitions can—and did—serve as both a surrogate and a mode of training for military action for the ancient Greeks. We might then ask where, within the world of medieval Christendom and its neighbors, the line was drawn between these two activities? We might get a sense of how some in that world thought about this issue by first jumping forward— into the sixteenth century—and examining some passages from Niccolo Machiavelli's *The Prince*. In turning to a work of literature, we would also be consistent with our approach in discussing the Greek world.

The so-named discourse was written sometime shortly after the author's political exile from Florence in 1512, and intended to be read by the Medici prince, Lorenzo II. Machiavelli hoped that his guide for how to be a most effective leader would be received warmly and lead to his being recalled into the service of Lorenzo and the city he so loved, although it is doubtful that the ruler read the work before his death in 1519. *The Prince* was circulated only in manuscript form at first, and was not published until 1537—five years after Machiavelli's own death. A measure of its subsequent importance to Renaissance thinking can be found in the fact that, within 25 years of its publication, it went through 25 editions.

The prince who was most admired by Machiavelli, Cesare Borgia, was, to put it simply, not admired by the mid-sixteenth-century papacy, which saw him as a far from appropriate figure to offer as a model for the ideal prince.[1] As a consequence, Machiavelli's work was placed on the Vatican's list of "prohibited books" in 1559 and the Inquisitional authorities in fact decreed that *all* of Machiavelli's works be destroyed. So, in Italy itself the influence of *The Prince* would dissipate by default in the last third of the sixteenth century. Moreover, in 1576 a powerful refutation of the arguments in the book was written by a French Huguenot (i.e., a Protestant) that was widely circulated—and subsequently translated and also circulated in English.

Of course, the result of this later work was to spread the interest in, and potential influence on the part of the text it refuted! And, in fact, Elizabethan dramatists refer with considerable frequency to Machiavelli in a manner that suggests that "everyone knows who he is"—that his name had become an iconic byword for them. There were apparently translations of *Il Principe* into English as well as three published translations into French and even one into Latin.

My point in raising the subject of the widespread presence of *The Prince* across parts of Western Europe is to suggest that the awareness of Machiavelli's equation between sports and warfare may be understood to have been fairly widespread. And what exactly *is* that equation? We find it in chapter 14, "The Duties of a Prince with Regard to the Militia." There Machiavelli brings to a culmination his discussion of the various areas in which a successful prince must be accomplished, and observes that "a prince should... have no other aim or thought, nor take up any other thing for his study but war and its organization and discipline, for that is the only art that is necessary to one who commands..."

He then goes on to assert that "in peace he ought to practice it more than in war, which he can do in two ways: by action and by study. As to action, he must, besides keeping his men well-disciplined and exercised, engage continually in hunting, and thus accustom his body to hardships..." We can easily recognize the direct relationship that the author finds between the sport of hunting and success as a warrior. (We will later encounter a similar relational equation for Muslim thought). We must presume that the view of this relationship was at least as widespread as the copies of Machiavelli's book.

Of course, Machiavelli's discussion is not at all dependent on the presence or participation of God. His militarily successful prince will not only stay in good shape, but he will know the lay of the land where he might someday have to fight or, from observations of one territory, prepare his eyes and mind for similar and dissimilar landscapes in other territories. And he will reinforce both of these qualities by exercising his mind, reading "history and study[ing] the actions of eminent men, see[ing] how they acted in warfare, examin[ing] the causes of their victories and defeats in order to imitate the former and avoid the latter..." —none of which is dependent on or even related to God.

But one can surely suppose that the use of sports as preparation for skill in warfare within the realm of Christendom predated Machiavelli; here, as elsewhere in his work, he is drawing on history and its events. If we follow warfare in and by Christendom back through the millennium that preceded Machiavelli's time, then we move through the period of the medieval Crusades to the Holy Land, and further back to the time, during the Carolingian Frankish period and its successor Ottonian Saxon era, when Christianity was spreading throughout pagan Europe.

The Church's gradually triumph over the Roman world did not come without its traumas. To begin with, barely was it accepted by Rome as a *religio licita* through Constantine's edict of 313 CE, then the question of what, precisely, constitutes *proper* Christianity arose. By 325 a Council of Bishops was convened at Nicaea, over which the Emperor presided, at which that question was addressed, most importantly with regard to how God is to be understood. In brief, the Trinitarian view championed by Athanasius—that understands God to be triune, in which Father, Son, and Holy Spirit are both coequal and co-substantial elements of God's paradoxically indivisible Being—was deemed by that august council to be theologically correct. The view espoused by Arius—that saw the Father as separate from and superior to the Son and Holy Spirit (for, Arius reasoned, the Father is eternal and unchanging, whereas the Son is born, grows up and dies, thus both changing and exhibiting non-eternal attributes)—was pronounced heretical.

But the Arian heresy did not simply disappear or die out; it persisted and was indeed joined by other heresies over the next millennium or so. Meanwhile, from having been accepted as a *religio licita*, Christianity rose to become the only acceptable form of faith—*the religio* of the empire—by about 381 CE, under Emperor Theodosius, as we have previously noted. Other forms of faith—Judaism and Zoroastrianism, for example, to say nothing of the various forms of paganism that had long histories in the Near East and East Mediterranean—all came to be regarded, in effect, as *superstitiones*.

By the time the Western Empire collapsed in 476 CE, the sort of leadership role that the emperor had once played was taken over by the bishop of Rome who, in his capacity as the father-guide of the increasingly far-flung Church, was referred to as *papa*—Latin for "father," and eventually rendered in English as "Pope." It was Pope Gregory ("The Great") who, at the end of the sixth century, came out of the walls of Rome to stare down the Lombard chieftain Ariulf of Spoleto, who was planning to sack the city. It was Gregory who worked out a *modus vivendi* with the surviving Roman government in Byzantium-Constantinople. It was he who used his personal wealth to feed the poor in the still-large city. He also wrote at length, hagiography, liturgy, and words against the heretics whose beliefs still plagued the Church.

But heresy, one might say, would shrink as a spiritual issue in comparison with the force that emerged in the following century, and moved into direct contact and conflict with Christianity from one end of the Mediterranean to the other between the mid-seventh and early eighth centuries: Islam. The relationship between Christendom and the *Dar al-Islam* would be varied over the centuries that followed. Later tradition might retrofit onto the late eighth/early ninth-century career of Charlemagne a series of vicious confrontations with Muslim chieftains across the Pyrenees in Spain. Although Charlemagne was both a champion of the Church and a promoter of writing and the arts to assist the Church narrative in its forward progress, he was also a man of broad spiritual interest and acceptance. He established warm diplomatic relations with the Muslim Abbasid Caliph in Baghdad, Haroun al-Rashid, through an ambassadorial trio that travelled all the way from Aachen—and that included, possibly as its leader, Isaac the Jew, the only one of the three diplomats, as it turns out, to survive the rigors of the journey.

Having been converted by the Franks, the Ottonian Saxons, who, in turn, dominated Western Europe in the tenth century, were intensely focused on converting others by the sword. And they were really only echoing the mood of the first decades of Charlemagne's own rule during which the Saxons had been force-converted. As noted in the previous paragraph, Charlemagne arguably became more tolerant only after he had achieved success at widening and securing his empire. Thus, one of the important historiographers of the early part of that era, Eigil, in his "Life of Sturmi, Abbot of Fulda,"[2] wrote of how "[w]hen the Lord King Charles [Charlemagne] had happily reigned for four years the Saxon people were still savage and most hostile in any way and wholly given over to heathen practices. So he brought together a great army to cause this people to take upon them the mild and gentle yoke of Christ."

This sort of text is typical, presenting slaughter as a primary method of enforcing the embrace of the God of love. The culmination of this modus operandi would arrive with a yet more hostile relationship with the Muslim world that would emerge by the end of the eleventh century—in part, no doubt, thanks to the great schism that split the Church into eastern and western branches in 1054, and the severe challenge to papal authority mounted by the young German Emperor, Henry IV, in 1075-77. Moreover, the Byzantine army had been emphatically defeated by the Seljuks, who had recently embraced Islam, in 1071, at the Battle of Manzikert. In this atmosphere of religious uncertainty, Pope Urban II declared the first Crusade to retake the Holy Land from the infidel Muslims in 1095.

In fact, in the period between the First Crusade at the end of the eleventh century and the seventh (or by some counts, the eighth or even ninth) and last "official" Crusade led by French King Louis IX (Saint Louis) in 1270, we move through a series of centuries in which Christians fight wars against the *Dar al-Islam* in God's loving yet emphatically and paradoxically violence-approving name—not only in the Middle East and East Mediterranean but in Spain and Sicily (in which case, one must really continue the Crusade timeline at least to the end of the fifteenth century).

Indeed, until Pope Urban II's sermon calling for a cross-bearing war—hence the term "crusade," from the Latin, *crux*, meaning "cross"—to free Christian sites in the Holy Land from the Muslims, the Christian knight's service to the Faith remained largely an abstraction. But the enthusiasm with which the Pope's words were received set in motion no fewer than seven—or eight or nine, depending upon how one views them—major campaigns over the next nearly 200 years, that extended not only into the Holy Land itself, but into parts of North Africa (specifically, what is today Tunisia, where the pious King Louis IX died) and Asia Minor (today's Turkey) with a goal of suppressing the misguided, misbelieving enemies of Christendom.

Knights pledging themselves to serve and obey the Church often formed distinct groups of soldier-monks, such as the Templar Knights. One of the great ironies of the extended crusader narrative is the savage ferocity with which these men fought, claiming that it was in the name of the God. The notion of a chivalric code, or even a code of conduct in war wherein one respects one's enemies, played very little role in the behavior of many of them as warriors.

In one instance, they used human heads as ammunition in their catapults in the siege of Nicaea (western Turkey) in 1097. Godfrey of Bouillon and the other leaders of the first Crusade wrote to the Pope with great relish regarding how the blood of Muslims and Jews flowed along the streets of Jerusalem in 1099: "...in the portico of Solomon's Temple, our men rode in the blood of the Saracens up to the knees of their horses." After Jerusalem fell, the dead bodies were so numerous that the funeral pyres were "as big as houses."

The wars fought in God's name, for which diverse sporting events were part of a training program, extended to the opposite side of the Mediterranean, as well. In Spain, since the arrival of the Muslim Arabs and Berbers under Tariq and Musa al-Nasir, between 711 and 718, Christian ideologues and warriors were variously engaged in trying to drive them back out. The nearly eight centuries of that effort are commonly referred to from a Eurocentric perspective as the *reconquista*—"reconquest." That extended enterprise yielded, aside from an array of battles, stunning works of literature, musical and visual art that reflect not only spiritual fervor but the reality of centuries of positive cultural interaction among the Christians, Muslims, and Jews of Spain.

Among the most important literary works is the anonymous *Chanson de Roland*, the first major poem within emerging French literature.[3] In that poem, Roland, the beloved nephew of Charlemagne, leads a desperate and furious defense of the rear guard of Charlemagne's army on its return through the Pyrenees from northeastern Spain into France. By Roland's side, helping to lead the fight against the Muslim ambush is the warrior-bishop, Turpin: the tangible symbol of the legitimacy of synthesizing spiritual with military goals. Bishop Turpin is the personification of God's word assuming the form of action.

Somewhat analogously, the appearance of the apostle *Santia-*

go el Mayor—Saint James the Greater—on a great white steed at the Battle of Clavijo in 844, scattering the enemy infidel forces that had been on the verge of victory over their Christian foes, was understood as a clear demonstration of God's distinctive role in influencing the outcome of battles in favor of God's preferred devotees. Saint James became the patron saint of Spain, who is otherwise known not as a warrior—*matamoro*, "moor-slayer"—but as a pilgrim to his own shrine at Santiago de Compostela in the northwest corner of Spain.

Roland will also play a role in later literary representations of military action in the ongoing Christian-Muslim conflict. Thus, Ludovico Ariosto penned a renowned poem in the early sixteenth century, called *Orlando Furioso*, in which, against the background of the same *reconquista* conflict of which Charlemagne is the key figure, the hero ("Orlando" is the Italian version of the name, "Roland") is driven mad through unrequited love for a pagan (read: Muslim) princess. Ariosto's fantastical and very long poem was written during the period after the completion of the *reconquista*, when the Ottoman Turks under Suleiman the Magnificent were otherwise advancing into Europe.[4] They would arrive as far as the gates of Vienna in 1527—the same year in which the Spanish sacked the Vatican in Rome during the third of four intra-Catholic, French-Spanish wars fought during the early sixteenth century.

The elements of history reviewed here offer a particular focus on the relationship between war and art—literary art, in this case—but ultimately we want to distinguish how this all, in turn, ties in to sports and its own relationship to religion. We do so by returning to the historical matter of a knight—any knight—such as Roland/Orlando. In theory, at least, by the time of Charlemagne and, later, the time of the Crusades, the overall program of training a knight encompassed his physical skills with various weapons and instruments. It included a moral commitment to a chivalric code that obligated him to serve not only his feudal lord and also an idealized lady—not his wife but someone else who was difficult if not impossible to obtain—but the Christian faith and its God.

Indeed, the ceremony of ordination as a knight was a solemn affair that emphasized the spiritual side of the knight's development. He pledged his life to the Faith and to the upholding of Christian moral precepts. Illuminated manuscripts that depict such ceremonies offer the knight with his arms and face upraised toward the heavens in a manner that anticipates modern athletes displaying similar heavenward gestures. (See below, chapter 13, 243-44).

But in order to achieve victory in combat, more than spiritual discipline was required—a good deal of physical training was necessary, too. The would-be knight (usually, the son of a knight) would spend about half his life studying and developing his skills in the art of war. At age seven, he was sent off to serve as a page in the castle of a greater knight, and by age 14, he was attached as a squire to another knight. Already as pages, young would-be knights practiced and sought to hone their skills by engaging each other with toy swords and shields, then graduating to real lances, swords, and battle-axes in an exercise called a "quintain."[5] The term refers not only to the training exercise but to the space where the exercise takes place, and also, sometimes, to the central element of the target toward which the young warrior directed his energies.[6]

For the target was usually a post—also called a "pell" (from the Latin word, *palum*, meaning "[pointed] post/stake"). The post—also, to repeat, often confusingly referred to as the *quintain*—was typically mounted with a shield or board. The pole, "attired" in armor—sometimes even to the point of offering a life-sized dummy, would provide an aspiring knight with a somewhat realistic object against which to practice his sword strokes and shield strikes either on foot or on horseback.

As a squire, he would also focus much of his effort during his late teenaged years on caring for his master's horse and weapons. At age 21, he would be ordained as a knight. By that time, he would be presumed capable of tending to his own horse and armor thanks to his experience as a squire; in addition, he was deemed ready to take the field, whether in friendly competition or war, due to his training as a page and as a squire.

Even in peacetime—as Machiavelli would prescribe, centuries later—a knight would remain in constant training, by way most obviously of spectacular tournaments. In the earlier stages of developing the idea of such knightly contests, a bloody free-for-all between two groups of knights would take place. In the beginning, the number of those engaged sometimes mounted into the thousands—an entire mock battle. Subsequently, the tournaments turned toward more "civilized" confrontations in which individuals would joust. By the beginning of the First Crusade, couched lances were part of a new war and sport technology: the bearer could strike at his opponent from a distance of about five feet, rather than being limited to the hand-to-hand close-up combat that knives and swords entailed.

But such an unwieldy weapon required a good deal of practice to be able to be used effectively. Hence, the peacetime contests—not only to *remain* in battle shape, but to get *into* shape in the first place. In a joust, the two knights charged each other, their blunted but still dangerous lances extended so as to meet at a headlong gallup (they placed caps called "coronels" on the lance ends to limit the impact of a direct hit). As the formalities of jousting evolved, a system of points was used to determine winners, on a sliding scale. Thus, a man who knocked his opponent off his horse was awarded the most points; one who broke his lance against his foe or landed a blow to his foe's helmet but failed to knock him from his mount received fewer points. So, too, as jousting continued to develop, so did the nature of the protective armor that the knights wore.

Ultimately, the victor would extract that armor and a "ransom" from his defeated opponent, so that a successful competitor, going from tournament to tournament, could amass a considerable fortune. An entire series of these one-on-one contests would shape a tournament. So, too, a knight who was successful at tournaments might attract the eye of a wealthy nobleman who might bid for his services on the battlefield.

By the middle of the era of the Crusades, Christian Europe was becoming increasingly *internally* secure, wealthy knights were evolving from roving sportsmen-warriors toward being a more settled nobility, and while jousting continued, other sports-like pastimes came into increasing popularity, such as hunting—particularly with falcons—and the more cerebral game of chess, which had been learned by Europeans from Muslims even earlier than the time of the Crusades and imported from the Middle East.

And meanwhile, the jousts evolved as more pageant than blood-rite, with large audiences and detailed codes of conduct. Jousts were sometimes used in judicial contexts. That is, disputes would be settled by a contest in which the outcome was believed to be effected by God: the victor, with God on his side, prevailed, and the dispute was settled in his favor. Thus, this kind of direct correlation between success in sports and divine involvement and favor echoed the relationship between success in war and divine favor.

Jousting combats also became entertainments used to help celebrate diverse religious and quasi-religious occasions such as births, baptisms, and marriages. Perhaps the most famous of these was one that ended, in the summer of 1559, in disaster. French King Henry II, as part of the celebrations for two impending marriages—of his sister, Marguerite, to the Duke of Savoy; and of his daughter Elizabeth to the Spanish king Philip II—was jousting against the Comte de Montgomery. The Comte's lance pierced Henry's helmet and shattered. Fragments entered the king's right eye and temple, and, although attended by the most eminent physicians in Europe at the time, he died 11 days later.[7]

By the beginning of the Thirty Years' War, in 1618—an internal Christian affair in which there was virtually no Muslim involvement—tournaments and jousts had begun to fade as a popular source of sports entertainment, no doubt because the perceived need for such events as training grounds for successful warfare had begun to dissipate. Rather than being due to a sense of a diminished Muslim threat to Europe (the Ottomans would besiege Vienna for the second and last time as late as 1683), this shift was more likely the result of the development of new technology for foot soldiers, which undercut the advantage that the horse-mounted warrior had long enjoyed. So, too, the nobility seems to have turned its back on a form of entertainment that they now regarded as too barbaric and, therefore, beneath them.

Then again, of course, fighting with a lance, and training with it, was by no means the only sport and the only mode of making war within medieval Christendom. Indeed, while skill in such fighting, and its accompanying aspects—fighting with heavy swords, with daggers, and battle-axes—were associated with the upper classes, the peasantry that fought on foot were, in some instances, also formally trained in sports in order to serve their masters on the battlefield. Thus archery, for instance, was recognized as sufficiently important in England, that in 1252 a law was passed requiring all males between the ages of 15 and 60 to equip themselves with some form of bow and arrows and to appear for practice training at the Butts, as the practice field for archery was then called.

The consequences of such a law would be singularly felt nearly a century later when, at the Battle of Crecy in 1346, some 2,000 enemy Frenchmen perished through the power and skill of English longbows. In that same battle—in which the English were outnumbered by three to six times the number of Frenchmen (depending upon the source one reads)—a mere 50 Englishmen are said to have died. If the victorious English King Edward III perhaps believed that God had been on his side, he surely understood that the technology of the longbow had given him a singular advantage in securing his stunning victory.

That battle also offered a turning point in history. Not only were horse-mounted French noblemen cut down by English (actually, mostly Welsh) foot soldiers, but, mired in mud, the wounded were slaughtered rather than taken prisoner, thus contradicting and in effect ending the prevailing chivalric code, according to the God-given dictates of which the wounded nobility were never willfully killed. We might presume that God was assumed to have abandoned the battlefield after the success of the English archers, leaving the disposition of the defeated to human victors and their mode of operation.

By that time, the ongoing military conflicts in God's name between Christendom and the *Dar al-Islam* in the Eastern Mediterranean were entering what we might call their penultimate phase. About a century after the English victory at Crecy, Byzantine Constantinople fell to the Muslim Ottoman Turks in 1453. From that epochal event until World War I, Christian efforts became defensive. They were directed either toward preventing *further* Muslim incursions into southern and eastern Europe or to pushing *back* the already-arrived Ottoman Muslims.

On the other hand, horse-racing—aside from that with a specific war-directed rationale for which the Battle of Crecy marks a distinct end point—may also be seen to have a specifically religious, Christian context in some parts of Europe during these same centuries. Certainly, the most renowned of these is the *Palio di Siena*—a horse-racing competition for a banner (*palio*) of painted silk that has been taking place in Siena, Italy, since the fourteenth—some would assert, the eleventh—century.

At that time,[8] the 17 *contrade* (city wards, but which function essentially as parishes, centered around one church in particular within the ward in which births, baptisms, confirmations, weddings, and funerals are celebrated) of Siena organized public races across the city. Meanwhile other sorts of sports competitions, ranging from many-sided, team-boxing matches (*pugna*) to jousting to bullfights, took place in the grand, ovoid main piazza, the *Piazza del Campo*, at the center of town.

But when the Grand Duke of Tuscany outlawed bullfighting in his domains, in 1590, (about halfway between the disastrous joust that claimed Henri II's life and the beginning of the Thirty Years'

War), the *contrade* began to organize their horse races in the *Piazza del Campo*. These were first conducted on buffalo-back and then on donkey-back, until the event evolved by about 1650 into the horse racing that continues to this day. Each parish is symbolized by its own totem—an eagle, a caterpillar, a snail, an owl, a panther, the forest, a tortoise, and so on. In each race, only 10 of the 17 *contrade* may participate, presumably due to space considerations. The seven that do not participate in a given race are automatically included in the next one, and the remaining three places are selected by lot from the remaining ten parishes.

Initially, one race was held per year, on July 2, marking both the Feast of the Visitation (the meeting described in Luke 1:39-56 between the Virgin Mary and what some have taken to be her cousin, Saint Elizabeth, in which their respective pregnancies with Jesus and John the Baptist were announced to each other). This also turns out to be the date of a local festival that honors the Madonna of Provenanzo (referring to a painting that once belonged to a Sienese leader, Provenanzo Salvani, which was believed to have miraculous curative powers). Eventually, a second annual race was added, on August 16, the day after the Feast of the Assumption, marking the bearing of the Virgin's soul (and body, as understood in most Catholic circles) up to heaven in the arms of her Son, according to a centuries-long interpretation of John 14:3.

Whatever the beginning point of the competitions—it is not inconceivable that they ultimately connect back to the chariot competitions held throughout the Roman empire in elongated stadia (hippodromes) very different from the sort of spaces in which gladiatorial and similar games took place—by the time they had emerged as public races in towns like Siena there was a consistent relationship between the double event and the calendar of Christian religious celebrations. For starters, the very date(s) of the running of the *Palio di Siena* reflect(s) a sense of connection between the competition and the concerns of religion. For both of these events are markers in the life and death cycle of the Virgin Mary, to whose honor the two races are dedicated — the point and purpose of which may be ultimately construed as the desire for the protection of the Mother of Christ for the city overall.

But the relationship between sport and divine patronage extended (and continues to extend) to encompass more specific details regarding how the race is run. Thus, the devout inhabitants of every *contrada* invoke the sacred aid of its patron saint toward both the horse that will run and the jockey who will ride. That prayerful process begins, in fact, a good four months before the race is run, continuing up to the day of the race. On that morning, the horse — one chosen for each competing *contrada* by lot from among a series of presumably equally strong and fast steeds — is brought into the main church of the parish and led, by its rider, up to the altar to be blessed by the priest. And should it happen to defecate while standing on such hallowed ground, that act is considered good luck, a superb harbinger of divinely aided success in the race to follow.

The 90-second race is preceded by a splendid pageant in which the *palio* and emblems associated with the Virgin Mary are paraded around the *Piazza del Campo*. After the race, the winner and his *contrada* supporters march to the exquisite Gothic-style cathedral that overlooks the *Piazza del Campo* to thank God for the victory. The nine losing *contrade* (together with the seven that did not compete) begin the long process of praying and preparing for the victory that they hope and expect will be theirs the next time out.

While both the Crusades and the jousting-based struggle with non-Christians were moving through the centuries in the eastern Mediterranean, and the horse-riding competitions of Italy were evolving in the central Mediterranean, at the far western end of the Mediterranean, there continued the previously noted enterprise of the *reconquista* — the process of reclaiming the Iberian Peninsula from Muslim political control, which had been initially achieved between 711 and 718.

Interestingly, it was on that peninsula, in Spain, sometime during the course of these centuries that a chivalric style of combat that specifically connected sports, warfare, and God could be most distinctly found. The medieval Spanish schools of fencing offered a kind of parallel as a martial art to the East Asian schools (see chapter 7), with the latter's strong, systematic spiritual and religious influences. While the Spanish style was admired by other European students of the sword, its metaphysical approach was ultimately regarded by most of them as impractical.[9]

Sword fighting in Europe would eventually disappear from the battlefield altogether and be relegated entirely to the sports arena as firearms came into use. Perhaps because life and death were no longer as clearly at issue, the change seems to have diminished, rather than to have increased, the level of association between spiritual and physical discipline in pursuit of success.[10]

In any case, when Ferdinand of Aragon managed to wrest Granada from Muslim control in January, 1492, the process of the *reconquista* was complete. Ferdinand failed to fulfill his promise of a religiously open nation-state. Instead, he introduced a policy of *un rey, un ley, un fey*—"one king, one law, one faith"—and thus the defeated Muslims would eventually be expelled. More immediately, by August 3, 1492—hours after Columbus set sail toward what would prove to be a new world for most Europeans—the Jews were expelled from Ferdinand's Spain.

This triple event—the expulsion of the Jews and Columbus's setting sail on his first voyage, and the eventual expulsion of the Muslims as well—leads us to three questions. First, what is the historical relationship between Islam and sports, and how will that relationship be affected by athletic engagement within the international arena, particularly in the modern era? Second, what is the historical relationship between Judaism and sports: do sports and God—or sports, politics, and God—share any common ground in the Jewish religious tradition, and how might that ground shift between the medieval and modern worlds? And finally, is there a relationship between sports and the concerns of religion in the world of the Native Americans that Columbus and his successor explorers from Europe would swallow up so quickly?

Notes

1. Even without the papacy's perspective, Cesare Borgia was pretty notorious as a cruel, tyrannical sort of leader.

2. One may find this document translated in J.T. Addison, *The Medieval Missionary* (1936), 49.

3. From a series of oral troubadour narratives, the *Chanson de Roland* makes its way into a somewhat definitive written form by the eleventh century.

4. The functional unification of the Christian provinces in Iberia by Fernando and Isabel helped make possible the taking of the last major Muslim province, Andalusia, and its capital, Granada, in January, 1492. By August 3—the day after Columbus and his crew set sail to the West for points unknown, Fernando and Isabel had expelled openly-professing Jews from the peninsula; the Muslim expulsion would follow not too long thereafter. The Ottomans, like their Seljuk Turkic predecessors, had embraced Islam when they conquered parts of the Middle East; by 1453 they had conquered Constantinople (that soon thereafter came to be known as Istanbul) and definitively ended the Byzantine empire; and had already begun incursions into the Balkans in southeastern Europe.

5. The term derives from Middle English *quintaine*, in turn adopted from Old French, and ultimately derived from Latin *quīntāna*, meaning "fifth," referring to the fifth street of a Roman camp, where war exercises took place.

6. One might suppose that such training customs for young would-be warriors had a long history, given a version of their presence, as we have noted, in *Aeneid* V and the funeral games for Anchises recounted there.

7. This death had been allegedly prophesized by the renowned Michel de Nostradamus (1503-66) in his 1555 volume, written in quatrains, *Les Propheties*. One of Nostradamus's most believing fans was Catherine de Medici, wife (and then widow) of Henry II.

8. "That time" would be around the time of the Battle of Crecy, if the beginning point is the fourteenth century; before the First Crusade if the beginning point is the eleventh century.

9. See Hall, "Marishiten," 107-8.

10 See Stephen G. Voss, "Kendo and Fencing: A Comparative Study in their Practice and Philosophy," in *Japanese Martial Arts and American Sports: The Historical and Cultural Background on Teaching Methods*, 28.

CHAPTER SEVEN
Sports and Spirituality from
the Ancient Near East to the Far East and Back

*L*et's take a few more historical steps backward in order to take two geographical leaps—one eastward and one back toward the west. One obvious area of sports that interweaves physical with spiritual focus is the martial arts. That they are, in English, called *martial* underscores the fact that they were understood to be a sport that had a larger purpose, for which the context was war.[1] But at the same time, these arts, as they evolved well before their relatively recent transplantation to the West, have had a decidedly *unmartial* goal.

In fact, the "martial arts" that we associate with China and Japan—as they have developed historically, and not to be confused with the fairly two-dimensional portrayal of them provided by Hollywood—are said, interestingly, to have originated not in the Far East, but in the Middle East.[2] Such arts—called *budo* in Japanese; and *wudao* in Chinese; meaning "the way" (*do, dao*) of "[stopping the] spear" (*bu, wu*)—seem clearly to have had, from the outset, a religious and philosophical component. What may have originated in Sumer of the twenty-sixth through twenty-fourth centuries BCE offered an emphasis on breath and breathing, which would be carried east through India to China and eventually to Korea and Japan.

The discussions of techniques for breathing and the association between breath and the soul instilled within us as a connec-
tive to God are both expressed in Mesopotamian literature and
are also articulated in the Bible in Genesis 1 and 2, where God
breathes Its spirit (Hebrew: *n'shama*) into that clod of earth (Hebrew: *adamah*; hence: Adam) and animates (from Latin: *anima*)
and besouls it. This association (breath-soul-God) was repeated
in analogous contexts that related to warrior capability, in descriptions found eastward from the Tigris-Euphrates River valley.
Most obviously, Gauthama Buddha, founder of the Buddhist tradition, came from a noble family of the warrior—*kshatriya*—class.
So, not surprisingly, he is said to have studied and excelled at
the arts of war before leaving home at age 29 and withdrawing
into the woods to meditate. And proper breathing techniques are
a distinct part of the meditation style that he ends up using, which
will be emulated by his followers.

Thus, the variously articulated Buddhist prescriptions for
proper breathing in association with both physical and mental/
spiritual exercises (*asanas*)—that in turn would achieve particularized articulations in various forms of yoga—transformed a physical warrior into a spiritual warrior, just as skills with implements
of warfare could be transferred to the competitive, but not lethal,
sport of martial arts.[3]

As we have already observed a strong relationship between
sports and warfare, the shaping of the martial arts as a war-based
series of sporting events should hardly be surprising. Moreover,
this relationship takes on a strong spiritual direction. This direction may be understood to be both *broadly* spiritual, with a code of
ethics and morality as its centerpiece, and *narrowly and specifically*
religious. By this last turn of phrase I mean that some form of divinity is included in the thinking that motivates the moral and ethical
code; I am distinguishing it from forms of spirituality that don't
necessarily imply the presence of (a) god(s), such as Buddhism.[4]

In any case, as the discipline of the martial arts makes its way from the Middle East through India to arrive into East Asia we may read about the beginnings of *wushu* (as the martial arts are also called) in China in the Shaolin Monastery in the Sung Mountains of Henan Province. There, in the sixth century CE, a monk from India named Bodhidharma is said to have introduced physical exercises together with meditation exercises to improve the physical and spiritual stamina of his followers. From these beginnings, the Shaolin monks eventually shape self-defense applications, which ultimately lead to variously formed Chinese, Korean, and Japanese martial arts.[5]

Others have asserted that the martial arts were already practiced in China for centuries before the arrival of Bodhidharma. But these sources first of all refer to influence from Confucian and Taoist thinking and second of all suggest that the "myth" connecting the origins of Shaolin martial arts to Bodhidharma was part of an attempt to invest them with more of a "magical and mystical" aura.[6] So, both of these comments, as far as our own subject is concerned, accomplish the same end of asserting a long chronological connection between the sport and the realm of the spirit. Whether or not Bodhidharma is historically responsible for engendering that connection is immaterial for our purposes.

However, some scholars have recognized a long-standing tradition of the warrior-monk/priest, who by definition simultaneously embodies athletic and spiritual skills,[7] although others have asserted that this idea is self-contradictory, since to fight and kill would contradict Buddhist principles.[8] But a Buddhist perspective can encompass the "benevolent taking of life" under prescribed conditions, such as those in which one is engaged in protecting someone. And if larger monasteries and temple complexes ended up maintaining private armies of warrior-monk/priests (*sohei*) to protect their lands, can we distinguish the spirituality of this group from that of the non-warrior monks residing in the same complexes? Indeed, the very existence of a word, *sohei*, that we translate *as* "warrior-monk/priest" to refer to such a monastic subgroup, would seem to make it clear that there was at least a subset of monks who were warriors and yet also monks.

Some have asserted that the *sohei* actually had very little to do with the day-to-day monastic living of the orders for which they served as a protective force.[9] But I am reminded of Western monastic orders, which have included members who subscribed to the order's principles while not living within the monastery's walls; in this case, perhaps there was a somewhat reversed idea: the *sohei* dwelt within the compound but didn't subscribe to all of the principles of the non-warrior monks. In any case, that they were not entirely disconnected might also be suggested by the myriad accounts of warriors from the outside who in their later years became monks.

This principle carries into the present era. One might note the renowned martial-arts master, Toshitsugu Takamatsu (1887-1972) who, upon retiring from active practice of the sport in 1970, announced that he would be devoting all of his time to the spiritual training that had played only a partial role in his activities previously. A virtually immediate consequence of that announcement was that a number of his non-religious students began to think for "a long time about the importance of balance between religious study and martial-arts practice."[10]

In fact, in some cases one can recognize an even broader mode of continuing a centuries-long tradition of relationship between the martial arts and spirituality. Thus, in the *Kukishin ryu*, the headmaster (*soke*) of the school is also the head of the Kumano grand Shinto shrine—as his predecessors have been for nearly 700 years.[11] Of more limited chronological import, the founder of the contemporary Japanese martial art of *aikido*, Morihei Ueshiba (1883-1969), reported that three moments of spiritual awakening between 1925 and 1942 led him to found his art,[12] which is referred to by one scholar as "a spiritual discipline...that embodies the essence of Shinto, the indigenous religion and spiritual foundation of Japan."[13] And further, Jigoro Kano, (1860-1938), twentieth-century founder of *kodokan judo*, established his "school" *within* the Eishoji Buddhist temple in Kamakura.[14]

Perhaps most intriguing, we find this war/sports-spirituality connection carried into the very process of manufacturing the *implements* used in Chinese and Japanese martial arts. Thus, for example, during the Kamakura Period (1192-1333) in Japan, those who smithed swords were either Tendai Buddhist priests or *Yamabushi* ("mountain ascetics" who followed Shugendo, a form of spirituality that blends elements of Shinto, Buddhist, Taoist, and folk-religious thinking). One category of swordsmiths would dress in the ceremonial robes of the Shinto priesthood while forging a blade,[15] and in any case the smith was expected to lead "a more or less religious life, abstaining from excesses of all kinds."[16] The art of fashioning a sword came to be understood as an act "pleasing to the gods;" the process of forging was deemed possible only in a workshop that had been purified with rituals that included prayers to the gods and to the divine spirit of the sword itself.

On the one hand, the workshop where such weaponry was forged assumed the conceptual properties of a kind of temple. On the other hand, there existed specific martial shrines at places such as Katori and Kashima and the Tendai temple on Mount Kurama that were revered as sites where revelations of a specifically martial sort had been received, the result of which had been the shaping of various martial-art systems.[17]

Unique among the array of martial arts associated with the Far East is the mode of wrestling known as *sumo* that is practiced professionally only in Japan. The goal of the match between two contestants is for one *rikishi* (wrestler) to push the other out of a circular ring (*dohyo*) or to force him to touch the ground with any part of his body besides the soles of the feet. The sport has ancient roots—tradition associates its beginnings with the legendary Nomi no Sukune, a wrestler under the equally legendary eleventh Japanese Emperor Suinin (29 BCE-70 CE). Emperor Suinin is said to have instructed his star athlete to kick and thereby kill his opponent, Taima no Kehaya. However, the sport clearly evolved away from such an extreme desired outcome.

Most of the current aspects of sumo wrestling began in the seventeenth century, during the early Edo period (1603-1867; thus, in spite of more ancient roots, sumo is typically referred to as a *gendai budo*: a "modern martial art"). The first professional tournaments took place in the Tomioka Hachiman Shrine in 1684. By then, the custom was already in place of requiring professional sumo wrestlers to live in communal "training stables"—*heya*—where every aspect of their daily lives, from food to dress, is governed by strict traditions.[18] Today, sumo wrestlers are still expected to grow their hair long to be tied up in a topknot (*chonmage*), as was common in the Edo period, and when in public to wear traditional Japanese garb. Among the many other aspects of strictly governed lifestyle, young, lower-ranking sumo wrestlers typically end their daily workout routines with a ritualized circle dance that requires coordination as a team and is thus intended to emphasize community.

In fact, sumo wrestling may have begun as part of a Shinto ritual dance in which human protagonists wrestle with a *kami* (a divine spirit). The sport offers a strong spiritual component—i.e., a good deal of ritual—somewhat reminiscent of what we have discussed for Roman arena competitors. The sumo traditions are more formalized and uniform, though, as they were originally (and still are) associated with the Shinto religion. Today, as in the past, before a tournament, two of the referees—*gyoji*—serving as Shinto priests, consecrate the newly shaped *dohyo*, and an array of traditions governs the competitions.

Contending wrestlers will not see each other prior to their matches, but prepare in either "East" or "West" changing rooms. They first don ornate silk aprons (*kesho-mawashi*) for the ring-entering ceremony (*dohyo-iri*). There are four of these on each day of a 15-day tournament, two for more advanced wrestlers and two for less advanced wrestlers; and in each of these, one procession enters from the east and one from the west. The procession presents all of the athletes in a circle, around the periphery of the *dohyo*, first facing out to the audience, and then in toward the center of the *dohyo*, performing a brief ritual—all of which is ultimately a Shinto purification ritual—before exiting back to the changing rooms.

There, the competitors change into their fighting, loin-cloth-like *mawashi*, each returning to the ring two bouts before his own. Entering the *dohyo*, each wrestler faces the audience, clapping his hands and then performing a leg-stomping *shiko* exercise. These Shinto-derived rituals drive evil spirits from the *dohyo*. Returning to his corner, each fighter is given a ladleful of water—"power water" (*chikara mizu*)—with which he rinses his mouth, and a paper tissue—"power paper" (*chikara kami*)—with which he dries his lips. The two fighters step back into the ring, facing each other in a squat, clapping their hands and spreading their arms wide—to show that they carry no weapons—and then return to their corners, where each picks up a handful of salt and tosses it into the ring to purify it.

All of this elaborate ritual precedes a confrontation that may last no more than 10 or 20 seconds. So, too, all of this is part of what is intelligible as a series of ceremonies in which the sports element seems almost subsidiary to the religious element. But the sports component is sufficient so that successful practitioners can ultimately expect extensive material rewards to accompany whatever spiritual well-being is achieved by the enactment of such ongoing discipline.[19]

Thus one may observe a diversity of different spiritual directions that may be associated with varied forms of the martial arts—as a sport and also as training for combat—as they developed in the Far East, geographically and chronologically "culminating" in Japan.[20] But if we circle back to the putative geographic place of origin of the martial arts—the Middle East—we might recall that by late antiquity, not only had much of it come under the power of Rome, but that by the early Middle Ages, Rome had become Christian. We might further recall that, as time moved forward, a new religious idea emerged within the Middle East—Islam—that would sweep across the region, westward as far as Spain and eastward as far as Southeast Asia, in the seventh and eighth centuries and beyond.

More precisely, Islam had emerged out of the *hijaz* — the southwest coastal region of the Arabian peninsula — within a few years of the Prophet Muhammad's death in 632. By 643, it had dismantled the last of the great Persian empires to the East, the Sassanian Empire, and begun its conquest by word and sword across North Africa, so that by 711 a Muslim force led by Tariq had entered into Spain, most of which would fall to Muslim conquerors in the course of the seven years that followed. From the Middle East to the western edge of the Mediterranean, Islam would abut the Christian world by the early eighth century, with consequences for both war and peace.

What is the relationship between Islam and sports as the centuries move forward? It is appropriate, in addressing this question, that we begin by recalling an all-important principle of religious thinking: that even as God is understood and believed to have been revealed to particular individuals — prophets, priests, heroes, and the like — at different times and places, and even though the words God expressed through individuals may eventually be written down, their *meaning* may not always be clear to all who read them. The world of religious thought is a world not only of revelation but of interpretation, as we have previously noted.

In Christianity and Judaism, the revealed word of God is understood to be found in the Bible. The two faiths differ from one another not only in *how* they interpret the biblical texts that they share in common, but in *what* they interpret and accept to *be* God's revealed word. Thus, for Jews that word is limited to the Hebrew Bible, whereas the Hebrew Bible is, for Christians, merely the Old Testament, the primary role of which is to anticipate the New Testament: it is the record of an old Covenant that anticipates the New Covenant. Catholics and Orthodox Christians embrace Deuterocanonical or Intertestamental texts as part of the biblical canon, but

Protestants reject these texts as apocryphal.[21] And both Judaism and Christianity yield oceans of literature over the centuries that comments on and interprets the divine revelations so that they may effectively guide Jews and Christians in how to live a life that is pleasing and not offensive to God.

The word of God as Islam understands it to be most effectively expressed is found in the Qur'an, revealed to and through the prophet Muhammad.[22] Islam also embraces a rich array of stories and sayings either ascribed to the Prophet—in his own capacity, as opposed to his capacity as the conduit through which God speaks—or that speak *about* the Prophet, or both. That literature is called *hadith*. There is, as well, a sea of Muslim commentary on both the Qur'an and the *hadith* that is as diverse and argumentative as are the Jewish rabbinic commentaries and the Christian patristic and scholastic commentaries. The overall scope of Muslim thinking on any issue, informed by the Qur'an and the *hadith*, but encompassing the varied scholarly viewpoints of diverse schools of thought, is called *shari'a*.[23]

Shari'a includes a range of features—its authorities are understood to be both learned in the primary texts and insightful with regard to their interpretations, and their discussions include disagreements that they resolve, in a given school of thought, by reaching a consensus (*ijma*). What might one find within the diverse arena of sports that is conceptually or historically part of Islam? How, if at all, might a Muslim protagonist associate his or her activity with religion in the course of history, beginning with the primary pair of Muslim literatures and encompassing the scholarly analyses of them that filled out what in sum becomes *shari'a*?

In a *hadith* from the highly regarded collection organized by the ninth-century Persian Sunni theologian, Muhammad al-Bukhari, we read that the Prophet says to "entertain your hearts; for hearts become blind when they are tired."[24] The question is: what does it mean to "entertain your hearts"? Could it encompass the idea of participating in sporting events or to be entertained by watching them? At least some Muslim jurists have understood this passage to mean just that. Thus, the notion of the legitimacy of sports from a Muslim perspective is evident from the words of God's own Messenger. Furthermore, a contemporary sheikh, 'Atiyyah Saqr, observes that "Muslims are commanded to be of sound bodies and sound minds in addition to having sound morals"—and to validate that perspective he quotes a *hadith* reported by a second great compiler of *hadiths*, the mid-ninth-century imam, Muslim Ibn al-Hajjaj: "A strong believer is better and more beloved to God than a weak one."[25]

If we are divinely commanded to be of sound bodies, then sporting events are a reasonable means of fulfilling that commandment. Moreover, since we have observed that in antiquity there was a correlation between sports activities and warrior activities, so the same was true in the Muslim world, since "a nation where fighting and battles are the norm, sports like weightlifting, archery and dueling would be very common, while swimming became the favorite sport to people living on sea-shores. In the Arabian peninsula, people got used to hunting and horse-riding due to their conditions of frequent traveling and moving from one place to another."[26]

The Imam Ibnul–Qayyam, in his well-regarded volume, *Zad al-Ma'am*, notes that movement is the essential core aspect of sports, and observes that such activity assists the body in ridding itself of waste and in fighting disease. For each organ may be associated with a particular sport that is most useful to its health, and some sports—he mentions archery, wrestling, and horseback-riding—offer overall benefits to the entire body. The act of pilgrimage, so essential to Islam—the last of the Five Pillars fundamental to Islamic life is *hajj*, making the pilgrimage to Makka, and ideally recapitulating the Prophet Muhammad's journey (in 622 CE) from Makka to Madina and back again (in 627-8 CE) to Makka—can be and has been construed, if not, of course, as a competitive sport, then as an exercise as physical as it is spiritual.[27]

Indeed, where in the more formal, competitive sense, sports

plays a role in Muslim life, the training to succeed in them, it is stressed, must include *spiritual* and *moral* training. By the same token, supporters and observers are not expected to be unduly unruly or violent against the opposition, nor should competitors insult each other, nor should a victor gloat in his triumph, nor should a loser be consumed by angry envy. After all, the victory is understood to be as much a function of *God's will in action* as it is a result of the athletes' skill and determination. There is a *hadith* that tells of how the camel of another rider outraced the camel of Muhammad—whose camel had always been first in every race, and had developed the reputation of being invincible. The Prophet's followers became saddened or even angry at what they construed to somehow be an injustice. But the Prophet calmly observed that "[a] lmighty God has decreed that nothing have permanent glory"—no situation, not even one associated with the Seal of the Prophets, is intended to last forever.

It may be fair to say that no athletic endeavor is undertaken in accordance with Islamic principles for the sake merely of the nature or success of that endeavor, or for the simple joy of competing. Certain sports—those, like boxing, that deliberately inflict pain and in which one can seriously harm one's opponent, for purely entertainment purposes—are regarded as unacceptable by most serious traditional Muslims. Muslims are also enjoined not to allow sports ever to obscure or neglect the performance of religious—or other—duties, or to involve foul behavior, to say nothing of inflicting harm on others, be they fellow competitors or fellow observers. Thus, the underlying principle of sports participation is that it be undertaken within a solid moral framework, that it not contradict the injunction that on the one hand enjoins us to "forbid not the good things that God has made lawful for you" but on the other, also commands us to "...transgress not. For lo! God does not love transgressors." (These are two parts of *Qur'an* 5:87.)

If sports, like physical activity in general, is acceptable within the proper framework, then one might wonder what sports, both conceptually and historically, might be particularly endemic to and/ or particularly embraced by the Islamic world, as suggested by the observation offered (a few paragraphs back) through the comments by Sheikh 'Atiyyah Saqr and Imam Ibnul-Qayyam. A starting point may be found much further back in history than either of these leaders, all the way to the time shortly after Muhammad's death. The Prophet's immediate successor, according to the Sunni tradition, was his father-in-law, Abu Bakr, (the Shi'i tradition recognizes Muhammad's son-in-law and cousin/nephew, 'Ali as his legitimate successor), who was succeeded two years later, by the Caliph Umar.

Umar (r. 634-44) is said to have stated: "Teach your sons the arts of swimming, sharp-shooting and horseback riding." His purpose in enjoining such instruction was to prepare them for life's requirements, in the realms of leadership, business, and war. Thus, even as the earlier-noted *hadith* speaks of camel-racing as an activity in which even the Prophet himself participated, racing was a particularly well appreciated sport in medieval Islam.

Indeed, racing was not limited to camels, of course. Upper-echelon Arabs were riders of horses, as were the Mongols and Turks who arrived later on from south central Asia and embraced Islam in the thirteenth century. What were important instruments of war were also important instruments of athletic competition—or rather, the sport of horse racing, like that of camel racing, was a means of helping to prepare riders to participate in the cavalry as part of the military. On the coasts of the Red Sea and Indian Ocean boat racing was also practiced, although there was a far lower frequency of their use in warfare than was true for horses and camels.

The sharpshooting to which Caliph 'Umar refers was most likely archery, which would have had an obvious and significant use in warfare. The interest in archery as a skill blossomed exponentially with the arrival of the Mongols and Turks. Within the world of Turkish manuscript illumination, there are miniatures that portray the *combination* of shooting and equestrian skills, as competitors sought to outdo each other in hitting a target while riding at top speed around the goal.[28] Many centuries later, archery would be complemented and ultimately supplanted by sharpshooting with firearms.

Horses can be used and have been used in other ways as part of the sports scene within the Muslim world. The game of polo, which may well have originated half a millennium before the Christian era in Central Asia and grew to great popularity in medieval Persia, involves the engagement of *teams* of riders trying to move a wooden ball across the playing field with a long wooden mallet. What began among Iranian tribesmen as a pastime of soldiers and wandering nomads emerged by the medieval period as a sport of kings.

As with riding and shooting, we can find a good number of illuminated manuscripts—Persian, in this case—that depict shahs and their entourages playing polo. Similarly, Muslim poetry focuses on this noble enterprise. Thus, the renowned late tenth/early eleventh-century Persian poet and historian, Firdawsi, writes about royal polo tournaments in his own era. His masterpiece, the *Shahnameh*, is a poetic revision and expansion of a narrative that had evolved over many centuries (perhaps as much as a thousand years) regarding the lives of the Persian kings. Firdawsi's poetic narratives are somewhat reminiscent of those written by the Greek lyric poet Pindar, in the latter's odes to victorious charioteers. But Firdawsi also focused on earlier eras—writing, for example, about a Sassanid shah of the fourth century who learned to play polo by the time he was seven years old.

So, too, the great thirteenth-century poet Nizami, in offering a love story about a king and his beloved consort, centers his tale around that consort's abilities on the polo field. Nizami describes matches that pit the king and his courtiers against his consort and her ladies-in-waiting. Among the obvious interesting elements of this description, and its illustrated accompaniment in the Persian illuminated manuscript tradition, is that it presents women engaged in athletic competition, underscoring a range of views within the Muslim world with regard to both female participation and even combined male and female interaction in sports events under what are deemed appropriate conditions. (These were, after all, part of a royal entourage, not part of the common people, for whom such mixing of genders for the purpose of sports competition would be far from embraced.)

Like riding and shooting from horseback, polo may be viewed as a form of competition that uses horses in a manner that relates both to warfare and to the sport of hunting and *its* relationship to warfare. There are other kinds of hunting, using animals other than horses as instruments—such as trained falcons—that were popular among the upper classes within the Muslim world (as in the Christian world). While the use of birds for hunting has a history that goes back to antiquity—Homer mentions the use of birds that hunt (in *Odyssey* 5:52-3)—one finds a particularly interesting reference to it in the mid-thirteenth-century tale regarding the young Borjugin Mongol prince, Temujin.[29]

He and a fellow young prince are lost in the desert, after having been defeated in battle, when they see a wild hawk gorging itself on its prey. The other prince suggests that they drive the bird away and eat its food, but Temujin responds that "we must earn our food," thinking in a more farsighted manner than his companion with regard to satisfying their hunger. So, they capture the bird instead, train it to hunt, and share the ongoing gastronomic results with it. Temujin[30] grows up to be the great conquering warrior and lawgiver, Chingis (Ghengis) Khan. Falcon hunting is thus thought of within this tale as part of a double moral lesson regarding how to be in the world.

Moral lessons are a consistent feature of the sports competitions that develop in the Muslim world, which is not surprising given the conscious placement of sports within a God-approved framework that is understood to have its starting point in the Qur'an itself. We can—and shall—follow this deliberate rendering of moral lessons along various paths to the present day.

Notes

1. The word "martial," of course, derives from a Latin adjective in turn derived from the name of the Roman god of war, Mars.

2. See Howard Reid and Michael Croucher, *The Way of the Warrior: The Paradox of the Martial Arts* (Woodstock, NY: The Overlook Press, 1986), 18.

3. It should be noted that the very term "yoga"—from a Sanskrit root (*yuj*) cognate with the English word "yoke"—refers ultimately to the idea of reining in one's uncontrolled impulses, the end point of which is to transcend one's ego and experience one's true identity of consonance with the godhead, and ultimately with the absolute realm of True Being. (See, among many others, Gavin Flood, *An Introduction to Hinduism* (Cambridge: Cambridge University Press, 1996), 93-6.

4. I do not define most forms of Buddhism as *religious*, per se, since they do not include reference to a named, personified *god*. The Buddha is merely an individual who offers a model to others in having achieved perfect enlightenment; he is analogous neither to Muhammad, a prophet through whom God is understood by his constituents to speak, nor to Jesus, understood by his constituents to *be* God. Thus, while emphatically *spiritual*, Buddhism would not be a *religion*.

5. See Herman Kauz, *The Martial Spirit: An Introduction to the Origin, Philosophy and Psychology of the Martial Arts*, 93; and Reid and Croucher, *The Way of the Warrior*, 20-5, 30.

6. See Stewart McFarlane, "Mushin, Morals and Martial Arts—A Discussion of Keenan's *Yogacara* Critique," *Japanese Journal of Religious Studies* 17, no. 4 (1990): 402. Note that both Confucianism and Taoism fall into the category that I have previously defined to include Buddhism as "spiritual" rather than "religious."

7. Thomas Cleary, *Code of the Samurai: A Modern Translation of the* Budo Shoshinshu, 14-18.

8. Thus, King, *Zen and the Way of the Sword*, 40-41.

9. Thus, Karl Friday, *Legacies of the Sword*, 121, asserts minimalist involvement.

10. Stephen K. Hayes and Masaaki Hatsumi, *Secrets from the Ninja Grandmaster* (Boulder, CO: Paladin Press, 2003), 14.

11. *Kukishin Ryu* (also called *Kukishinden Ryu*)—translated as "Nine Gods Spirit School," or "Nine Demon Gods School" (for reasons beyond this discussion)—is a Japanese martial art said to have been founded by Kuki Yakushimaru in the fourteenth century. It teaches a range of six different disciplines with diverse weapons, such as *taijitsu, bojutsu, kempo, sojutsu, hanbo,* and *naginata,* supplemented by *heiho* (military strategy). *Kukishin Ryu* practitioners also study esoteric teachings and Onakatomi Shinto (*Ko*-Shinto) practices. See: http://www.shinjin.co.jp/kuki/hyoho/index_e.html (History and Genealogical Section).

12. Kisshomaru Ueshiba, *Aikido* (Tokyo: Hozansha Publications), 1985), 153-4; and Morihei Ueshiba, *The Art of Peace*, transl. John Stevens (Boston, MA: Shambhala Publications, 1992), 5-10.

13. William Gleason, *The Spiritual Foundations of Aikido* (Rochester, VT: Destiny Books, 1995), 1-22.

14. See http://en.wikipedia.org/wiki/Jigoro_Kano, citing an article that appeared in *The Japan Times* on March 30, 1913.

15. Reid and Croucher, the *Way of the Warrior*, 141.

16. Winston L. King, *Zen and the Way of the Sword: Arming the Samurai Psyche*, 71-3.

17. Hall, "Marishiten," 103-5.

18. One might note, by way of comparison with Roman arena fighters, that the sumo gastronomy regulated by the *heya*, both in terms of content and in terms of structure—large lunch and long nap immediately following—is designed to produce heavier competitors. But the purpose is not to protect internal organs from weapon wounds, but to make it more difficult for a fighter to be thrown by his opponent.

19. For more information on sumo wrestling, one might look to *The Beginner's Guide to Sumo*, published by the Japan Sumo Association; to Mina Hall, *The Big Book of Sumo: History, Practice, Ritual, Fight*, (Stone Bridge Press, 1997); or to Lora Sharnoff, *Grand Sumo*, (Weatherhill Press, 1993).

20. I am grateful to my friend and colleague Ilan Weinberger at Georgetown University for allowing me to read his unpublished 2008 Master's Thesis, "Japanese *Budo*: An East Asian Religious Paradigm for Self-Cultivation, Morality and Conflict Resolution," from which I have drawn much of the detail pertinent to the story of the relationship between the Far Eastern martial arts and spirituality. A reader of his thesis will find a good deal more information and further discussion there than that which I have provided here. It is available from Georgetown University's Lauinger Library.

21. Books such as Maccabees I and II, Judith, Tobit, and The Wisdom of Ben Sirach, among others, are considered part of the Bible by the Catholic and Orthodox Churches—placed between the Old and New Testaments (hence "intertestamental"), which also makes them the second ("deutero,"in Greek) part of the canon, after the Old Testament but before the New Testament.

22. A technically more accurate translation of the Arabic *rasul* is "messenger."

23. The term itself means "path," referring specifically to the kind of path (*shar*) that leads to water in the wilderness.

24. The *Sahih ("authentic"/"correct") al-Bukhari* is one of six major hadith collections in Sunni Islam. It is one of the three most trusted collections, and is considered by some to be second only to the Qur'an in spiritual significance and reliability. The compilation, completed in 846 CE, contains some 2,602 traditions that al-Bukhari culled from over 300,000 that he is said to have heard as he moved about through the Abbasid Empire.

25. With the incredibly rapid spread of Islam in the seventh and eighth centuries, it soon became apparent that some so-called *hadiths* were not legitimate, but were created by individuals with their own political motives for representing them as telling about or being ascribed to Muhammad. The process of examining and compiling legitimate, reliable collections included, among early efforts, the work by the scholar commonly and simply referred to as Muslim (ca 821-75), who gathered some 9,000 *hadiths* into a compilation so revered that it is known as *Sahih Muslim*: "[the] authentic Muslim [collection]." In Arabic, "muslim" means "one who submits [to God's will]." Thus the term which comes to be used more broadly was taken as a proper name by Muslim and in this context, the title of his compilation puns on the work with him as its author and as a guide for the attentive reader. Al-Bukhari's compilation, as we have noted, is the other widely revered one, among the six major Sunni collections overall.

26. The quote in this from comes specifically from the December 18, 2010, weekly internet blog, *The Muslim Voice*, answering a question regarding the role of sports in Islam. The comment was written by the blog founder, Sa'ad Riazuddin; however, Riazuddin's response reflects a number of hadiths such as al-Bukhari's *Maghazi* 18 and *Jihad* 78.

27. The most fundamental aspects of Islam are based on five obligations, known as the Five Pillars. The first is the *shahada*, the expression of belief in one God and the prophets (whose final and definitive exemplar is Muhammad), as well as in angels and demons, reward and punishment, heaven and hell following final judgment—and in a profound tension between the contending notions of predetermination and free will. The second is *salat*, praying five times daily between sunrise and going to sleep. The third is *sawm*, fasting from sunrise to sunset during the month of Ramadan. The fourth is *sadaka*, the tithing from one's self in order to provide for those in the community possessing less than one has. The fifth is *hajj*, the effort, if at all possible, to make the pilgrimage to Makka once in the course of one's lifetime. A fuller *hajj* would also include emulating Muhammad's journey from Makka to al'Madina in 622. The latter city was called Yathrib at that time, but its significance in Muhammad's life eventually yielded the new name, al'Madina, meaning "the city." Muhammad's journey from Makka to Yathrib is known as the *Hijra*, and marks the beginning of the Muslim calendar. For simplicity's sake, I have been using and shall continue to use the Gregorian

calendar as my chronological reference point, whether discussing pre-Christian, Christian, Jewish, Muslim, or other groups.

28. As, for example, in the miniature from the *Huner-Nama* (*The Book of Skills*), painted in 1584 and depicting Sultan Murat II practicing this very skill. See below, Epilogues, 310.

29. The name means "best iron/steel" in Chinese, and puns nicely with Turkish *temurdji*, meaning "smith"—and thus, with the tradition that Chingis Khan was originally a smith by trade. The original tale, composed at the behest of his successors sometime after the death of Chingis Khan (better known to English-speakers as Ghengis Khan) in 1227 CE , was written in Mongol, making use of a script borrowed from the Uighur Turks. That original text no longer exists; the earliest extant version is in a Chinese translation, *Yuan Ch'ao Pi Shih* (usually translated as *The Secret History of the Mongols*), of which the earliest extant version is from the Ming Dynasty period, after the Mongols had already been driven from China. For the hunting anecdote, see Francis Woodman Cleaves's English-language translation of *The Secret History of the Mongols* (Cambridge, MA: Harvard University Press, 1982); Erich Haenisch's German translation (Leipzig, 1941) 31ff; and for a concise discussion of the issue of textual transmission, William Hung, "The Transmission of the Book Known as *The Secret History of the Mongols*," *Harvard Journal of Asiatic Studies*, (Vol 14, 1951), 433-92.

Chapter Eight
Religion and Sports Within
and Beyond the Muslim World

*A*mong other sports that one may recognize as having
a beginning deep in antiquity, as evidenced by the
literature from Egypt, Mesopotamia, Greece and Rome,
from the *Epic of Gilgamesh* to the *Aeneid*, none is more familiar
than wrestling. By the time of medieval Persia, such a sport was
extremely popular—the competitors were covered in olive oil,
which presented more of a challenge as they tried to grasp each
other in order to triumph, either by lifting an opponent above
one's head or by pinning him. Firdawsi also writes about this
important sport in his *Shahnameh*: the hero, Rostam, is a *pahvlivan*:
a mighty wrestler and warrior who, like Herakles in the Greek
tradition, is constantly engaged in ridding the countryside of
negative and chaotic powers.

Eventually, the Persian Empire, in its medieval, Islamic form,
would fall into the ambit of the expanding Seljuk Turkic (1037)
and Mongolian (1219) Empires (before re-asserting itself as the
Persian Safavid Empire in 1500). While the Turks may have embraced wrestling as a sport received from their conquered foe—
the term for a wrestling champion in Persian, *pahlivan*, is hardly

altered when, in speaking Turkish one says *pehlivan*—the Turkish tradition itself suggests a different beginning to a particular history that shaped oil wrestling as the Turkish national sport. It is said to have begun with the first *kirkpinar* tournament some seven centuries ago.

The story has it that the tournament emerged after a group of 40 victorious Turkish soldiers made camp but were too energized by their victories to settle down, so they decided to expend some of their excess energy in wrestling matches. While others won or lost and in any case ended their matches, one pair continued. Neither competitor could overcome the other. Both protagonists refused to accept a draw, so they continued to wrestle into and throughout the night. At dawn, as others awoke and prepared for morning prayers, they passed by the spot where the two wrestlers had been engaged, curious to see what the outcome was.

The two were still engaged, but stock still, standing up, locked in a wrestling embrace—they had both died rather than give in to the other. Their bereaved companions buried them under a fig tree. Some time thereafter, visitors to the site, drawn by the unusual story, noted that a spring had begun to gush forth from the earth between the two gravestones. The spring came to be called *Kirk Pinar*, meaning "Spring of the Forty." The site evolved as a center for wrestling where a tournament by that name developed in tribute to those two unnamed wrestlers who refused to give up.

Here, too, we have ample evidence of the spread of a passion for the sport of wrestling across Persia and Ottoman Turkey in illuminated manuscripts. One miniature of about 1525, from the era of Sultan Suleiman the Magnificent, depicts the sultan seated on a throne observing a series of wrestling matches in one of the courtyards of his Topkapi palace complex.[1] Indeed, not only did the interest in wrestling continue into the era of modern Turkey, but the style remained constant. Today, as then, the wrestlers are clothed only in leather pants that extend from waist to knee (in Iran the pants are similar, but made of silk rather than leather) and olive oil is poured on the contestants to make their bodies more slippery and difficult to grasp, bring down (or lift up), and pin.

This national Turkish sport (known not only as *kirkpinar*, but also as *yagli gures* in modern Turkish) leads to a three-day-long nationwide competition every late June to early July. The beginning of the competition includes a visit to the graves of Adali Halil and Kara Emin, two important modern-era champion wrestlers—as if their double gravesite might serve as a surrogate for the one where two unnamed wrestlers, who inspired the annual *kirkpinar* competition nearly 700 years ago, are buried. Each year, a prayer service is held, thus confirming an important connection between the athletic efforts about to be expended and the spiritual sense of God's power and presence within that athletic context.

Not only is the annual *kirkpinar* competition the oldest ongoing, internationally sanctioned sports competition, having continued without interruption since its official beginning in 1360 or 1362, but *kirkpinar* wrestling is considered by many to be the most macho of sports. The sense of a religious component to this emphatically physical sport is evidenced in at least two clear ways. The first is that, throughout the Ottoman era, would-be wrestlers trained in schools, called *tekke* in Turkish (the notion is reminiscent, in a broad sense, of the gladiatorial training schools in ancient Rome). These were special training centers that taught both physical and spiritual skills, based on the conviction that the successful human being cannot separate the corporeal from the spiritual within him/herself.

One might infer that, whereas Roman arena-competitors addressed diverse gods, both in hope and expectation and in gratitude for victory or remorse in defeat, *kirkpinar* competitors would—and do—direct themselves toward God as God is conceived in Islam: as singular, merciful, and compassionate; as all-powerful, all-knowing, and all-good; and as interested and involved in human affairs. Moreover, the prizes awarded not only recognize an athlete's success as a wrestler but also sportsmanship, suggesting that the Muslim emphasis on proper behavior in the context of athletic competition is very much part of *kirkpinar.*

Indeed, one of the important literary descriptions of oil wrestling is found in a story from one of the most famous Persian works of literature: the *Gulistan* (*The Rose Garden*) by Mushrif ud-Din Abdallah Sa'di. Written in 1258, this combination of maxims and didactic tales offers, in section XXVII, a moral that reflects a sense of the importance of proper conduct and the consequences of improper conduct and attitude in the context of a wrestling competition. In that story, a *pahlivan* knows 360 wrestling tricks, each of which could lead to victory. He teaches 359 of these to a favorite student who, with increasing—and increasingly excessive—pride that accompany his expanding success, arrives at the point of asserting to the shah that he is superior to his master in strength and equal to him in skill. "I have not challenged him [in order to supplant him as the reigning *pahlivan*] out of respect for his age."

The shah is displeased by what he understands to be a lack of respect, so he commands that a wrestling match be held in a spacious, fenced-in outside area, attended by everyone of consequence in the empire. The young wrestler charges into the arena of competition with the force and fury of an enraged bull elephant—the very mountains would have been moved by the force of his strength and ferocity, our author writes. The master, knowing that he lacks the youthful strength of his opponent, calmly engages him by way of the single stratagem that he has not taught his student and easily defeats him. Where the *pahlivan* is rewarded by the shah with handsome gifts, the youth receives a reproachful speech in which he is scolded for having been, in effect, a traitor to his own teacher and then failing in his presumption to challenge him.

The youth replies: "Oh sire! My master did not overcome me by strength and ability, but one cunning trick in the art of wrestling was left that he refrained from teaching me, and by that little feat he defeated me today." To this, the *pahlivan* responds: "I indeed prepared myself for just such a day as this. For as the wise have told us, 'put not so much into a friend's power that, should he become angry, he can do you an injury.' Have you not heard what the man who was dealt with treacherously by his own pupil said: 'Either in fact there is no good faith in this world, or perhaps nobody practices it in our own time. No person learned the art of archery from me who did not in the end make me his target.'?"

So the moral of the story is, on the one hand, in the most specific sense, what is expressed in the words spoken by the master, and those he repeats from "the wise men"—that one should always hold something back from friends just in case they become enemies at some point. On the other hand, the more general moral pertains to the canon of proper behavior toward others.[2] In this case, then, a moral regarding general attitude that is part of (if by no means limited to) Muslim ethos has been contextualized by reference to the ultimate sport, wherein it's expected to prevail. If all that prevails is disrespect toward teachers and competitors, as well as arrogance on the playing field, and outside it, then it undermines the spirit that is implanted within the body, and will inevitably lead that body to defeat. One might argue that all moral guidance originates from God in this tradition, so God occupies an implicit place in the tale as well.

The second way in which the religion-sports connection is evident is this: the wrestling championships that are held all over Turkey (in addition to the national championship competition at Edirne) enjoy a particular focus in the context of religious festivals—including during the month-long fast of Ramadan—when special contests are held during the evening *iftar* (the feasting that follows each sunrise-to-sunset-long fast)—as well as at life-cycle events such as circumcisions and weddings.

The notion of sports events as conceptually related to or even originating as religious ritual is evident in this last context. But there are still broader contexts to explore with regard to the specific relationship between sports competitions and religious concerns, both within the Muslim world and on the borders between it and Christendom. The picture that I have been endeavoring to paint in this overall narrative has taken us some distance from the sort of relational ground on which we stood in discussing Greek athletic competitions, beginning with the *Iliad*'s account of the funeral games for Patroklos. For we have no texts in the vast sea of Muslim literature that present an athlete, per se, as competing and turning to God either for help or after having succeeded. Still, we have returned to the same sort of ground whereon we stood with the Greeks.

We observe, first of all, within the discussion of the validity of athletic competitions in Islamic literature the assumption that an athlete will recognize God's role in his victory — or his defeat. Then, by noting the frequency with which the Muslim tradition contains instances of individuals offering *du'a* (informal, on-the-spot prayers for the success of all kinds of enterprises), we can certainly infer that no Muslim athlete worth his (or her) salt, whether in the medieval or the modern era would be likely to engage in competition without offering a brief *du'a* in God's direction or would fail to address God in thanksgiving after success or in humility after lack of success.

Finally, just as, in looking at Greek (and other) literature and art and recognizing obvious inherent parallels between the hero on the battlefield and the hero on the playing field, we must look into poetry and parables and also into that branch of Muslim literature that focuses specifically on the hero, and find that sort of parallel. An obvious place to start would be in the lengthy classic, *A Thousand and One Nights*. There, for instance, we find the hero, Sinbad, telling tales of having engaged in a series of seven adventures. While it is more the strength of his character than of his body that is emphasized (but that is part of the point, isn't it?), one may at least entertain the thought that, were he insufficiently athletic and strong, he would surely have perished in any number of his encounters.

In Sinbad's second voyage, could he have managed to cling,

even with the assistance of his unraveled turban, to the leg of the gigantic *rukh* as it soared and swooped from the abyss of diamonds to its eerie, if he lacked muscle? Conversely, might Sinbad have been among those quickly devoured, as some of his companions were, in his third voyage, by a giant (reminiscent of the Polyphemos episode in Book IX of the *Odyssey*), had he been overweight—the juiciest among them being consumed first by the ogre? It's reasonable to imagine that Sinbad is not just morally fit and luck-laden, but he's probably physically up to the challenge, as well.

There are further elements that might be added to this discussion. One—apropos both of the sense of body-spirit or body-mind continuity and of the importance of sporting competitions as training for the larger competitive worlds of business and warfare—is that "sports" competitions in the Islamic world are not limited *to* those of the *body*. Mental competitions—board games, such as chess and backgammon—were also deemed to prepare the mind for successful strategic behavior in both business and war. Chess, for instance, first developed in western India sometime before 500 CE, as a game called *"chatur-anga,"* meaning "four [military] divisions" in Sanskrit (referring to infantry, cavalry, elephants, and chariotry that, on the chess board would evolve as pawns, knights, bishops, and rooks).

The game arrived into Persia by about 600 CE—where the Middle Persian name for it was *shatranj* (an exact rendering of the Sanskrit name)—and with the overwhelming of Persia by Islam in the mid-seventh century, it soon spread throughout the Islamic world. By the eighth century, it had entered Christian Europe, in most of the countries of which the name of the game is a variant form—like the word "chess"—of the Persian word *shah*, meaning "king," that offers a pun on the word *shat* ("four"). While obviously not a physical sport, as a mental exercise that can be said to train the mind for strategizing against an opponent in either peacetime or warfare, the game certainly parallels the physical sports as a surrogate for war.

Yet another element to this discussion of Islam and sports, particularly as the *dar al-Islam* has variously interacted with Christendom over the past fourteen centuries, is the idea that, in the modern era—most specifically in the last decades of the twentieth century and the beginning of the twenty-first century—the question of the participation of Muslim *women* in sports competitions has raised new issues with respect to how to fit that engagement into the canons of acceptability within the canons of Islam's religious tradition. The issue is not that of participation per se, or of participation together with men, for as we have seen, for example in polo, the Persian literary, illustrational, and apparently historical tradition (at least with regard to the upper classes) countenanced both. Of course, given the far-flung and diverse world of Islam, there may well be imams and mullahs who have objected to Nijami's description and the accompanying illuminations of the thirteenth century and would today object to both.

But a more fundamental question, stemming from the orthodox Muslim view of how female modesty is expressed—among other ways, by clothing that covers both body and head hair—is how such an expression of modesty may coexist with participation in sports. In the case of shooting, for example, one can readily see how that coexistence is possible. Iranian sharpshooter Lida Fariman competed in both the 1992 and 1996 Olympic Games, and was able to wear traditional robes and head cover. Similarly, Iranian Manje Kazemi competed in the 2000 Olympic Games in Sydney while dressed in a traditional manner, as did her countrywoman, Nassim Hassanpour, competing in the 10-meter air-pistol event four years later in Athens.

But for someone such as Algerian Hassiba Boulmerka, who won the gold medal in the 1500 meters in the 1992 Barcelona Olympics, it would have been difficult if not impossible to compete in such garments.[3] Her decision to run in standard runner's garb led to her being denounced by an Algerian mullah—who took the opportunity to condemn all those who "dare display their nudity before all the world." In Boulmerka's case, she became fearful of returning to the country that she had represented with such pride as an athletic competitor, due to the vehemence of the mullah's denunciation and the explicit threats against her that his outcry yielded and encouraged.

Thus, the matter of dress codes in international sports competitions is one that warrants discussion—after all, one-fourth of the world's female population is Muslim, and many of these women sacrifice the opportunity to compete lest it undercut aspects of their religion. Can their form of faith be reconciled with the demands of sports? If the sartorial terms of international foot-racing since the advent of the Modern Olympics in 1896 have been Eurocentric and secularly Christian, can and should they change to accommodate the needs of a Muslim runner?

Does the will to institute changes require a critical mass of competitors who are not secular Christians? If a single *observant* Christian cannot compete on Sunday and be consistent with his faith, or a single observant *Jew* cannot compete on Saturday and be consistent with her faith, or a single observant *Muslim* woman cannot compete in a bikini-like outfit and be consistent with her faith—and they are world-class athletes who, aside from these considerations, *can* and *desire* to compete—should the Olympic authorities consider measures to accommodate their needs? What sort of measures could be put into the field of play? These are questions that connect past to present and future.[4]

In the last decades, an almost opposite matter has evolved: how many Muslim countries will *countenance* participation by women in their Olympic delegations? The simple answer is that the number has been slowly increasing since Iran sent its first female athlete to compete back in 1964. The North African Muslim countries have typically led the way—Morocco's 38-person delegation in the 2008 games in Beijing included 11 women; Tunisia had women competitors in eight different kinds of sports, from track and field to wrestling; and Algeria, where Hassiba Boumerka was denounced by a mullah back in 1992, was represented by another woman, Nahida Touhami, in the 1500 meters in 2008—and, for the first time, Algeria also fielded a woman's volleyball team.

Still more statistically impressive, the Hashemite Kingdom of Jordan arrived in Beijing with women not only as part, but as a *majority*, of its Olympic delegation—four out of the seven-athlete group were female, two of whom in fact carried the Jordanian flag during the opening ceremonies. Symptomatic of evident changes in the Muslim world of international sports participation, even among the more socially conservative Gulf countries, women were allowed to compete for the first time in the 2008 Beijing Olympics. Thus, for example, Buthaina Yaqoubi arrived to compete in the 100-meter dash and the long jump as part of Oman's Olympic team. And the United Arab Emirates was represented by Sheikha Maitha Muhammad Rasheed Al-Maktoum—the daughter of the ruling family's Sheikh Muhammad—in *tae kwan do*; her cousin represented the UAE in equestrian show jumping.[5]

One might look at the Muslim/non-Muslim sports interaction from a still different angle of focus, in asking how any Muslim athlete, of either gender—say, a male athlete and superstar, such as former NBA basketball player, Hakeem Olajuwon—might maintain certain fundamental tenets of his Muslim faith at times and places of athletic competition in which that would be inconvenient to his life as an athlete. Could Olajuwon—who is, to date, the tenth-highest scorer in the history of the National Basketball Association—manage to practice the *sawm*, the sunrise-to-sunset fast during the month of Ramadan, even when that fast falls in the middle of the professional basketball season? Olajuwon, a Muslim from Nigeria, came to the United States and emerged as a star playing first for the University of Houston and then as an NBA basketball player from 1985, as well as on the U.S. Olympic "Dream Team" of 1996.

But Olajuwon remained unwavering in—and even grew increasingly devoted to—fulfilling the requirements of his faith. Clearly, choosing to fast all day often made competition, whether in practices or in games, a much greater physical challenge during the years when Ramadan fell during the basketball season.[6] Interestingly, though, his teammates often commented that he played harder and more sharply at those times. So the answer for him was yes: he could maintain a strict Muslim gastronomic regimen while competing at the highest level in his sport.

In the matter of the intersection between sports and religion, the angle of our discussion has been shifting. We have considered the relationship between sports and war and how, as mirrors of each other, both involve the realm of the sacred, whether it's gods in antiquity or the Christian God in the medieval era of jousts and Crusades. We have pondered the broad issue of athletes competing in the gladiatorial arena and how, on the one hand, the audience becomes briefly but significantly godlike, and how, on the other hand and in a variety of ways, the athletes themselves count upon divine intervention to assist them.

In turning to the world of Islam, our initial focus has been on those sports that have come to be accepted, preferred, or glorified *within* the Muslim world except for the context of sports/war intersection that carries Islam into contention with the world of Christendom, as in the era of the Crusades. Thus, training and competing in horsemanship, say, which makes one a more effective cavalry warrior, involves religion as well when the battle is understood to be on behalf of God—and is, therefore, undertaken with divine support.

But in shifting toward the modern world we have found that the *intersection* of the Muslim and Christian worlds offers a different set of complications with respect to the meeting of personal faith and public athletic performance. That intersection is not necessarily simple or one-sided in its emphases—confined, that is, to the question of how Muslim competitors in various international or American athletic events avoid abandoning various Muslim principles when those principles run up against the needs of the sport in question. For example, we might note that there emerged, particularly by the late twentieth century, a burgeoning interest on the part of the occasional European *Christian* to compete in the theretofore strictly Persian or Turkish *Muslim kirkpinar* competition.

At Edirne at the end of the twentieth century, that ambition was thwarted. In the year 2000, Dutch oil-wrestler Melvin Witteveen's proposed entry into the competition was rejected by the Turkish wrestling authorities. Witteveen's interest to compete had been piqued by the arrival of the *kirkpinar* competition in Western Europe—specifically, in Amsterdam—for the first time in 1997. By the following year, the Amsterdam competition had gone international, but clearly the sentiment in 2000 was that the Edirne competition should be true to its national roots.

That condition will almost certainly change. It's likely that Turkish authorities won't continue to support the irony that their competition is merely national and therefore of less worldwide athletic significance than the Amsterdam competition, which is truly international—to say nothing of the competitions that have come to be held elsewhere in the last few years, including as far away as Japan.[7] But the point is that in the current era, the national and/or religious *borders* of sports competition are, ideally, in the process of continuous shift or even erasure. With that reality in mind, the question becomes: how does one accommodate as wide an array as possible, not only of international but of interreligious competitors?

This leads to yet one further issue within the discussion of Islam, sports, and international competitions: the creation, in 1953, of the Pan Arab Games. These competitions are of interest to this narrative precisely because, in theory, at least, they consciously *ignore* the issue of religion. They are not pan-*Islamic* games—for they exclude Muslims not only from beyond the Middle East (such as those in nearby Pakistan or Afghanistan and distant Indonesia) but also those from within the region but outside the specifically "Arab" ambit—Iran and Turkey, for example, which are not Arab states. Conversely, at least in theory, they could include not only Arab Christians (most obviously from Lebanon) but even Arab

Jews, since from Morocco to Yemen to Iraq there have been Jews—for virtually as long as Islam has been present in these areas—and there continue to be some Jews as well as a fair number of Christians who, as inhabitants of the region, would be called *Arabs*.[8]

The configuration of the Pan Arab Games, held, like the Olympics, every four years—except when political events have made this impossible—offers interesting twists to the political shaping of the modern world, in sports as elsewhere. For the word "Arab" would originally have referred to anyone who is from or traces his or her ancestry to the *'arav*—the southwestern area of the Arabian peninsula. This is why, although since the mid-seventh century the majority of such individuals have been Muslim, there could be, have been, and are Christian and Jewish Arabs.[9] But in the context of the twentieth century, "Arab" has acquired a political, rather than geo-ethnic connotation, so that the Arab world extends, politically, from Morocco at the farthest western edge of North Africa to Iraq, and the language, Arabic, is found as the primary language across that extensive realm.

Turkey has its foundations in south central Asia, and its primary language, Turkish, could not be farther from Arabic in its phonological and grammatical structure.[10] This is why the modern Turkish state, created in the 1920s by Atatürk, turned away from the Arabic writing system that had been in use through the Ottoman centuries; he viewed it as a nonconductive mechanism for effectively expressing the sounds of the Turkish language. Conversely, although modern Persian—Farsi—continues to use the Arabic writing system, as did its medieval linguistic ancestor, the language itself is also distant from Arabic and the inhabitants of the primary Farsi-speaking region—currently called Iranians but since biblical times called Persians—are as ethnically different from Arabs as are the Turks.

Yet most Westerners, and certainly most Americans, tend to treat the terms "Arab" and "Muslim" as synonymous and think of Jordanians, Egyptians, Turks, and Iranians not only as Muslims but as Arabs. In any case, the definition of "Arab" and "Arabic" is hardly simple; it is perhaps safer to rely on the language as the reference-point for definition, rather than to pretend that ethnicity, nationality, or even point of geographic origin can be clearly discerned.

Where the Pan Arab Games are concerned, not only were the first series of competitions held in Alexandria, Egypt, but to date Egyptian athletes have won the most medals by far of all the participating countries.[11] Yet, it might be noted, that while Egypt is generally considered an "Arab" country—and not only for the purpose of the games—nonetheless, when its president, Anwar Sadat, made his historic visit to Jerusalem to speak before the Israeli *Knesset* (Parliament) in 1977, part of his argument in favor of pursuing peace with his erstwhile enemies was that Egypt had spilled too much blood and spent too much energy fighting *on behalf of the Arabs.* In other words, he saw Egypt as non-Arab, in essentially ethnic and national terms.[12] So, the breadth and ambiguity of the term "Arab" lends itself well to the breadth and varied ambiguities of our discussion.

Two other related and interesting details regarding the Pan Arab Games might be worth noting. The first is that the competitions included female participation beginning only with the sixth series, held in 1985 in Rabat, Morocco. Thus, the issue regarding female Muslim participation in the Olympic Games and World Games, as it relates to both clothing and modesty, offers a particular twist with regard to the Pan Arab Games. For, in spite of my comments belaboring the difference between "Arabs" and "Muslims" in the past few paragraphs, the participants in the Pan Arab Games are nearly all Muslim, and thus the issue of how female participation might be possible without offending the sensibilities of certain Orthodox Muslim leaders—and, in their view, offending God— must be addressed from within a largely *intra*-Muslim context.

The second significant detail to be noted is that in the ninth Pan Arab Games of 1999, the number of participating countries grew to

21 with the inclusion of a Palestinian delegation. This participation was interesting, from the perspective of our discussion, in several ways. Because within the political configuration of the Middle East it marked recognition by the Arab states of a *de facto* Palestinian state—side-by-side with the (non-Arab) State of Israel—at a time when the rest of the world was only beginning to move actively in that direction and when such statehood had (and has) yet to be an accomplished fact.[13]

Because the games that year were held in Amman, Jordan, and Jordan had laid political claim to that part of Palestine popularly known as the West Bank since the end of the first Arab-Israeli war of 1947-9, but had by 1999 completely renounced its political interest in that territory, leaving the West Bank Palestinians to work out their political destiny in conjunction with the Gaza Strip and through discussions with Israel and the world at large.[14] It is also of incidental interest that the Palestinians fielded a soccer team that made it all the way to the Pan Arab Games semifinals, in which they were eventually defeated—by the Jordanians.

Thus, an array of interrelated issues centered on athletic competition arises from the reality of religious—specifically Muslim-Christian—interaction in the modern era. But we are reminded of the fact that across history (and literature), sports has been inspired by and most often been a surrogate or training ground for war. If we think of early Christian-Muslim encounters along sports/war lines, we inevitably think of the Crusades, in which the skills of a warrior fighting battles in God's name might be enhanced by his training as a competitive athlete.

In the modern era, such Muslim-Christian conflicts have turned from the battlefield to the sports arena, at least for the most part. But the reference to Palestine in its Pan Arab Games relationship to Jordan provoked references to Israel—usually referred to in common parlance as "the Jewish State." This turns our focus to the third among the Abrahamic siblings, along with Islam and Christianity, and the question: what are the angles from which we might approach the subject of the relationship between sports and religion in the context of Jews and Judaism, from antiquity to the modern era?

Notes

1 See below, Epilogues, 310.

2 For the entire narrative, see Mushrif ud-Din Abdallah Sa'di, *Gulistan* (*The Rose Garden*), (section one, "Of the Customs of Kings"), section XXVII. In the English edition based on the translation by James Ross (Ames, Iowa: Omphaloskepsis), 2000, this will be found on pages 37-8.

3 The first Muslim woman to win a gold medal in Olympic competition was Morocco's Nawal El Moutawakal, the 1984 track and field 400-meter champion. I am not aware of any religious leader in her country publicly objecting to her running attire.

4 One can see how relatively easy flexibility can and sometimes already does operate within the specific sartorial arena in the small—one-paragraph-long— article in the *New York Times'* sports section on Thursday, June 30, 2011 that noted that "Weight lifting's world governing body agreed to modify its clothing rules to accommodate a Muslim woman competing for the United States." Kulsoom Abdullah had been barred from competing because her religious need to cover her head, legs and arms would produce a violation of international weight lifting rules regarding attire. The rules modification allows a unitard—a one-piece, full-body, tight-fitted garment—to be worn.

5 As the 2012 London Olympics were approaching, another watershed was reported in a March 20 article by Jere Longman and Mary Pilon, in the *New York Times*. The article observed that "every participating nation is expected to field at least one female athlete, including three Muslim countries—Saudi Arabia, Qatar and Brunei—that have previously sent only male competitors." The article refers to an article that appeared that same day in *Al-Hayat*, a London-based, Arabic-language newspaper, that "the Saudi Crown Prince Nayef bin Abdul Aziz has approved the participation of female athletes in London as long as their sports 'meet the standards of women's decency and don't contradict Islamic laws'." A smaller byline by Mary Pilon in the *Times* sports section the following day names the two competing women from Saudi Arabia: Sarah Attar (800 meters—which most likely would mean that the sartorial issue will have needed some flexibility) and Wodjan Ali Seraj Abdulrahim Shahrkhani (judo). Thus—aside from obviously not-yet-resolved gender issues and how they impinge, or should impinge, on the shaping of Olympic competition and the alleged standards of equality officially articulated by the I.O.C.—one sees clearly how religion remains a distinctive factor

in sports competition from a particular angle in this story. Later, in a July 30, 2912 article by Jere Longman entitled "A Giant Leap for Women, but Hurdles Remain," which featured a photo of Attar at the opening ceremony (wearing a *hijab*—a head scarf) two points particularly noteworthy for this discussion were made. One was that the Saudi women walked behind, not together with their male counterparts; the second was that there was a possibility that Shahrkhani would withdraw from the judo competition if she were not permitted to wear a *hijab*. Christoph Wilcke, "a Saudi expert for Human Rights Watch [is quoted as observing that i]t seems strange that the I.O.C. wouldn't have contemplated clothing."

6. In the book *A Different Kind of Superstar*, by Brad Darrach, Olajuwon is interestingly quoted as referring to playing basketball as an act of worship for him. If Hank Greenberg and Sandy Koufax are the one-two punch of Jewish athletic decisions not to play on Yom Kippur, as we shall see, then Hakeem's second punch is Husain Abdullah, a Vikings defensive back at the time of this writing who fasts daily during Ramadan—and has done so since he was seven years old. Both he and his older brother, Hamza, at this time a defensive back from the Arizona Cardinals, are discussed in Pat Borzi's article, "In the Heat of Camp, the Hunger of Faith," the *New York Times* (Monday, September 6, 2010, D1).

7. This last detail offers an ironic contrast to the internationalization process of Sumo wrestling competition that has increasingly troubled Japanese nationalist purists in the last few decades.

8. The number of Christians has, alas, significantly dwindled in the last decade, thanks largely to ISIS.

9. For clarity on this issue, see Ori Z Soltes, *Untangling the Web: A Thinking Person's Guide to Why the Middle East is a Mess and Always Has Been* (Savage, MD: Bartleby Press, 2011).

10. Farsi is also not a relative of Arabic, nor are the languages spoken in Uzbekistan, Kazakhstan, Kyrgizstan, Afghanistan and Pakistan, to name some neighbors near to the region. Conversely, Hebrew and Aramaic are, and so is Amharic.

11. As of the end of the eleventh Pan Arab Games, held in 2007 in Cairo, Egypt, the Egyptians had won a total of 985 medals in all—504 gold, 319 silver, and 162 bronze. The second-largest overall haul has been achieved by Syria, with 692 medals, 213 of them gold, 216 of them silver, and 263 of them bronze. Morocco has won the third largest overall total—519 medals—and the second largest number of gold medals: 222.

12. The language of the Egyptian hieroglyphs is not Semitic; it was referred to in previous eras as "Hamitic," whereas Arabic, Hebrew, Ethiopic, and other languages were called "Semitic." More recently, all of these have been labeled

"Afro-Asiatic," but the language of the hieroglyphs is understood to be more different from Arabic than are Hebrew, Ethiopic, or any of the other languages formerly called "Semitic." The most "modern" version of the Egyptian language initially written in hieroglyphic form is, in fact, Coptic—a language that is no longer in everyday use, though it is the liturgical language of the Coptic Church, which is, of course, Christian and not Muslim at all.

13. Since that time, another important "first" took place on March 9, 2011, in which a Palestinian national team met Thailand in a qualification match toward the 2012 Olympic Games—the first global qualifier to have taken place on the West Bank since 1948. Part of the significance of this event was that the organization of the team was facilitated not only by Jibril Rajoub, who had spent 17 years in an Israeli prison for tossing a grenade at Israeli soldiers as a teenager, but also by Zvi Varshaviak, Israel's Olympic committee president. Both leaders were very conscious of—inspired by—Nelson Mandela's statement that "sport has the power to change the world." While neither of them is naïve about this, both see the sports development as a potentially large step that can help lead the Israeli-Palestinian relationship in the right, peace-bound direction. See Rob Hughes, "In the West Bank, Openly Political Soccer," in the *New York Times* (Wednesday, March 9, 2011), B11-12. See also below, chapter 10, 180-81, chapter 11, 249-50.

14. To date, the matter of Palestinian statehood—of any sort—has yet to be achieved nor have the details of its parameters been agreed upon by the Palestinians themselves, the Israelis themselves, or the two groups in joint discussion.

CHAPTER NINE
Jews in Sports from Nahmanides in Barcelona to Mendoza in England

*T*here is surely no stereotype more widespread than that which disassociates Jews and the Jewish tradition from sports or from physicality in general. On the one hand, there is a certain logic to that. Physical strength and speed were not likely to be a key to survival for Jewish communities that functioned as a series of far-flung islands in vast non-Jewish seas of Christians, Muslims and others—at best tolerant (as opposed to embracing), at worst murderously disposed toward their Jewish neighbors from late antiquity to the early modern period.

Simple arithmetic in most situations made the pointlessness of a physical approach to survival clear, as the words "physical approach" pertained to sports as a surrogate and preparation for war and to war itself. And where that phrase might apply to living close to the earth as peasants and farmers do, or as a nobleman might— at least according to the sort of ideal sketched out by the likes of Machiavelli—the likelihood of Jewish engagement would also be necessarily slim. Jews could not own land, did not fit within either the earth-working or leisure-hunting population—and would be better served for their own protection, in most cases, by living close together in more urbanized settings, rather than by being spread out and isolated from each other across rural landscapes.[1]

Indeed, by the late medieval period, as the majority of Jews did live in urbanized settings, at least in central and western Europe, they tended, both by preference and by compulsion, to inhabit prescribed parts of the villages, town and cities in which they lived. The official term for such a section of town in the Muslim world came to be *mellah*. In the Christian world, the official term came to be *ghetto*—a Venetian-dialect equivalent of the broader Italian word, *gietto*, meaning "foundry." It refered to the Jewish quarter in Venice, located near a key iron foundry, where Jews were first officially confined under the Doge Leonardo Loredan in 1516; they were required to live there and to spend their time there between nightfall and dawn—the area was gated to keep them in and others out. As the medieval Christian world moved through the Renaissance toward modernity, the limited living location of the Jews became more stringent and official in most places, until the late eighteenth century.[2]

By further paradox—given the transformation of Western versus Eastern European Christendom during and following the late eighteenth century—one of the areas where such restrictions were less stringent was in the Polish Empire of the fourteenth century, under Kazimier the Great. Since, for reasons beyond this discussion, Jews tended to own and run inns both within and outside urban environments throughout Kazimier's domains, there was a good number of more ruralized Jews in Poland (and after the breakdown and break-up of the Polish Empire between the mid-seventeenth and late eighteenth century, throughout the parts of Eastern Europe that were now part of other polities, such as Romanov Russia). Nonetheless, even such rural Jews rarely turned to physicality as a way of life or as a way to remain alive.

It was wiser and safer, by and large, to use the mind rather than the body to make it from one year to the next. Whether it was within the context of the Crusades, which so decimated the

Rhineland Jewish communities during the late eleventh through mid-fourteenth centuries, or in the century in Spain that extended from 1391 to the expulsion of 1492, in which entire Jewish communities disappeared through a combination of forced departures and forced conversions, Jews were far more wont to turn to their wits than their brawn as a survival strategy. In any case, sports was largely anonymous in the medieval period as far as our current knowledge of who was doing what is concerned—and for Jews it was certainly not a hurried-to source of entertainment, self-expression, or preparation for weapon-wielding adventures.

Nonetheless, Jews might well look to their biblical roots, should they choose to do so, for inspiration regarding athletic activity and success. For example, there is the model of Jacob, as we have noted previously, whose all-night wrestling match with an angel (Gen. 32:25-30) ends in both victory and the transformation of the patriarch's very name—from Jacob, the "heel-grabber," to Israel, "one who has striven with God."

So, too, Jews might have looked to the shepherd, David son of Jesse, not only as a skilled practitioner of the sling shot when dealing with wild animals who might threaten his flocks, but also when he encounters the gigantic Philistine warrior-athlete, Goliath. And of course there was the ultimate strongman, Samson, who uses the jawbone of an ass to slay hordes of Philistines and, with his physical might, brings down their house of feasting. Moreover, as we have seen in chapter 1, this last pair of athlete-heroes fight with a distinct sense of having God at their backs as a partner in the otherwise uneven battles in which they are ultimately victorious.[3]

Should Jews of the medieval era have chosen to look just beyond the pages of the Hebrew Bible, they could have referred to the first two Books of the Maccabees. While outside the Jewish canon, these offer the textual foundation of the Hanukkah story, and Jews could certainly find in them the basis for redemptive inspiration along military lines. For in those two narratives one finds a combination of physical and spiritual strength in the Judaeans as they engaged in a three-year-long conflict with the Seleucids.[4] But in any case, since both volumes do fall outside the canon, we cannot expect most Jews in a premodern era to have turned to them. Yet those who did would have no doubt appreciated the descriptions of Judah and his brothers as physically strong and mentally brave, powerful warriors and brilliant guerilla tacticians—succeeding against a force much larger and better equipped than they are. Their physicality did not detract from the spiritual purpose for which they were fighting: the right to retain a sense of God and how to address that God that distinguished the Judaeans from the Seleucids and other pagans around them.

Interestingly, the two Books of the Maccabees differ most obviously from each other in that the first emphasizes the accomplishments of these men—human accomplishments—whereas the second emphasizes the divine role in the Hasmonean victory, and is fraught with miraculous occurrences. It is Second Maccabees that most specifically alludes to sports as an aspect of the problem-ridden relationship between the Judaeans of the mid-second century BCE and the Hellenistic culture surrounding them, of which the Seleucids were only part. It details the eagerness of the High Priest Joshua—his Hellenistic Greek name was Jason—to build a *gymnasion*—a facility in which athletes could exercise in the nude, in the Greek style—in Jerusalem (2 Maccabees 4:9-15).

The text also refers to his having sponsored a delegation of participants in athletic games taking place north, in the coastal city of Tyre.[5] Such games would have been modeled on the four types of competitions native to Greece discussed earlier.[6] The issue implied in both these would-be acts by Joshua/Jason is of how spiritually corrupt the High Priesthood had become by his time, as they sought to become involved in activities that, attached as they were to pagan gods, seemed absolutely antithetical to what the God of Israel would approve as Judaean behavior.

The notion that God was an athlete-warrior of sorts[7] and could thus be counted upon to support those who fought in Its Name, which we have already seen exemplified in the ideology of the Christian Crusades, might be seen to have distinct roots in the Hebrew Bible. In the stirring vision of seraphim swooping around the Throne of God articulated in Isaiah 6:1-4, the so-named angelic beings are heard to be intoning "Holy, holy, holy, the Lord of *armies*, the whole earth is full of His glory!" Admittedly, the word that I have rendered as "armies" is conventionally translated as "hosts" but not only might we ask, "hosts of what? Are these not hosts of warriors in the ongoing struggle against evil in its various manifestations, in which struggle the prophet is being called to serve?" Moreover, the Hebrew word, *tzva'ot*, in fact *does* mean armies — it is the word one uses in modern Hebrew to translate that term from English, for example.

More to the point, in a number of times and places in the Hebrew Bible, God is shown in action as a Lord of armies, albeit functioning in an unconventional manner. Thus, when the Israelites are attacked in the wilderness, barely out of Egypt, at Rephidim, by the Amalekites (Exodus 17:8ff), God assists them toward a victorious outcome as long as Moses is able to keep his God-directed arms and staff raised toward the heavens. (When his arms grow heavy, his brother, Aaron, and Hur, father of Joshua, help him to keep them raised.) After the eventual Joshua-led Israelite victory, the Lord instructs Moses to record the divine intention of liquidating the Amalekites altogether, and Moses builds an altar, "and called the name of it *Adonai-nissi* (verse 15)." The name means "the Lord is my banner."

There would be far-reaching ramifications for this initial confrontation between the Israelites and the Amalekites. They would extend to the beginning of the end of the kingship of Saul, who, as we are told in I Samuel 15, either misunderstood or simply disobeyed God's command by failing to wipe out all of the Amalekite descendants of those who attacked the Israelites in the wilderness, falling upon "the hindmost of thee, all that were enfeebled in the rear, when thou were faint and weary" (as the text of Deuteronomy 25:18 explains).

In addition, the effects of conflict between the Israelites and the Amalekites is also evident in the Book of Esther, the only narrative within the Hebrew Bible that focuses on Judaean descendants of the Israelites who live in the Diaspora. In the Persia described in that narrative, the villain, Haman, who sought to exterminate all of the Judaeans, is referred to as an Agagite—in other words, an Amalekite, since the kings of Amalek were all called by the name, Agag. Thus, the rabbinic commentators observe, Saul's failure to obey the command of "the Lord of hosts (armies)" led to a near-disaster for Saul's descendants some 600 years later.

The direct reference to God as a Lord of hosts in these battle contexts suggests—and suggested to medieval Jewish interpreters—a concept of a Lord of armies, and that God is repeatedly seen to be militarily engaged on behalf of the Israelites and their Judaean descendants. Moreover, in the era just prior to the destruction of the Second Temple, when the Hebrew-Israelite-Judaean continuum was on the verge of bifurcating toward Judaism and Christianity, there were several key political and spiritual factions within Judaea. There was at least one that withdrew from the mainstream Judaean community, convinced that the general population was failing to uphold God's covenant and that an apocalypse was imminent that would leave only the members of their splinter faction as survivors.

The faction, identified by some scholars as the Essenes, became rather well-known in the modern era after the discovery in 1947 of a large group of parchment scrolls, found in the Judaean desert in a series of caves not far from the northwest corner of the Dead Sea. The "Dead Sea Scrolls," as they are popularly called, are understood to have been written by that outsider group of Judaeans and hidden for safety's sake at the time of the rebellion against Roman power that culminated with the destruction of the Second Temple (65-70 CE).

Among the non-biblical texts is one commonly called the "Battle Scroll" that describes an apocalyptic, final confrontation between the "Sons of Light" (the forces for good), led by "The Good

Teacher," and the "Sons of Darkness" (the forces for evil), led by "The Wicked Priest." The forces for good would ultimately have God, as an explicit Lord of armies, at its back. Its troops would carry banners inscribed with quotations from the Psalms, signifying God's active support in the struggle. Indeed, in the seventh and final battle, we read, "the great hand of God shall overcome [Belial and all] the angels of his dominion, and all the men of [his forces shall be destroyed forever]" (IQM 1:14-15).[8]

Thus, the long sweep of Hebrew-Israelite-Judaean history could and perhaps sometimes did offer itself to Jews as a potential inspiration to God-supported military activity—and perhaps the various sports related to such activity—during the centuries since the Jewish-Christian schism and what later followed as the beginning of the Jewish dispersion among the nations. But even in the context of the Book of Esther, where, in the end, the Judaeans are permitted to arm themselves and then display the ability not only to defend themselves but to destroy their enemies, (see Esther 5), the path to that moment is opened up by acts of Esther and Mordecai that are strategically skillful and based on wiles and words, not feats of arms and athletic prowess.[9]

If the Hebrew Bible was the foundation-stone of the edifice of Judaism, then the structure that was built on that foundation began its construction with the evolution of rabbinic literature—around the time of the Dead Sea Scrolls and the shaping of the so-called Essene community, when the Hebrew-Israelite-Judaean continuum was beginning to split into Judaism and Christianity—and it progressed all the way through the five centuries or so that followed that era. Thus, rabbinic literature, which both directly interprets the word of God as traditionalists understand it to be found in the Hebrew Bible and addresses everyday problems for everyday Jews by reference to that word, emerged in layers, first oral and then written, between the last few pre-Christian centuries and ca 500 CE. In that literature of interpretation, shaped during the era connecting antiquity to the medieval period, we note the articulation of a Jewish ethos that sees itself in contrast to that of the pagan Greeks and Romans who are in the majority as Judaeanism starts to become Judaism (and Christianity).[10]

That Jews were at least somewhat interested in sports in antiquity is suggested by the passage in the Talmudic tractate *Kiddushin*, 29A, where it is stated that a father ought to teach his son how to swim. Conversely, the warning offered in section 18B of tractate *Avodah Zarah*—the name of which refers to its primary subject, "idol worship" and its concomitants—not to go to stadia, because they are "the seat of the scornful," suggests that there were plenty of Jews who did go, although whether as audience or participants is not clear. So, too, the denunciation of Jews who play ball games on the Sabbath suggests that there was a significant mass of Jews who either were willing to abrogate the Sabbath in favor of sports or who interpreted such games as a non-abrogation.

Broadly, then, a "Jewish ethos" looks down on what its rabbinic leaders see as a material-obsessed physicality exemplified by exercising and competing in the nude (in the Greek context) or near-nude (in the Roman context). The rabbis associated what they saw as the glorification of the body as directly connected to the religious sexuality of the distantly ancient Canaanites, whose fertility rituals directed toward Ba'al, Ashtoret, and other gods and goddesses were a constant temptation and threat to the survival of the Israelite religion that the prophets, from Elijah to Ezekiel, were championing. The fear of assimilation or worse, apostasy, helped to govern this rabbinic disdain. *Their* God, rather than a gendered physical being, was a metaphysical one that did not enjoin Its constituents to bring offerings as much as to "do justly, love mercy and walk humbly with thy God."[11] *Their* God asserted that the world itself stands not on sacrifices of animal—or human—bodies, but on three things: "Torah, worship and good works."[12]

Rabbinic examination of the Torah understands it to offer not only the Ten Commandments articulated in Exodus 20 and Deuteronomy 5, but also no less than a total of 613 commandments that a Jewish male is expected to seek to fulfill; so, too, a Jewish male is expected to pray no less than three times a day, regardless of daily-life complications—two challenges (particularly the first, fulfilling all those commandments), that may be viewed as far more rigorous a lifelong enterprise than, say, running the 26 miles and 385 yards of a marathon or slashing with a sword at another man armed with a trident and net. Passages attributed to different prophets within the biblical tradition became the basis for rabbinical *dicta* that take an antithetical approach to seeing physical strength and speed as admired attributes. For that most singular of Talmudic tomes, the Pirkei Avot ("Sayings of the Fathers"), enjoins Jews to recognize that the proper response to the rhetorical question, "Who is strong?" is a spiritual, not a physical answer; it is: "He who controls his own impulses."[13]

Such convictions fulfill what the rabbinical tradition recognizes as an obligation imposed by God not merely on the Israelites, but on the Jews as the descendants of the Israelites, to be "a Light unto the Nations." This is the centerpiece of an ethos that began to be shaped as Judaism itself was being shaped within the pagan world. For the majority of Jews, it was a world that would ultimately be dominated by Christian and Muslim populations.[14] The reality of such convictions, in combination with the reality of being a minority living under consistently tenuous conditions, made for a minimal rather than maximal focus on physical prowess within the far-flung diaspora of Jewish communities.

It is interesting to note, given this reality, that the 1329 work by the French Jewish philosopher-theologian and scientist, Levi Ben Gershon (Gershonides)—focusing on immortality, prophecy, divine knowledge, divine providence, astronomy/astrology, and creation—is entitled *The Book of the Wars of the Lord* (*Sefer Milham-ot Adonai*). Particularly given that much of his effort is directed at refuting points made by the preeminent Jewish medieval thinker, Maimonides (1135-1204), in the latter's *Guide for the Perplexed* (*Moreh Nekukhim*),[15] it would seem that the choice of the title offers an emphatic conceptual transfer of a material, physical idea to a spiritual, metaphysical realm.

The title surely derives from the conviction that the struggle to understand God, and what and how it is that God would have us be, must be seen as a virtual apocalyptic conflict, a war *for* the Lord—a war for proper understanding of how to grasp God—the outcome of which will determine the future condition of the human (or at least the Jewish) Being. At issue is not God as a warrior on behalf of the Jews in defending them against their enemies, but on behalf of the Jews in defending them against themselves with respect to being the "light onto the nations" that, as God-guided, they can and must be.

However, records from the medieval period show that active Jewish conflict with non-Jews was of the verbal sort, in which prominent Jewish leaders were forced into the position of a public debate—the proper term was "disputation"—against representatives of the Church, who were determined to prove the spiritual superiority of Christianity over Judaism. Perhaps the most famous of these medieval disputations occurred in Barcelona in 1263, when the Jewish scholar, Nahmanides, was commanded to appear to debate the verities of the two faiths with one Pablo Christiani.

Without belaboring details:[16] three days into the process, as it appeared that Nahmanides was getting the upper hand in the argument, the Jews of Barcelona begged him to desist, as they feared the consequences of angering the Dominicans who had sponsored the debate. Thus, we are reminded that the Jewish condition was usually fragile enough even to fear words, to say nothing of mounting physical opposition to their majority neighbors. However, the king himself asked the Jewish scholar to continue. And in the end King James I of Aragon rewarded Nahmanides with a prize of "300 dinars," declaring that he had never before heard "an unjust cause so nobly defended."

Royal support seems to have protected the community from violence against it or expulsion, which might otherwise have been expected as the "normal" outcome of a Christian-Jewish disputation—but it was insufficient to help Nahmanides himself, at least once he put his words into written form. Pablo Christiani selected certain passages from what Nahmanides put into writing, and construed them as anti-Christian blasphemies. Nahmanides argued that he had not written down anything that he had not openly argued before the king, who had granted him freedom of speech during the disputation. Nonetheless, the compromise arrived at to satisfy the Dominicans included banishing Nahmanides for a two-year period. Ultimately, though, Pope Clement IV was convinced to extend Nahmanides's two-year exile into a permanent one and King James was either unable or unwilling to argue the point against the Pope.

We are thus reminded that the position of Jews as a scattered archipelago of islands in seas politically and otherwise controlled by others had, among its effects, the ever-present possibility of expulsion, and together with that, a condition of nonparticipation in many of the ordinary walks of Christian (or, across the "border," Muslim) life, from owning and working land to participating in various crafts—to engaging in sports, military, and related activities.

Given all the obstacles discussed above, the occasional appearance of a noteworthy and gifted physical figure within the premodern Jewish world is all the more compelling—and ultimately problematic. One might consider a character who may, first of all, be mythical rather than historical, whose recorded (real or imagined) presence was viewed in the local Jewish sense as virtually *messianic*—and in the end, in a kind of moral warning lesson, needed to disappear and go back, as it were, from whence he had come. That figure is the Golem of Prague, created, it is said, by Rabbi Judah Loew of Prague (1512/25-1609) sometime toward the end of the sixteenth or the beginning of the seventeenth century.

Rabbi Loew was revered as a Talmudist and mathematician, and as the author of an important commentary on the renowned eleventh-century French Jewish Bible commentator, Rashi;[17] in kabbalistic circles, he was renowned for his complex mystical writings. He became most widely known for the story of how he allegedly used his esoteric knowledge—his access to secrets associated with Creation—to devise a creature that protected the Jewish community of Prague from its enemies in an era when potential attacks and threats of expulsion were rampant. The creature has been referred to through history simply as the "Golem"—from a word that appears once in the book of Psalms (139:16) and means "unformed/shapeless [mass]."

As a localized "messianic" guardian, the Golem served the Jewish community and protected it from hostile Christians. The tradition regarding the manner of its creation and its very existence is, to say the least, extraordinary.

Rabbi Loew is said to have shaped his creature out of earth, on the banks of the Vltava River, creating the anthropomorphic figure by reciting prescribed, esoteric, mystical formulae as he walked around it seven times in the appropriate direction.[18] The process culminated with the placement of the Ineffable Name of God, either (depending upon which version of the story) written on a piece of parchment and placed within the creature's mouth, or inscribed directly on its forehead.[19] Thus, we recognize that Rabbi Loew was recapitulating the original culminating creative act of God, taking earth (*adamah*) as God did in creating the first human being (*adam*) and, as God breathed life into the being that was thus *be-souled* with God's own breath, so Judah Loew breathed life into the Golem by using the true, hidden, secret, ineffable Name of which he (Rabbi Loew) was a master.

Although the preternaturally large and strong result of this process—one envisions a Herakles-Samson sort of athlete, as it were—was a creature who served and, according to tradition, often saved the Jewish community of Prague from potentially harmful enemies, the downside of the story soon evidenced itself. Inevitably, the Golem got out of hand—for only Rabbi Loew truly understood how to control it; others could command it and it would respond, but they neither appreciated the manner in which it would respond literally to every command nor understood how to make it desist, when necessary, from whatever action had been demanded of it.

So, its creator had to deactivate it. Rabbi Loew did so by removing the name of God (or the word, "truth")[20] from its mouth (or its forehead), whereby it returned to a condition of being a lump of earth. This culmination of the Golem's career thereby offers a concrete reminder of the dangers attached to using mystical formulae, and in the case of our narrative, also perhaps represents the inadvisability for European Jews of relying on *physical* prowess to enhance their chances for survival.

We are back, so to speak, where we began.[21] But the Christian world and its attitude both toward its own certain sense of God and toward the Jewish community was undergoing a slow series of changes, at least in Western Europe, at around the very same time during which Judah Loew was meddling with the creative process through esoteric mystical formulae. For the Protestant reformation of the first half of the sixteenth century had torn western Christendom into a series of schismatic fragments, and by the last part of the century—and continuing all the way into the early eighteenth century—Protestants and Catholics were engaged in the kind of bloody conflicts with each other that had been reserved for Christian wars against the Muslims during the previous half-millennium.

In such an Age of Religious Wars, as that period is called by historians, there was an increasing number of intellectuals who began to doubt the traditional conception of God as all-powerful, all-good, all-knowing as well as interested, involved, and interventionist in human affairs. One of the eventual ramifications of such doubt was a shift in the Christian European sensibility. That sensibility had prescribed a marginalization of non-Christian populations, such as the Jews, throughout Europe for the previous fifteen centuries. In contrast, by the late eighteenth century, Jews were beginning to find their way into the European mainstream, with a range of consequences, not least of which was growing participation in sports.

Notes

1. As a spiritual matter, although Jews can and do pray individually, there is a strong sense that God prefers communal prayer—particularly for life-cycle events—and prayer is traditionally offered three times a day. Combined with practical matters such as finding food that is kosher, this would also militate in favor of living in proximity to other Jews.

2. It might also be noted that living in a Jewish ghetto by no means suggested the negative connotation that it came to have by the late eighteenth century. See Robert C. Davis & Benjamin Ravid, eds, *The Jews of Early Modern Venice* (Baltimore and London: Johns Hopkins University Press, 2001). There is a good summary of this in a not-yet-published paper by my colleague in Georgetown University's German Department, Hillah Cullman, *Ghetto als Heimat: Frankfurter Ghetto als Juedische Heimat—in Heinrich Heines "der Rabbi von Bacharach."* ("Ghetto as Home: the Frankfurt Ghetto as a Jewish Home—in Heinrich Heine's 'The Rabbi of Bacharach'.") That paper will no doubt soon appear as a journal article, although I cannot predict in which journal. It is meanwhile available at Georgetown's Lauinger Library.

3. See the more detailed discussion of Jacob, Samson and David above in chapter 1, 23-31.

4. Named for Seleukos, one of Alexander the Great's favorite friends and generals, the Seleucids shaped one of the post-Alexander Hellenistic kingdoms, in and around what is now Syria. Their relations with the Judaeans were fairly calm until the advent of the King Antiokhos V, who demanded that his image be placed in the Temple in Jerusalem and that his cult as a god be included in the cult of the Judaean God. This eventually led to the revolt (ca 168-65 BCE) that gained religious freedom and, as an unanticipated by-product, political freedom for Judaea.

5. 2 Maccabees 4:18-20. The mode of participation was specified as providing extensive funds for offerings at the Temple of Herakles—which, since the bearers of the funds themselves thought this singularly inappropriate, ended up being used to outfit warships known as triremes.

6. See chapter 4, 65-6.

7. God, who is emphatically nonphysical in the Jewish tradition, would be a unique "athlete-warrior."

8. Belial is the key figure opposing God; his name translates as "without God."

9. Mordecai, overhearing a plot against the king, is able to warn him about it; the king asks Haman how to honor someone beyond measure and Haman, thinking that he will himself be honored, unwittingly provides that honor for Mordecai. Esther, having risked her position as royal favorite, invites the king and Haman to a series of private dinners that end up leading to Haman's demise at the hand of the king.

10. See above, chapter 6, 94 for a brief discussion of Judaean gladiatorial participation.

11. Micah 6:8.

12. Pirkei Avot I.2

13. See Pirkei Avot ("Sayings of the Fathers"), IV:1. The word *"pirkei"* is somewhat awkward to translate. It is more usually rendered in general contexts as "chapters of," but in the title of this rabbinic text is more often rendered as "sayings of," to underscore that this is what the content of the book is: sayings, statements, comments, observations made by a series of key figures in the early Jewish tradition.

14. There are, of course, Jews who live or who have lived among Hindus, Buddhists, Confucians, and practitioners of other faiths and philosophies, but the majority have been dispersed islands within either Christian or Muslim seas.

15. The term "perplexed" in the title of Maimonides's work refers to Jews trying to figure out how to live their lives in a God-pleasing manner in a world often hostile to them and to some of the key customs deemed necessary to living such lives.

16. For a fuller account of the Nahmanides Disputation, see Ori Z Soltes, *Famous Jewish Trials: From Jesus to Jonathan Pollard* (Bartleby Press, 2013).

17. Rashi is the acronym of an eleventh-century (1040-1105) rabbi from northern France who authored the first comprehensive commentaries on the Talmud and the Hebrew Bible.

18. More precisely: he is said to have used two assistants, with whom he prepared all four elements. His son-in-law, a Kohayn, and a pupil who was a Levite, prepared fire and water; Rabbi Loew prepared air; the Golem itself was made of earth. After purifying themselves and studying the *Sepher Yetzirah* ("The Book of Formation," a mystical text that seeks to answer the question of how God created the universe), they began the process at midnight of the prescribed day. While reciting combinations of letters and words—*tzerufim*—the Kohayn walked around the creature seven times from right to left, after which the Levite walked

around it seven times from left to right, after which Rabbi Loew walked around it once, then placed the Name within its mouth (or upon its brow) that caused it to open its eyes.

19. Yet another variant suggests that the word written down by Rabbi Loew was the Hebrew word for "truth": *emet*, contrived of the first (*aleph*) and last (*tav*) letters of the Hebrew alphabet with a middle letter (*mem*) in the middle, thus signifying the notion that truth encompasses all. And "Truth" is in any case a synonym for God's Ineffable Name.

20. A further variant: that by simply erasing the *aleph* from the beginning of the three-consonantal word, *emet*, one could instantly deactivate the Golem, since the remaining two consonants spell the word *met*, meaning "dead."

21. The narrative, well-known within both the Jewish and the Christian communities of central Europe, may well have inspired cautionary tales such as Mary Shelley's *Frankenstein*.

CHAPTER TEN
Sports and Judaism Since Emancipation

*B*y the time the Age of Religious Wars had ended (the conventional date that is usually offered is 1715, the year in which the French "Sun King," Louis XIV, died after a reign of 70 years) the God-question had begun an insistent rise among the existential inquiries that were making their way through Western thought. In brief, the seventeenth century was marked by new discussions—new angles of questioning and seeking answers—regarding God's existence, in the hands of figures such as the French Catholic, Descartes; the German Protestant, Leibnitz; and the Dutch Jew, Spinoza. It is not that any of these individuals doubted the existence of an all-powerful God, but the way in which they reexamined and/or rephrased questions about God opened the door for others who *would* doubt.

Thus, by the end of the following century—in part, perhaps, also because of the array of revolutions that marked the period of ca. 1760 to 1820: industrial, technological, scientific as well as political and philosophical—two views of how the world functions began to stand in distinct opposition to each other. The one, the *teleological* view, maintains that an all-powerful and presumably all-good, all-knowing as well as involved God created us for a purpose—the Greek word for "purpose" is *telos*, hence this worldview is a teleo-

171

logical one—and that a key part of our human purpose is to figure out what that divinely imposed purpose *is*.

In opposition to this essentially traditional Jewish-Christian-Muslim viewpoint stands the *mechanistic* view, arriving into Western European discourse by the late eighteenth century. The mechanistic view asserts either that God created the universe, wound it up, as it were, like a finely wrought machine, and turned away—or that, (in a more extreme variant of this view), the universe is simply here, it got started somehow, it keeps going, there is no God of even a disengaged sort. No God, period. In either variant, we need to find human purpose from within ourselves, and not from some metaphysical superstructure.

The French philosopher Voltaire was an example of a thinker who asserted that the convictions of traditional religion are out of date and irrational. He most famously parodied Leibnitz, as well as anything resembling a teleological worldview, in his *Candide*. The German philosopher Immanuel Kant, on the other hand, offered a less extreme certainty, but in his *Groundwork of the Metaphysics of Morals* he sought to shape a moral code—he called it the "Categorical Imperative"—that does not depend at all on the conviction that there is a God out there commanding moral behavior (i.e., who decrees that "thou shall not murder; thou shall not commit adultery," etc). Such thinkers considered themselves enlightened, secularized Christians and called their era the Age of Enlightenment: their world, as far as they were concerned, had arrived out of a dark age of irrational thought into one of clear, rational thinking.

The point of this brief theological-philosophical digression is this: that in the context of shifting convictions with regard to the nature or even the very existence of God, the traditional religion-based foundations of Jew-hatred and Jew-persecution began to be undermined in many parts of Western and Central Europe. A growing array of thinkers began to ask whether, as Christians, they could be so certain that the Jewish belief system is wrong, much less threatening to Christians, if one cannot be certain about the nature and possibly even the existence of the God who has been approached some-what differently by Jews and Christians (and Muslims) over the past many centuries. The practical consequence in this shift in thinking was a series of acts that removed the social, economic, and also cultural (and even, eventually, political) limitations that had kept Jews out of the mainstream for so many centuries.

The English first sought to open the doors to Jewish involvement in the secular Christian world with a "Jew Bill" of 1753, though its passage failed at that time. The Hapsburg Empire that dominated much of central Europe began a process of tolerance toward its Jewish citizenry in 1782, under Emperor Joseph II, culminating with the entrance of Jews into the Hapsburg armies by 1788. The French, after the revolution of 1789, debated the question of whether the Jews of France were Jews who happened to live in France or Frenchmen who happened to be Jewish rather than Catholic. They embraced the second of these perspectives, and on September 28, 1791, declared as much in an official edict. The Prussian state finally climbed onto a similar bandwagon by 1812.[1]

In brief, Emancipation, as Jewish historiographers typically call this era, gradually made it possible for there to be all sorts of Jewish participation in the mainstream, including in the world of sports. This development also signaled a shift in the way religion and sports were perceived; instead of a focus that was limited to God's presumed presence in athletic aspiration or accomplishment, it encompassed the fact of Jewish involvement in sports, regardless of whether those participating thought of themselves more as Jews by faith rather than by culture, ethnicity, or some other definitional marker (or more than one of these).

Specifically, Daniel Mendoza, who was born in 1764 in the East End of London to a poor Sephardic[2] Jewish family, and left school at age 13 to work for a tea dealer, was drawn—after winning a fist-fight with a porter who had insulted his employer—to a sport that was beginning to emerge at that time in England: boxing. Boxing as a form of athletic competition that was governed by specific rules (as opposed to fighting by whatever means to settle some dispute) had begun a rise to popularity only in the early 18th century. The first British heavyweight champ, James Figg, was crowned in 1719. Figg popularized sparring exhibitions and after his death in 1740 he was followed as boxing's king by his former pupil, George Taylor, who, in turn, was followed by Jack Broughton. By 1734, Broughton had already formulated the first set of rules for boxing—they would remain in place, unchanged, until 1838. He created the first boxing gloves and imposed style, rather than simply brute strength, on the burgeoning sport.

In the generation that followed Broughton's predominance, the level of corruption grew as part of the context of boxing. A generation after that, a number of figures came to prominence, including the first Irish champion of England, Peter Corcoran, and, in 1791, "Battling" Mendoza. Mendoza had been taken under the wing of "gentleman boxer" Richard Humphreys, who both made boxing acceptable to the gentry and introduced Mendoza to a number of well-heeled fans and patrons who helped his rapid rise to fame. Strong but typically lighter than the opponents he faced, Mendoza is usually credited with developing defensive moves—side-stepping, "guarding," and jabbing with the left hand in a straight motion—that would enable him to avoid getting hit by larger, stronger opponents.

He is therefore referred to as the father of "scientific" boxing. In an era when fighters usually stood face to face and traded punches, Mendoza's formula for success was designed around footwork, weaving in and out and attacking one's opponent quickly and from diverse angles.[3] So, he earned the heavyweight title and held it for four years. One might say that his social rise, that paralleled his athletic success—he was the first Jew in England to meet the king (George III)—was possible in spite of continuing social restrictions on Jews, and also that his rise helped to undercut those restrictive attitudes and laws.[4]

In any case, the book that he wrote in 1789, *The Art of Boxing* found a substantial audience, and many young Jews—and non-

Jews—were drawn to the school for boxers that he founded after his retirement from the ring. His technique, based on speed, finesse, and well-honed moves became the basis for the "Mendoza School"—also known as "the Jewish School"—that is the ancestor of the kind of style brought to such perfection by Muhammad Ali in the second half of the twentieth century.

As mentioned, by the time of Mendoza's writing and teaching, the world was beginning to open up for Jews on both sides of the Atlantic, with new possibilities and also definitional problems. Permitting Jews into the mainstream, say, within the socioeconomic and educational systems of France, had practical complications. Jewish children could now attend state-run public schools, rather than privately run Jewish schools but, although the public schools were part of a theoretically secular state, they were closed on Sundays (the Christian Sabbath) and Christian holidays, and open on Saturdays (the Jewish Sabbath) and Jewish holidays.

So, would those Jewish children stay home on Saturdays? Go to school but not write—or participate in ball games (because both of these are considered "work" and one may not work on the Sabbath within the Jewish tradition)? Would they only be able to write if an examination was being administered that day? Would they only play if there was a championship match that required their participation? And what would they do if the first day of Passover fell on a Tuesday? And what of the shopkeeper who, by law, had to close his shop on Sunday—would he keep it open on Saturday as his Christian competitors naturally did, in order not to sacrifice one-sixth of his business—but thereby abrogating *his* Sabbath—or would he close it to keep the Sabbath but thereby sacrifice much of his business?

The answer to this layered question would depend in part on how one defined oneself as a Jew at that time. If the definition was based purely on *religious* identity, and in turn connected to religious *observance*, then how could one abrogate the Sabbath, since that would be to undercut one's religion? Unless, that is—as was beginning to happen in Germany by 1810 or so—a reshaping of the religion of Judaism, called Reform, was taking place, and one were drawn into the Reform circle. In that case, a range of traditional commandments might be viewed as no longer *relevant* to Jewish life in the modern world.

But other possibilities, outside the definition of Judaism as a religion, were also beginning to present themselves, both positive and negative. One might begin to define oneself as a *cultural* Jew, rather than as a religious Jew, in keeping with the expanding secular sensibility within the Western world—although articulating one's Judaism as "cultural," much less as "secular" would not really flourish for another century and a half. (In that case, where the issue of religion—and therefore, Judaism in the strict sense as a religion—and sports is concerned, would this part of our discussion become functionally irrelevant?)

Since during this same period, also known as a period of romantic nationalism, other groups were asserting a reinvigorated sense of *nationality*, might Jews do the same? But then, the very conditions under which they were emancipated, say, in France—because they were adjudged Frenchmen first, who happened to be Jewish, rather than being perceived first as Jews who happened to live in France rather than Germany or Italy—would be undercut. If I were to declare myself a Jew by nationality, then what rights, tied to citizenship considerations, could I reasonably expect within France or Germany, no matter how long my family and its ancestors had dwelled in such countries?

It turns out that this sort of question remained on the minds of the Christian inhabitants of these countries long after Emancipation theoretically answered it. And with the Jewish response to both this condition (and with it, a seemingly impossible-to-kill anti-Judaism), and to the ideas of romantic nationalism in general combining to produce a Jewish nationalist movement by the end of the century, the issue becomes further complex.

Among the responses from within the Jewish communities of Europe to the definitional question within the extended Romantic nationalist context was to *embrace* the notion of nationality. Thus, beginning with a book penned by the German Jewish writer, Moses Hess, in 1862, called *Rome and Jerusalem*, not only was modern Jewish nationalism born. More than a vague birthing concept, Jews were enjoined — and therefore the title of Hess's book — to think forward by thinking backward. They were encouraged to aspire to reclaim the great and glorious days of the Israelite kingdom of David and Solomon, in a manner similar to that according to which Italians of the mid-nineteenth century were being encouraged by their primary Romantic nationalist theorist, Giuseppe Mazzini, to think forward by thinking back to the great and glorious days of Imperial Rome. The culmination of Hess's idea may be seen in the work of Theodor Herzl at the end of the nineteenth century — most specifically, with his convening of the First Zionist Congress, in 1897, in Basel, Switzerland.

In fact, another late 19th-century viewpoint was supplied by the anti-Jewish German pamphleteer and politician, Wilhelm Marr, who in 1879 began to refer to Jews as "Semites" — extracting that term from the vocabulary of comparative philology — to suggest that they were altogether a *race* apart from the European "race." His desire to push Jews once more back, away from the mainstream toward the fringe of European society, opened up a genealogical, bloodline, and ethnic category that would have profound implications for Jews in Europe, most obviously in Germany itself two generations later. Herzl's work was in part an attempt to respond to the new anti-Semitism by suggesting a program that would remove most Jews from Europe and make it clear that those who chose not to leave made that choice because they were unequivocally self-identified as Frenchmen, Germans, Italians or whatever. This would hardly change the viewpoint of the followers of Marr, of course, but perhaps some of them could at least be satisfied that most Jews would be leaving Europe.

By that time, a growing array of Jews had been making a mark on the expanding world of European and American sports. Lipman Pike — about whom more in the next chapter of this narrative — became the first professional baseball player in the mid-1860s, as that sport emerged in the United States after the Civil War. Lon Myers became renowned as a runner in the 1880s and Lewis Rubenstein, from Canada, won the first world title in figure skating, in 1890. It is not altogether surprising, then, that with the emergence—or reemergence after a dormancy of seventeen centuries—of Jewish nationalism, a sports-inspired physicality should be a more than incidental aspect of its early development.

Modern Jewish nationalism—Zionism—was in the process of being born through the efforts of Herzl and others, and with it a replenished focus on physicality and its virtues, in the century following Daniel Mendoza's bringing such virtues to the fore for the European Jewish community. Thus, among the definitional aspects of Zionism—what exactly should be its essence and its goals?—there arose what has been called a kind of "muscular Zionism." To be more precise, Max Nordau, one of the first champions of Theodore Herzl's work, in speaking at the Second Zionist Congress of 1898, called for the shaping of a "new Jew" marked by a "muscular Judaism."

This movement placed a decisive emphasis not only on returning to an engagement of the earth after forced exile from earth-directed living for the better part of 15 centuries—to being "rebuilt" by plowing and sowing and building the land of *Eretz Yisrael*—but on developing a strong interest to engage in, and gaining the prowess to succeed in physical culture in general and sports competitions in particular.

With strong physical ambitions, the "muscular Jews," both Zionist and not, founded an entire series of gymnastic clubs. The Bar Kokhba Club was established in Berlin in the year of Nordau's address (1898)—named for the physically imposing warrior and brilliant strategist who had led the Jews for three years in a revolt against Roman power in 132-35 CE. Soon, dozens of gymnastic clubs were springing up—not all necessarily connected to the Zionist movement—so that by 1903 there was an umbrella organization to encompass them all. More broadly—if not related to muscular Zionism, then no doubt a further outgrowth of its ideology—by 1906, there emerged a wide range of different *kinds* of sports clubs and organizations within the European Jewish world.

In Vienna, Austria-Hungary, for instance, the *HaKoah* ("The Power/Strength") club, founded mainly by Hungarian Jews in 1909, was the best-known of these sports clubs. Soon, there were more clubs and teams of that name. The *HaKoah* teams would become remarkably accomplished in international competitions, particularly in swimming and track and field, and the jewel in their collective crown was the 1925 soccer team that won the Austrian national championship—and brought a new sense of pride to Jewish communities throughout the wide world in which the team played.

On the other hand, by 1915, in Germany, the first of the *Maccabi* clubs came into being. They were named after Judah Maccabee and his four brothers, heroes of the Hanukkah story—whose exploits as guerilla warriors against the Seleucid Empire, which ultimately led to Judaean political independence, we recall, were glorified in the First Book of Maccabees. While this text remained apocryphal in the Jewish biblical tradition, as we have noted, its message grew over time in its capacity to inspire Jews—particularly in the modern era of Emancipation. The perceived need for a counterweight to Christmas, in countries which, while nominally secular, still operated in part according to a Christian calendar, and for which Christmas offered itself as the ultimate children's holiday, helped spur the growth of Hanukkah as a popular Jewish celebration.

The Maccabi Club in Berlin would become the largest Jewish athletic club in Europe between the wars. In 1921, an entire Maccabi World Union was founded to unite most of the clubs of this name, and the Maccabi World Union expanded its activities to encompass communities as far away as Australia and South America. In fact, the enthusiasm for sports among Jews led to the development of an entire para-Olympic movement, created by the Maccabi World Union and designed for worldwide, entirely Jewish participation, and called the Maccabiah Games.

After 14 years of discussing plans for such a competition, the Union held the first Maccabiah Games in Tel Aviv in 1932, with about 400 athletes participating. The second games took place about a year later, with nearly 1,350 athletes participating. The decision to host such games in Palestine must be understood, in part, in political terms: it was an aspect of the statement by Jewish nationalists—Zionists—that the reemergent Jewish presence in the ancestral homeland was not temporary or offhanded, but deliberate and permanent. It was shaped in the context of the post-World War I world, and power-jockeying from without by the British and the French; and from within by the various Middle Eastern Arab, Egyptian, Persian, Turkish, and Kurdish peoples to reconfigure the region along new, post-Ottoman lines. The Maccabiah statement may be understood as part of the larger Zionist vision of recreating a Jewish nationalist sensibility along lines that would encompass not only the political or the spiritual but the cultural as well.

In any case, the creation of the Maccabiah Games would have other, related implications as the Nazi party swallowed up Germany and then its neighbors, and the world moved gradually toward the second of the twentieth century's world wars. The second Maccabiah Games, of 1935, took place in the shadow of Hitler's ascension and his articulation of the Nuremberg Laws depriving Jews in Germany of citizenship rights. Several Maccabiah delegations, seeing the writing on the wall, chose not to return to the countries that they had represented, but to remain in Palestine. Due to the Arab riots of 1936-9 against the Jewish communities in Palestine, World War II (1939-45), and the struggles against the British that followed the war, the third Maccabiah Games were not held for another 15 years—two years after the independent State of Israel had come into existence.

In fact those 1950 games came in the aftermath of the International Olympic Committee's decision to deny Israeli participation in the 1948 Olympics on the grounds that, at the time those games were being organized, the state did not yet exist and so its delegation was not able to be officially recognized by the Olympic Committee. The third Maccabiah Games were also held under the cloud of the mourning that gripped the world Jewish community in the aftermath of the Holocaust, which claimed many Jewish athletes and Jewish athletic club members among its six million victims. These games marked a new departure point for both the nascent state of Israel and the world Jewish community. For the state, they offered a sibling to a second set of international Jewish games held in Israel, the *HaPoel* ("The Worker") Games—that grew out of a sports club and competition movement founded back in 1923 by the Socialist Labor Movement in Palestine. They also came to represent a national, regional prelude, by the 1960s, to the Olympic Games.

Both the HaPoel Games and the Maccabiah Games were originally to take place every four years, like the Olympic Games. But, whereas, from the beginning the Maccabiah Games have been competitive and have drawn champion athletes from around the world to participate, the HaPoel Games were originally directed more towards mass participation—in other words, by more "everyday" competitors. Nonetheless, after the 1935 second Maccabiah, with so many of those world-class athletes remaining in Palestine and joining the HaPoel Organization, the HaPoel Games became somewhat more focused on competition. In effect, by the time of the third Maccabiah, HaPoel athletes competed in the Maccabiah, so that the two organizations, the Socialist Labor Movement's HaPoel Games and the Maccabi World Union's Maccabiah Games) now both fed into the Maccabiah. In turn, since the 1952 Olympics were approaching, they also became part of the regional pre-Olympic preparation and try-out competitions.

One might recognize parallels to the discussion at the end of chapter 6 regarding the Pan Arab Games. There is the definitional issue—what defines an Arab as opposed to a Muslim and how are those two terms are regularly confused and conflated, similar to the question of what defines a Jew, and the varied answers to that question offered at different times and places. A second parallel is seen with regard to the establishment of Olympic-like competitions by these two groups, games both in their own right and as a kind of testing ground for would-be Olympians—and both taking place in the Middle East.

And indeed, to backtrack chronologically, while the Jewish nationalist movement was emerging and evolving,[5] the modern Olympics themselves—inspired by a romanticized European cultural memory of ancient Greece at its most elegant—had emerged in 1896. In those first games, a German Jew, Alfred Flatow, participated as a gymnast, winning three gold medals and a silver; Gustav Felix Flatow, also from Germany and also a gymnast, won two golds.[6] With these athletes one might say that the arrival of Jews into the mainstream world-sports arena had begun. In fact, from the opening of the modern Olympic Games, Jews began a noteworthy history of participation and success, fraught, however, with particular issues and complications.[7] Where we have seen, for instance, that the Muslim participation in the Olympics or other modes of sports events has presented challenges regarding how to maintain the tenets of Ramadan at that time of year, or the question of sartorial correctness for Muslim women, the Jewish issues have been in some cases parallel and in others very different.

For the sake of convenience, we might divide those Jewish issues into three categories. The first and simplest is the raw statistics of participation and success, an issue trebly interesting: first, because the non-physically-focused history of Jews discussed in the previous chapter makes such accomplishment rather startling; second, because sports fans, at least in the modern era, are obsessed with statistics; and third, because Jews in the modern era—particularly in the era since (and perhaps in part as a consequence of) the Holocaust—are as concerned as any ethnic, national, racial, or religious group with the question of who, in a given category of accomplishment, is one of "us."

Thus, one of the interesting things in this discussion is that, statistically, the overall Jewish participation rate in the Olympics and other international competitions is at least equal to the overall percentage of Jews in the population of the planet at large. The overall success rate, similarly, in statistical terms, corresponds more than respectably to the number of Jewish participants in the games and, in turn, to the percentage of Jews in the overall planetary population.[8] And there have been outstanding champions from various countries. Many of these have been from Eastern Europe which, after World War II remained firmly implanted within the Soviet orbit until the last decade of the twentieth century.

The identities of these Eastern European athletes as Jews were never hidden but neither were they touted, and it is probably fair to say that their own sense of identity as Jews was viewed, by their countrymen and themselves, as somewhere between ethnic and religious — but not religious in a formal sense: most of them were not likely to attend synagogue or pray in a formal, congregational context very often, if at all, or worry about consuming kosher food. Needless to say, the Soviet-led Communist umbrella under which they all competed discouraged any sort of overt expression of religious identity.[9]

Interestingly, many of the most outstanding performers were women. To name a few of these — might we call them "stars of David"? — one might note the Hungarian Jewish swimmer, Eva Szekely, who won medals in both the 1952 and 1956 Olympics, and who, aside from her 101 Hungarian records, held 5 Olympic and 10 world records at one time to go with the 88 titles that she won. So, too, Hungarian Jewish gymnast Agnes Keleti won five gold, three silver, and two bronze medals in the Olympic Games of 1952 and 1956. Due to both the politics of war, which forced the cancellation of the 1940 and 1944 games, and an injury that Keleti suffered just prior to the 1948 games, she was already 31 years old when she won her first medal.

Then there was Irena Kirszenstein-Szewinska, who won Olympic medals — three golds, two silvers, and two bronzes — for Poland in the 1964, 1968, 1972, and 1976 Olympics in track, (variously for the 100-, 200-, and 400-meter runs and the long jump) to go along with 13 medals in the European championships and 26 Polish national titles. So, too, there was, among the men, Gyozo Victor Barna, the

Hungarian table tennis champion—for several decades, table tennis was regarded as a virtual "Jewish" sport, as was fencing—who also won 22 world championships in the 1920s and 1930s; and Angelica Rosenau, who won 17 world titles in table tennis for Rumania in the 1950s and early 1960s.

Recognition certainly arrived for these athletes and others with less extensive championship resumes in their own countries, but we are less likely in the West to be aware of them—much less of their religious identities, which, particularly in the context of the internal politics of the Soviet Union and its satellites, would, to repeat, hardly have been advertised. Nearer to home, the Canadian track and field star, Fanny Rosenfeld, (who won Olympic gold in 1928) was voted the outstanding Canadian athlete of the half-century in 1950.

By that year, Victor Hershkowitz was beginning his run of 9 straight titles in three-wall handball—a sport that had begun a long run of extreme popularity in New York City in the 1920s and 1930s—part of a cache of 43 titles that he held in a storied career matched only by that of Jimmy Jacobs, who earned 15 national handball titles of diverse sorts, both as a singles and as a doubles player. In fact, he and his doubles partner, Marty Decatur, played for 12 years together without ever losing a match. And there have been Jewish stars in even less obvious and mainstream kinds of sporting competitions, such as Brooklyn-born Sidney Franklin (his given name was Sidney Frumkin), who took up bullfighting, and rose to the status of a head-liner in the *Placa de los Toros* in Madrid, Spain, arguably the center of bullfighting, in 1945—an unusual direction not only because he was Jewish but because he was an American city boy!

Perhaps the most renowned Jewish Olympic star from the United States is Mark Spitz, who added to his "disappointing" haul in 1968—a mere two golds, one silver, and one bronze—a record-breaking seven gold medals in swimming, each a world record at the time, at the 1972 Olympics. (His total was finally supplanted by Michael Phelps's eight medals at the Beijing Olympics of 2008.)

The mention of Mark Spitz and the Munich Olympics of 1972

brings up a second category of particular focus or interest where the issue of Jews and sports in the past century is concerned. This category pertains to the ugly (as opposed to benign) relationship among religion, sports, and politics. For the 1972 Olympics will always be remembered, by Jews at least, for the tragic incident that championed impropriety and the abrogation of the fundamental Olympic principle of separating athletic competition and its camaraderie from political and related concerns.

The massacre of 11 Israeli athletes by Arab terrorists was an act symptomatic of the expanding arena of political conflict between Israel and its Arab neighbors out of the Middle East into the larger world and, from the perspective of this narrative, of carrying a political agenda—in this case a deadly, and not merely verbally or otherwise urgent agenda—from the battlefield into the temporary domiciles of the players, who were gunned down as if they were soldiers and not athletes. The irony was, of course, palpable, since the outcome was a mass-murder in the Olympic Village designed to be an international locus of friendly competition, transcending the political differences of its participants or of members of a particular group singled out for its national and, by definition, religious identity.

This last issue is a "by definition" given, since Israel's own identity from its inception—regardless of its structure as a democracy whose citizens include Christians, Muslims, Hindus, Baha'is, and others—is as "the Jewish State," and its role, both from its own and from the world's perspective, is to operate as such on the world stage. And thus, the irony was in fact exponentially increased by the fact that the murders took place in Munich, Germany, the heartland of Nazism in the late 1920s and early 1930s and the city in which Adolph Hitler effectively got his start in what would emerge over the following decade as the most stunning massacre of Jews the world had or has ever seen.

And in fact, both the politicization of the Olympics—which can be seen, lest we forget, to extend all the way back to their ancient iteration in Greece—and the specific politicization that focuses in a prejudicial manner on Jews and Jewish athletes, particularly in Germany, preceded the 1972 Munich Games. Most obviously, if we think back to the Nazi era, we arrive at the 1936 Berlin Olympics, presided over by none other than Adolph Hitler.[10] Part of Hitler's ambition at that moment was to demonstrate how civilized and well-ordered the new Germany was under his guidance, and part of his ambition was to demonstrate the physical predominance of what he had begun to call the "Aryan" race.

"Civilized" meant, among other things, that the "rumors" of his suppression of certain groups—primarily, but by no means limited to, the Jews—were false. There was a practical need to do this, since the protests in some corners of the globe against what could hardly be hidden with respect to suppression, had threatened to lead to the virtual cancellation of the Berlin Games. Thus, the Nazi overlords of Germany let it be known that, among others, some outstanding Jewish athletes would be joining in the competitions to determine who would represent Germany.

Among these was Margaret Bergmann, the outstanding female high jumper in Germany and a very likely candidate to win a gold medal were she to compete in Berlin. Much media focus was devoted to her return from England—where her parents had sent her soon after Hitler came to power, but from which she was called back by the regime under threats to the welfare of her family—to try out for the German track and field team. In the Olympic trials, Bergmann broke the German high-jump record—in fact, jumping higher than what turned out to be the gold-medal jump in Berlin. Astonishingly, however, at the last minute, she was removed from the team on the grounds that her performance at those trials had been subpar.

The real reason, of course, was that she had served her purpose for Hitler's propaganda machine and was no longer needed: having demonstrated that Jews were being allowed to compete, the Nazis had succeeded in inducing the Americans and other Western powers to participate in the games, thereby legitimizing the regime. Now, through the charade of Bergmann's tryout performance, they could eliminate her (and other Jews) from the German team.

As for the Americans, on the other hand, their—our—Olympic Committee offered no resistance to the barely disguised anti-Semitism of the Olympic hosts-to-be. On the contrary, Avery Brundage and his committee showed themselves eager to acquiesce to Nazi sensibilities—more concerned about the psychological condition of Hitler than the welfare of Jewish American athletes. Indeed, Brundage argued against the boycott of the games for which many Americans were calling, asserting that Jewish "special interests" were trying to push for that boycott in order to isolate a Hitlerian regime, which he felt was far more benign than those "special interest groups" were claiming.

Also at the last moment, Jewish runner Marty Glickman, whose times should have placed him on the gold-medal 4 x 100 meters sprinting team —and up to that moment *had* placed him on it—was pulled from the competition, in deference to the Nazis. The irony there was that the Americans substituted the African American Jesse Owens in Glickman's place. This ended up permitting Owens's brilliant track and field skills to be shown even more broadly than they would otherwise have been. As every schoolboy knows, Owens won four gold medals at the Berlin Olympics, demolishing the myth of "Aryan" superiority that Hitler had hoped to see paraded before the world—and causing the Füehrer to stomp angrily out of the enormous arena that had been built as the centerpiece of Nazi propaganda ambitions for those games.

Hitler was both antisemitic and a racist—and of course, since Wilhelm Marr's previously noted, 1879 publication, Jews were in any case primarily viewed as a race, not as a religion: both "Semites" and "Hamites" were understood to be inherently inferior to "Japhethites." In 1879, the anti-Jewish German pamphleteer and politician, Wilhelm Marr, in an essay/pamphlet designed to re-marginalize the Jews, particularly of Prussia, after a few generations in which they had been gradually allowed into the European mainstream through a series of emancipatory decrees by various central and western European states—began to refer to Jews as "Semites" (extracting that term from the vocabulary of comparative philology, where it referred to a group of languages of a particular "family" and type)—to suggest that they are altogether a race apart from the European "race"—and certainly not real Prussians, no matter how many centuries that may have been living in Prussia.[11]

This misconceived notion—that all Jews come from the Middle East and are therefore "Semites"—was an idea derived, paradoxically, by secular anthropology from the biblical text of Genesis 9, in which Noah's three sons are Shem, Ham, and Japheth: these were presented by anthropologists as the progenitors of Asians, Africans, and Europeans, respectively. Marr's desire to push Jews back away from the mainstream toward the fringes of Prussian and European society opened up a genealogical, bloodline, ethnic category—all Jews were viewed as Semites (and non-Jewish middle easterners, including most obviously Muslim and Christian Arabs, were simply left out of his formulation)—created the basis for racial (rather than religious) anti-Jewishness. There is obvious irony here, by the way: in Genesis, Shem is said to be the brother whose descendants will have authority over the descendants of his brothers, due to his moral superiority, but Marr and his colleagues ignored that part of the narrative in favor of diminishing "Shemites" in favor of "Japhethites."

Thus, for Hitler, Jews were as much as or more of a race than a religion. If the substitution of Owens for Glickman (and Metcalfe for Stoller) and the resounding victory of the American team that included two African Americans over his "Aryan" sprinting team perhaps enraged the Fuehrer only slightly less than had two Jews remained on the American team, it would only have been because, among the inferior races that he despised, he happened to have a particularly strong disaffection for the Jews—as, to repeat, a race.[12]

Owens' performance forced the Fuhrer (literally) out of the stadium in Munich (in dismay and disgust) at the blowing-up in his face of his plan: that the Games would offer a showcase for his racial notions. Brundage on the other hand proved himself more wedded to antisemitic prejudice than to anti-African American racial prejudices. He did not likely lack for the second of these perspectives, but, at this time at least, it took a back seat to the first.

Thus, within the context of the Olympics, the "Jewish Question" has had two particularly intense viewings, both situated in Germany, within the context of the two most astonishing aspects of Jewish historical experience: the Holocaust and the re-creation of an independent Jewish state after eighteen centuries of dispersion among the nations. In both cases, neither Jews who were caught in larger political webs nor a Jew like Mark Spitz, whom circumstances permitted to float above the web's complexities, were religiously traditional, formally practicing Jews, in the sense of thrice-daily prayers or frequent synagogue attendance.[13]

This observation leads to the third category of particular focus or interest where Jews and sports are concerned. This category runs on a track most obviously parallel (not identical) to those for Muslim participation in international sports events in the contemporary world. It is the issue of Jewish religious identity and how that identity might be maintained or compromised within a national or international arena of competition.

Thus, for example, where sartorial issues are concerned, worry regarding the maintenance of "modesty" such as we briefly discussed with respect to Muslim women could as easily pertain to traditional Jewish women—but as with their Muslim counterparts, any participant would decide for herself whether, say, participation in a track event that requires or expects minimum clothing *would* preclude involvement in that sport. Less stringently, traditional male headgear, such as a skullcap, might pose an issue for, say, a swimmer, but such an athlete might or might not be traditional enough for this to be an issue at all.

And for the Jewish athlete, there's the question of what to do about keeping the Sabbath and Jewish festivals while engaging in competitions that might impinge on them. This is analogous to the matter for a Muslim athlete of maintaining the daylight fasts of Ramadan as that month arrives in the midst of the season or more pressing, the play-offs in his or her particular sport. But I am reserving the discussion of this last issue, for reasons that will become obvious when we arrive at it, for the chapter that follows this, in which we consider sports, religion, and politics in America in general.

Notes

1 The English, in fact, repealed their Emancipation edict the following year, so that Emancipation for Jews arrived only much later and gradually. So, too, that process among the Hapsburg domains remained somewhat stagnant for several generations after Joseph's death, but the successor regime, the Austrian Empire, eventually and gradually abolished restrictive sociopolitical legislation for Jews between 1846 and 1867, by which year a new political arrangement that created Austro-Hungary further extended the Jewish right to participate in mainstream society. Similarly, the Prussian state would swing back and forth like a pendulum with regard to Jewish rights, changing its less restrictive 1812 perspective a number of times between that year and the Revolutions of 1848 and again through the final act of Emancipation of 1871 — but the details of that story are beyond the scope of our discussion.

2 "Sephardic" means that his family originated among the Jewish communities that were exiled from Spain in 1492 or Portugal (from which the Jews were exiled in 1496-7). *Sepharad* is the Hebrew-language word for "Spain" by the medieval period.

3 Pierce Egan, the British journalist in whose five volumes of essays, collectively called *Boxiana*, which appeared in 1813-28, the phrase "sweet science of bruising" was first used, arguably was inspired to think and write about the sport as other than violent due to Mendoza's innovations. The phrase re-emerged in A.J. Libeling's 1956 book, *The Sweet Science*, which anthologized essays that he wrote for the *New Yorker* between 1951 and 1955.

4 Mendoza was not the only Jewish boxer on the British scene at that time, only the best-known. Other Jewish fighters included Samuel Elias, Barney Aaron, the Belasco brothers, and Isaac Bitton.

5 As was the nationalist movement among the Arab peoples: the first Jewish Nationalist Congress met in Basel, Switzerland in August 1897; the first Arab Nationalist Congress met in Paris in July 1913. For more on this complicated story, see Soltes, *Untangling the Tangled Web: A Thinking Person's Guide to the Morass of the Middle East* (Bartleby Press, 2009).

6 Some sources suggest that the two Flatows were cousins, others that they were not related at all.

7 In the 1896 Olympics, Hungarian Jewish swimmer Alfred Hajos-Guttmann won two gold medals, Austrian Jewish swimmer Paul Neumann won one gold; and Otto Herschmann, also from Austria, won a bronze. Herschmann later won a silver medal in Olympic fencing, in 1912, making him the first athlete to medal in two different sports. Conversely, Hajos-Guttmann received a third medal in 1924—for his design of the sports facilities at that year's games.

8 Overall, as of 2008, Jewish athletes have won some 325 medals, 135 of them gold, in the course of the modern Olympic Games. I'll leave the math of success quotients to the reader to calculate.

9 Thus, their inclusion in this discussion, in fact, directly contradicts the relationship between sports and religion in the formal or traditional sense, and refracts an altogether different issue that is part of the religion-sports-politics matrix. That is, the definition of Judaism, particularly in the modern world, as ambiguous: is someone a Jew by religion? culture? ethnicity? nationality? race? civilization?—all of these definitions have been applied at various times under varying circumstances.

10 There are other instances of prejudice against Jews that may be noted at other times in modern Olympic history, and also instances of prejudice against members of other groups—just think of the bigotry-based stripping from Jim Thorpe, an incomparable Native American athlete, of his Decathlon and Pentathlon medals some time after the 1912 Olympics—but 1936 and 1972 vis-a-vis the Jews in particular stand out where our narrative is concerned. See the brief discussion of Thorpe below, in chapter 12, 217-18.

11 In his pamphlet *Der Weg zum Siege des Judenthum über das Germanenthums* ("The Way to Victory of Judaism over Germanism"), he introduced the idea that Germans and Jews were locked in a longstanding conflict, the origins of which he attributed to race—and that the Jews were winning. He argued that Jewish emancipation that resulted from German liberalism had allowed the Jews to control German finance and industry. Furthermore, since this conflict was based on the different qualities of the Jewish and German races, it could not be resolved even by the total assimilation—or even conversion—of the Jewish population. Among other things, these ideas would have powerful consequences (that, as we shall seem encompass the Olympic games) a few generations later in the Germany of Adolf Hitler.

12 The German team, in fact, came in third; it was also beaten by the Italians.

13 Such matters—the prevention of athletic participation on religious grounds and/or the interweaving of those grounds with political issues that either obscure

or actually replace the religious grounds — continue to be relevant in an unfortunate manner in present times. A February 16, 2009 *New York Times* front-page sports-section article detailed the last-minute denial of a visa to Shahar Peer, "a Jewish player traveling on an Israeli passport," to compete in the Barclays Dubai Tennis Championships, "a major stop on the early-season circuit that feature[d] all but one of the top-10 players" that year. While Dubai made its decision presumably because of Peer's passport — and argued that the visa denial was made out of concern for violent activity that might be provoked due to the Israeli military engagement in Gaza a few weeks earlier — it is interesting that the newspaper article made such clear reference to her religious identity *and* her passport, almost as if they were two separate, if related sources of that visa denial. While the Sony Ericsson WTA tour decided not to cancel the tournament and no other players withdrew (most of them were apparently already in Dubai by the time the last-minute action was taken by the government), they were all supportive of Peer and expressed dismay at the UAE. "All the players support Shahar," commented Venus Williams, one of the top players on the tour. Two days later, the Tennis Channel announced that it would not televise the Dubai Championships as an act of protest against the United Arab Emirates' action. Perhaps there have been some changes with regard to these sorts of sensibilities and how to respond to them since the 1930s. It might be yet further noted that a few days later, on February 20, another *New York Times* sports article noted that the government of Dubai had promised to extend a visa to the Israeli tennis player, Andy Ram, for the upcoming men's Barclays Dubai tournament. Moreover, in that same article, the head of the Women's Tennis Association indicated that the Dubai tournament would be removed from the following year's tour unless there was both a written guarantee given that Shahar Peer would not be denied a visa for that tour, and that Dubai would have to pay a fine — it was $300,000 — for having abrogated the rules of the WTA by denying her a visa in 2009. She did indeed play the following year, protected at all times by a phalanx of Arab guards.

CHAPTER ELEVEN:
America from the Maya
to the Birth of "The National Pastime"

One must begin the discussion of the relationship between sports, religion, and politics in the New World with reference to its oldest inhabitants. Not surprisingly, there is much to be found that is relevant to our narrative. Perhaps the most renowned of sports with a distinct religious and political set of connotations is the Mayan ball game known variously as *pok-a-tok* or *pok-to-pok*—or variously as *pitz, tlachco,* or *ulama*.[1] This may have been the first organized team sport in history. At the very least, we have direct evidence of it in the form of ball courts, going back in at least one instance to before the beginning of the Early Classic period (ca 200 CE)—there is a ball court at Cerros, for example, from perhaps 1000 BCE or earlier—the sophisticated contours of which suggest that the game and its settings had already been in process for several centuries.[2]

The game was most often played as the centerpiece of a religious ceremony or the culmination of a political or military event, or, not surprisingly, both. It was played on a stone court whose measurements varied,[3] the precise configuration of which changed over time but typically possessed walls that sloped inward and with elevated temple structures at the long ends. *Pitz* was played with a solid rubber ball, about 20 centimeters in diameter and weighing up to eight pounds.[4] Some apparently had human skulls at their core, wrapped in strips of rubber, perhaps attesting to the sacrifice-centered religious importance of the game.[5] The rubber for the ball came from the dwarf plant, "guayule," that is found in Vera Cruz and Northern Mexico.

While we have no documentary evidence to confirm exactly what the goal of the game was—some of the courts possessed large rings through which some have supposed the ball was to pass to bring victory—there are enough visual representations in surviving Mayan art, such as several carved vases from the Yucatan area, to suggest certain of the game's parameters. Thus, all scholars agree that one of goals was *not* to allow the ball to hit the ground, and that as each team of seven players—or perhaps two teams that, together, totaled seven players (the number may or may not have been absolute)—moved the ball around, none of them were permitted to touch the ball with their hands, calves, or feet. So, the ball had to be batted about using the hips, the upper parts of the legs, the elbows, the shoulders, or the head.

Apparently, as a consequence of this feature—and given that the ball was large, heavy, and fairly hard—players wore odd, protective gear. Around their waists, they sported yokes made of leather and/or basketry with a protruding palmate stone and a leather apron. They also wore protective gear around their chins and covering their cheeks, as well as hard leather gloves, quilted cotton elbow pads, and knee pads.

And while we cannot be certain as to the goal of the game as a *game*, we can be quite certain of its significance within the cosmic scheme of things—as a symbol of the working of the universe and thus, in a sense, as part of a *ritual*. The most renowned and complete Mayan text that has survived to us—it is popularly referred to as the Mayan Bible (a rather misleading phrase)—is a compilation of stories that offer an overarching interpretation of the world and the human place within it. That text, called the *Popol Vuh*—the Book of Council—is associated with that branch of the Maya known as K'iche' and originally written in the language of that name. Stories found within it are visually echoed on monuments from the Preclassic and Classic periods, as well as on Classic-period pottery and subsequent documents ranging from the Colonial period to the contemporary world in which oral traditions continue to be transmitted.

Within the *Popol Vuh*, the key figures are two sets of twins. The second set—the definitive pair of heroes—is called Hinahpu and Xbalanque by the time we encounter them in the seventeenth-century manuscript version from the Colonial period; in the Classic period, they are somewhat differently named, Hun-Ahau and Yax-Balam. In any case, these two are the progeny of a set of twins named Hun-Hunahpu (One Hinahpu) and Vucub-Hunahpu (Seven Hinahpu). These first two are called into the Mayan Underworld, Xibalba—the "other world," also interpreted as "the realm of death," but with neither the negative connotation of hell/Underworld nor the positive connotation of heaven—because they have been playing the ball game with such vigor and passion and have made so much noise that they have disturbed the Lords of Death below.

Called to Xibalba, this first set of twins is tricked by the Lords of Death into being defeated on the Underworld ball court and both are sacrificed. The Lords of Death bury one twin (Seven Hinahpu) underneath the ball court in Xibalba and hang the skull of the other (One Hinahpu) on a branch of the gourd tree—as a warning to others who might presume to disturb or otherwise offend the gods of Xibalba. But that hanging skull is found by a daughter of one of the Lords of Death, and it impregnates her by spitting into her hand. Her father is enraged (indeed he intends to cut out her heart and sacrifice her), which terrifies her, so she flees from Xibalba up to the Middleworld—our human reality, sandwiched between Xibalba and an Upper World—where she wanders rather aimlessly until she encounters the mother of the dead twins.[6]

Sheltered (reluctantly at first) by the mother, she soon gives

birth to the second pair of twins, Hunahpu (Hun-Ahau) and Xbalanque (Yax-Balam). So it is that, after a series of diverse adventures,
these twins find the ball-game paraphernalia of their deceased father and uncle that had been hidden by their grandmother after
the death of those first two. The two young heroes begin to use the
gear, to play the ball game—and become extremely proficient at
it. Soon, as with their father and uncle, their endless raucous playing begins to disturb the Lords of Xibalba who live directly under
the ball court. They are called down to Xibalba, as their father and
uncle had been, but—to make the heart of this story short—they
outwit the Lords of Death, not only surviving a series of trials but
ultimately defeating their would-be destroyers.

In one trial, Hunahpu is decapitated but Xbalanque manages
first to replace Hunahpu's head with a squash that he carves to
look like his brother's head, and subsequently to trick the Lords
of Death and reclaim and replace his brother's head where it be-
longs. In a second trial, the brothers leap into a pit of fire, have their
bones ground into powder and cast into the river, and are then
resurrected, first with the faces of catfish and then with their own
faces. Afterwards, disguised as traveling actors, they perform for
the Lords of Death, dancing a death-dance of sacrifice in which one
twin decapitates and dismembers the other and then brings him
back to life. The end of this part of the narrative is that the Lords of
Death are fooled into begging to be decapitated and dismembered,
expecting to be brought back to life.

The heroes accede to the first request by the Xibalbans, (decap-
itating and dismembering them), but then fail to bring them back
to life. The consequence is not only that the lords are more than defeated—they are dispatched summarily—but that the heroic twins
bring hope back with them to the Middleworld, for all of humankind. For anyone and everyone can hope that, when his/her soul is
called to Xibalba in death, s/he may succeed in outwitting the Lords
of Death and emerge as a triumphant hero like the twins did, to be
venerated by his or her heirs and descendants.

For our purposes, what is significant in this narrative is that the center of action—both above ground and below ground (Mayan artists portray Xibalba both as being underground and as being under the water)—is the ball court. Given the scant but significant imagery we have of players of the game of *pitz*, and the fact that branches of contemporary Maya play a game that closely resembles *pitz*, the narrative makes very clear that the ball game and its arenas have a spiritual/religious connotation. Moreover, the images of players that have emerged from within Mayan art include those with the kind of headgear that would identify them as kings, and others wearing the head gear of hunters or warriors—all categories of men who were delegated to mediate between their community and what existed outside it so that their world would survive.

As Linda Schele and David Freidel point out in their magisterial yet accessible work on the Maya, the story of the triumphant twins yields three axioms that "appear repeatedly in the imagery of Classic Maya *religion and politics* [emphasis added]. First, the Hero of the Maya vision did not overpower his enemies: He outwitted them... Secondly, resurrection and rebirth came through sacrifice—especially death by decapitation. The Hero Twins were conceived when the severed head of their father spit into the hand of their mother. They defeated death by submitting to decapitation and sacrifice. Finally, the place of confrontation and communication was the ball court. The ballgame...was the arena in which life and death, victory and defeat, rebirth and triumph played out their consequences."[7]

So, we are confronted with a sporting event that is deeply embedded in the political and spiritual reality of the Maya. Even as we remain uncertain as to precisely how the game was played, it is clear from literature and visual iconography that the game and the ball courts where it was played had a profoundly sacred quality to them and were the centerpiece of both religious and political life.

Indeed, there has been considerable discussion over the years as to the aftermath outcome of the ball game. Some have opined that the captain of the winning team offered his head to the losing captain, and that, thusly honored by being sacrificed, he in fact gained a direct, nonstop ticket to the uppermost heaven, rather than the 13-stop route ordinarily taken to get there in Mayan religious thought.[8] Most scholars of the Mayan cultures disagree emphatically, asserting that, on the contrary, sacrifice was the penalty for *defeat*, and not the reward for victory.

Of course, for our purposes, the question of who was beheaded and sacrificed is beside the point. The fact that there was a ceremony that followed the game, and that the details of its ritual depended upon the game's outcome, is the important issue: the intimate relationship between the game as a sport and the game as part of a larger religious reality is what is significant.

There is more. In a manner reminiscent of the way in which Roman audiences watched the gladiatorial and other games from above, like gods, the audiences of the Mayan games watched from stairs situated above the playing field. Moreover, if, as some archaeologists maintain, the ball being pushed around across the field and its walls symbolized the sun, so that the game offered a kind of microcosmic representation of the sun's orbit around the earth, then not only did the game present a ritual of praise to the sun-god, but the players who pushed the ball around became, during the time of the game, surrogates for the sun-god—*sacerdotes* (plural of *sacerdos*)—and the audience, too, observing the patterns of the ball's movement and the actions of the players, assumed a god-like position for the duration of the game.

More to the point, if the ball game was understood as a kind of allegory for the movement not only of the sun but of the celestial bodies in general, then it is perhaps not surprising that the number of players added up to seven in various combinations, recalling and representing the seven planets visible with the naked eye (the sun, the moon, and Mercury, Venus, Mars, Jupiter, and Saturn), the configuration of which shifted over the course of the months and the seasons.[9]

It is no accident, therefore, that both temples and astronomical observatories were part of the architectural complexes of which the ball courts were the centerpieces. One of the Preclassic-sites discussed in some detail by Schele and Freidel—Cerros, mentioned above as an important Early Preclassic (ca 2000-1000 BCE) site, located on an inlet along the southeast coast of the Yucatan peninsula—offered its main ball court as the central element of a tripartite subgroup of a large, sacred precinct. The ball court was sandwiched between two somewhat differently conceived platform structures, perhaps analogous to the manner in which the *Popol Vuh* describes our world—Middleworld—as sandwiched between Xibalba and the Upper World. In fact, the ball court complex resided at the axial opposite "end" of the sacred zone from the structure referred to by archaeologists as the "First Temple"; the latter was built at the water's edge and the former at the edge of a canal dug to define the southern boundary of the sacred zone.

One might say that this zone, in its entirety, mediated between the realms of sea and land as it marked the central axis of mediation between heaven and Xibalba. At one end of the horizontal axis—the First Temple, the carved décor of which emphasized the passage of the sun rising and setting and of the morning star rising and the evening star setting—the royal rituals were enacted that marked the king's journeys between our world and the sacred realms beyond our own. At the other end, the great ball game was played that marked the passage of the heavenly wanderers across the heavens and culminated with the offering of ballplayers as "gifts" to the powers of the sacred realm.[10] This symbolized the intermediating activity necessary for success in activities such as agriculture, which was, in turn, necessary for the survival of the community.

Nor is it surprising that all of these structures were adorned with such an elaborate array of imagery, both direct and symbolic, reflecting a tight interweaving of religious, agricultural, and political concerns. The extensive reliefs along the periphery of the Great Ball Court at Chichen Itza, a key site of the Early Postclassic period (ca 900/1000-1200 CE),[11] reflected the culmination of the game as ritual, depicting in stylized fashion the decapitation sacrifice (blood that spurts from the neck of the warrior-athlete who has just lost his head is symbolized by snakes) [fig 10]. This is, in turn, integrated and associated with the imagery of other rituals, such as the fire ritual.

Thus, the ball game was part of a ceremonial life that involved not only the community at large but its leadership in particular. It "provide[d] the metaphorical setting for the sacrificial events by which a king or heir promoted his legitimate authority. Whether the king was taking the role of supreme athlete, acting out the role of one of the Ancestral Twins [who defeated the Lords of Death in Xibalba, as described in the *Popol Vuh*], or sacrificing a captive king or noble, the ballgame had deep religious significance."[12]

Within the subsequent history of ball-centered sports, a number of epilogic comments might be offered. One is that the adoption of a rubber ball from the Native Central American tradition into European sports as well as the idea of coordinated cooperative team efforts may have influenced the shaping of European sports toward modernity. A second is that there seems to have been a variant form of the "classic" ball game, also invented by the Maya, in which a

Figure 10. Beheading of Mayan Player (detail)

much smaller hard-rubber ball (which could apparently reach very high speeds), was thrown and caught with a *cesta* (wicker basket) that was tied to the player's right hand. That game, subsequently known as *jai alai*, would have been imported back to Spain where it was most intensely taken up by the Spanish Basques.[13]

A third epilogic note is that, among other Mayan games was a board game called *bul* which, like *pitz*, functioned as a war game and offered itself as a microcosmic model connecting both to the macrocosmic operation of the universe at large and to the humans within it. *Bul* was played with 15 grains of corn in a row; the 14 spaces—twice 7—between the grains were the "playing field." Four flat grains of corn, each with one side burned, were tossed like dice in this game of chance. Such a mode of gambling might be seen to have a kind of ancestry in the *Popol Vuh* itself, where the cosmic grandparents of the human race, Xpiyacoc and Xmucane, make a prophetic deduction based on the calculations derived from corn grains.

Versions of this game were played among diverse Mesoameri-can peoples. Thus, the Azteca, for instance, played a version known as *patolli*—and the playing of *patolli* came to be criticized by Span-ish Catholic missionaries and their followers, in part because it had a clear religious significance for the Azteca.[14] It was treated as a visual articulation of the periodicity and details of movement of the stars and planets; the four-fold directionality possible for its pieces (the number of "dice" is also four) suggested the four directions of the world and the four seasons; the total number of possible posi-tions, 52, multiplied by 5, yields 260, the number of days in the Aztec ritual-cycle calendar; the surface onto which the four "dice" grains were tossed was a *"poop,"* a mat of woven straws.[15]

The Spaniards opposed playing the game specifically because it was said that players invoked the names of Aztec gods while en-gaged in it. *Patolli* was outlawed after the beginning of the Spanish conquest of 1521, but survived in areas distant from the Spanish presence—and is still played today. Like chess (as noted above in chapter 7), what is at issue is a board sport that carried with it implications for war and peace, and life and death—and the religious underpinnings of all four.

Within the sweep of pre-Columbian cultures that dotted the Americas prior to the European invasion, another indigenous group that invented a sport with both religious undertones and ramifications for the forward-moving history of sports—in this case, in the form of a direct continuation into the modern era—was the Iroquois, or possibly by their Algonquian neighbors just to the north. The sport is lacrosse, a game played by two teams in which the purpose is to shoot a small ball past a goalkeeper into a rectangular goal. Each player handles the ball by means of a long stick—between about 3 and 6 feet in length—with a small basket attached at the end. Today, the sport is played between teams of six to ten members (depending upon whether it is played indoors or outdoors) and the goal is a standard 4' x 4'9" surrounded by a circle 9 feet in diameter marking a zone—called the crease—into which an offensive player may not enter (although he may reach into it with his stick to gain possession of the ball).

The original game was somewhat different. Some have argued that it is based on the *jai alai* game invented in Mesoamerica and that it migrated north by the 1100s. If so, then it was radically transformed, and that transformation constituted a virtual re-invention by the six-nation amalgam[16] of the Iroquois confederacy whose tribal lands covered much of what is now southern Ontario in Canada and western New York State.

In its earliest mode, it seems to have been a major communal, religious event, sometimes lasting several days, and involving between a hundred and as many as a thousand players from opposing villages or tribes. Typically, the game would be played from sunrise to sunset in open plains between the two villages or tribes in question, and goals might be placed from about 500 yards to several miles apart. Generally, there were no out-of-bounds markers, the goals would be a clearly identifiable rock or tree—or perhaps a pair of wooden posts erected for that purpose—the ball could not be touched with the hands, and more precise rules would be agreed upon the day before the game began.

One might envision such a game—the ball initially tossed into the air and the two teams rushing forward from opposite sides to gain control of it—to involve a mass of players swarming the ball and trying to move it across the playing field, or in the absence of direct access to the ball, striking at opposing players to cut the size of their team down. Medicine men acted as coaches and women apparently served refreshments—although a separate woman's form of the game, called *amtah*, with much shorter sticks and larger ball-baskets, was also played. The Iroquois called the men's game *baggataway* ("bump hips") or *tewaraathon* ("little brother of war"), and eventually limited play to teams of 12 to 15 players on a field with defined boundaries and goals set about 120-feet apart.

Both within and beyond the Iroquois confederation the game and/or its variants also went by other names. Thus, the Onondaga (one of the six nations that comprise the Iroquois confederacy) also called it *dehuntshigwa'es* or *guh jee gwah ai* (both of these meaning "man hits a rounded object"). The Mohawk also called it *hon tis kwaks eks*, as well as *begadwe* ("little brother of war"). The Oneida also called it *gal ahs* or *ga-lahs*. Beyond the Iroquois Confederation, the Choctaw, located well southeast of the Iroquois, called it *kabucha*. The Ojibwe—one of the largest North American Native American tribes and originally located due west of the Iroquois—called their slightly different version of the game *baaga'adowe* (similar to the Iroquois term meaning "bump hips"). Underscoring the relationship between the game and warfare, the Eastern Cherokee[17] referred to their slightly different version as *da-nah-wah'uwsdi*, meaning "little war"—closest in meaning to the general name used by the Iroquois, *tewaraathon*.

With regard to the subject of our narrative, *baggataway/ tewaraathon/ da-nah-wah'uwsdi* served various purposes, aside from those of settling intertribal disputes and, given the diversity of national groups within the Iroquois, cementing a sense of commonality among those six nations that comprised the tribe. As with Mayan *pitz*, it varied from offering mere recreation to providing training in warfare for young braves—thus, recalling the funeral games of the ancient Greeks on the one hand and the early jousting events of the medieval Christians (and their chaotic, mob-like beginnings) on the other—to serving religious purposes. For, most fundamentally, the extended playing of the game was seen as a communal act of prayer and as an event enacted for the pleasure of the gods in general and the Great Spirit in particular.[18]

Not surprisingly, pregame rituals—rhythmic dances and chanting anchored by mesmerizing drumming sequences the evening before; the dipping of the players' sticks into water to purify them on the day of the game, a tobacco-burning ceremony—were essential elements in the shaping of the event. Players decorated themselves and their playing sticks with paints, cuts and scratches, and also symbols—totems—associated with the qualities needed to succeed, such as speed and strength.[19] Medicine men conferred ceremonial blessings on the players and their equipment, and sacrifices were offered to the Great Spirit. Indeed, lacrosse is the Creator's game.

Such a religious sensibility remains intact among a good number of contemporary Iroquois. Onondaga Chief Irving Powless, Jr., has observed that "when we play a game here on Mother Earth, a game is taking place up there in the Land of the Creator at the same time. So then, after we pass away and we are through, we have a means by which we can get our stick up into the Creator's world so that we'll play again."[20] At the time he made these remarks, Chief Powless had been playing lacrosse for 68 years—at least once a year in the traditional mode, with a wooden stick and without helmets and pads, without a time clock, on a field without boundaries.

The game was apparently first observed by Europeans when French Jesuit missionaries in the St. Lawrence River Valley (in what is now southeastern Canada, just north of New York State) wit-nessed a game in the 1630s. They condemned it as too violent; as corrupting, since all players were required to place bets on the out-come—and, most of all, as damnable because it was an important part of the ritual and ceremonial life of the Native American form of faith that they hoped to eradicate in favor of Christianity. One such missionary, Jean de Brebeuf, seems to have been the first to write about it after observing a game among the Huron Indians in 1636. He is credited with applying his own name to it. Some say the name was based on the French phrase for field hockey, *le jeu de la crosse* ("the game of the cross"); others (these are in the minority) that the stick reminded de Brebeuf or someone else among the Je-suits of a bishop's staff, a *crosier*.

In any case, not only is there an obvious irony to the sugges-tion that the French terminology ultimately reflects religious think-ing, but it is also ironic that European colonists themselves became interested in the sport, in spite of Jesuit opposition, so that a cen-tury later, by the 1740s, French colonists were taking up the game in substantial numbers. In another century, in 1844, a team was or-ganized in Montreal by the city's so-called Olympic Club specifi-cally to play against an indigenous team, and by 1856 the Montreal Lacrosse Club was formed and began to develop written rules for the game.

By that time, sports were moving in new directions in the New World, and an array of non-European kinds of events and compe-titions were in the process of, or on the verge of, taking shape, as apparently removed from the worlds of religion and politics as the United States had come to imagine it was from direct European *or* Native American roots. "New" sports that might be considered uniquely American were assuming shapes that continue to be rec-ognizable today.

Baseball naturally comes to mind first of all, with regard to those sports that are considered uniquely American—it is, after all, "the American pastime." The irony with respect to baseball's origins is not that the sport's beginnings have long been associated folklor-istically with Abner Doubleday in 1839, but that the evidence from all sides—including his own letters and papers—makes it clear that he was by no means baseball's ground zero. Rather, the game is now thought to have originated in the very England from which the American colonies so eagerly broke away in the 1770s—back in 1755. This was noted—referring specifically to a game played on Easter Monday of that year, in Guilford—in the diary of a lawyer of that period, William Bray. The consensus among historians is that, derived from bat-and-ball games such as cricket and rounders, the game arrived to North America with English and Irish immigrants, rather than having sprung full-grown from the American sports imagination.[21] How it became "the American pastime" will form the beginning of the discussion in the chapter that follows.

Notes

1. *Pitz* is really the proper Mayan term (usually translated simply as "ball"); *tlachco* is Nahuatl; and *ulama* is the name used in Western Mexico. The name *pok-a-tok* may have been made up by Western scholars. Strictly speaking, although we popularly refer to this as a specifically Mayan game, it is probably more accurate to label it as pan-Mesoamerican since the Olmec, for example, must have played it (there are ballplayer figurines and actual rubber balls from Olmec sites).

2. See the discussion of this in Vernon L. Scarborough & David R. Wilcox, eds, *The MesoAmerican Ballgame* (Tucson: University of Arizona Press, 1993).

3. The largest court, at Chichen Itza, measured 545 feet by 225 feet. Chichen Itza also offered 22 additional playing ball courts. In addition, smaller courts were found at other sites, notably Copan, (perhaps the most imposing and certainly the most decorated of ball courts) which, instead of the rings high up on the wall that are found on most Maya ball courts, offers six carved macaw heads at which players are believed by some scholars to have aimed the ball.

4. I will henceforth use *"pitz"* to refer to the game. See fn 1.

5. In fact, there's no absolute evidence that balls of this size and weight were actually used for play but may rather have been used strictly in the sacrificial contexts that followed the actual games.

6. In terms of the complexities of epic literature, and the prevalent motif of a hero who has a deity either as one of his parents (like the Greek Achilles) or

as a strong supporter (like the Greek Odysseus), there is wonderful irony—and paradox appropriate to the ambiguities both of the human condition and of the realm of the gods—that the second pair of twins should stem from the stock of Hun-Hunahpu and Vucub-Hunahpu (their father and uncle) *and* the stock (their mother) of a Lord of Death, who killed those first twins.

7. Linda Schele and David Freidel, *A Forest of Kings: The Untold Story of the Ancient Maya,* (New York: William Morrow and Co., Inc. 1990), 76.

8. This is asserted by Dee Finney in a website compilation called *Mayan Games: The Dream and the Reality.* There are 13 levels to heaven in Maya cosmology; I am not aware of other sources besides Finney that suggest a gradual ascent through them, but I like the idea that such a lengthy journey would be circumvented by the team captain who was sacrificed.

9. The term *"planetes"* means "wanderers" in Greek. See chapter 1, fn 7.

10. In fact, "often these sacrificial victims were bound into a ball-like form and hurled down the stairs of a temple." (Schele and Freidel, 126).

11. Ibid, 373 and footnote 54, which further details visual elements of religious significance—such as a skull with emerging water lilies as a symbol of fertility and renewal—and further notes the war-related significance of the Mayan ball courts. The Great Ball Court at Chichen Itza seems to have been constructed as a monument to the successful completion of the Itza's wars of conquest.

12. Ibid, 126.

13. An alternative theory is that the Basques invented *jai alai* in the seventeenth century or somewhat earlier but that the game changed with the introduction of rubber into Europe from South and Central America, so that it was merely the material and not the nature of the game that connected *pitz* and *jai alai.* But then, is it mere coincidence that the game is said to have been invented after the Spanish had established an extended conquistadorial presence in America? In any case, see Carmelo Uza's "The History of Basque Pelota in the Americas," in *The Journal of the Society of Basque Studies in America,* vol XV, 1995, 1-16.

14. I am using the term "Azteca," because it is commonly used. However, the term in Nahuatl is "Mexica" and otherwise, therefore, preferable in that it carries less Western scholarly baggage.

15. The full Aztec annual calendar was really a 365-day solar calendar that included the 260-day ritual cycle within an 18-month cycle of 20 days to each month, plus 5 nameless, unlucky days.

16. The confederacy, a melting pot that grew by the incorporation of other nations into its imperium, whose members became naturalized as full citizens of the tribe, originally (in 1451 or possibly even as early as 1142—

both of these were dates of significant solar eclipses) consisted of five nations: the Mohawk, the Oneida, the Onondaga, the Cayuga, and the Seneca. The Tuscarora, originally from the North Carolina area, joined later, in 1720. While they are known to most outsiders as the *Iroquois*, the Nations typically refer to themselves collectively as *Haudenosaunee*: "they [who] are building a Long House." The Seneca were the westernmost Nation within the confederacy—and hence were known as guardians of the western door of the Confederacy "Long House"—while the Mohawk, the easternmost inhabitants, were regarded as guardians of the eastern door. The centrally located Onondagas were keepers of the Long House's central flame.

17. The Cherokee are believed to have originally been a branch of the Iroquois; they consist of seven clans, the territories of the Cherokee nation extending from the Ohio River into South Carolina. The Eastern Band of Cherokees lived in the area now known as the Smoky Mountains National Park that straddles eastern Tennessee and western North Carolina; they were forced westward to Oklahoma by Euro-Americans who craved their lands in the infamous march in 1836 along what is known as the Trail of Tears.

18. To this day, special "medicine" games are organized throughout the year in a style that harks back to earlier times. "[A]n unlimited number of males from age seven to 70 ranges about, and the first team to score a certain number of goals—sometimes three, sometimes five—wins... The caller doesn't play, but he keeps the ball. 'The ball is the medicine,' [former all-American lacrosse player at Syracuse University and Faithkeeper of the Turtle Clan of the Onondaga Nation, as well as a Chief of the Onondaga Nation Council of Chiefs of the Six Nations of the Iroquois Confederacy Oren] Lyons says... Nationals offensive coach Freeman Bucktooth [observes:] 'Whatever illness you have, it pushes it away. It's amazing how well it cures you.'" See S.L. Price, "Pride of a Nation," *Sports Illustrated* (July 19, 2010) 60-71. This passage is on page 66, left column.

19. Humility and clean playing are also necessary—particularly given that the traditionally wooden stick is understood to be "a gift from Mother Earth, that a living thing died to make it and that its spirit has been transferred to the Iroquois player, who honors the tree's sacrifice by playing humbly, calmly, *'in a more spiritual manner'* [emphasis added]." Ibid, right column.

20. Chief Powless is quoted at the end of the article by Tom Rock, "More Than a Game: Lacrosse and the Onondaga Nation," in *Lacrosse Magazine*, November/December 2002. Virtually every Iroquois male has a small lacrosse stick placed in his crib and is buried with a full-size one—the first thing he will grab when he crosses to the Other Side.

21. Even the William Bray assertion falls short of certainty, if we are asking about the origin of the game in any sort of form, as opposed to the particular form

that the game came to take in America. Thus, there is mention of a bat-and-ball game traditionally played in Romania, mentioned for the first time in a document from the reign of King Vlaicu Voda, in 1364; and there is a description of a "baseball" game, together with a woodcut illustration of boys playing it in the 1744 publication, *A Pretty Pocket-Book*, by Englishman John Newberry—to offer two pre-William Bray (and certainly pre-Abner Doubleday) examples.

CHAPTER TWELVE:
Twentieth-Century American Sports and its Intersection Among Immigration, Religion, and Race

The first reference to a baseball game on American soil is a 1791 bylaw in the town of Pittsfield, Massachusetts, prohibiting the playing of baseball within 80 yards of the town's new meetinghouse. And the first documentation of an actual baseball game in North America is in Ontario, Canada. Dr. Adam Ford describes a contest that took place on June 4, 1838 in Beachville, Ontario. But seven years later, Alexander Cartwright of New York City led the process of codifying the rules of baseball, and the first game universally recognized as the first in U.S. history to be both officially recorded and to have followed those rules was played on June 19, 1846 in Hoboken, New Jersey, between the New York Nine and the New York Knickerbockers.[1] By the 1870s, the game was being referred to as the "national pastime"—and on June 3, 1953, Alexander Cartwright was officially recognized by the U.S. Congress as the inventor of modern baseball.

There is a good deal less controversy with regard to the origins of basketball. Historians pretty much agree that in early December 1891, Dr. James Naismith invented the game. Naismith was a Canadian from McGill University in Montreal, who, as a professor of physical education—at the time, he may still have been a graduate student—was teaching at Springfield College in Springfield, Massachusetts.[2] He was seeking an indoor form of exercise that would keep his students both interested and fit during the wintertime and came up with the idea of nailing a peach basket to a wall at precisely ten feet above floor level in the college gymnasium, and writing out a set of rules that would govern how the game would be played.

At first, the peach basket, with its bottom intact, yielded an inconvenient goal, since every time someone made a basket, it was necessary to retrieve the ball—a soccer ball, by the way—with a ladder. Soon thereafter, the bottoms of the peach baskets pressed into service were punched out so that the ball could simply fall through, but it was not until 1906 that the baskets were replaced by metal hoops and backboards. The first official game, played with nine players on a side in the Springfield College gymnasium in January 20, 1892, yielded a score of 1-0 on a shot made from 25 feet away— the same year in which Senda Berenson modified Naismith's rules somewhat in order to create a specifically women's game. By 1897-98, the five-man team had become the standard.

And so on—with incremental changes. The next truly important alteration was that soccer balls were replaced in the game by the sort of ball we would recognize today--one that, among other things, made dribbling an important part of the game. It's interesting to note that the discovery of the Maya and some sense of their ball courts had been around for about half a century before Naismith came up with his idea. Of course, the hoops on the Mayan ball courts were placed vertically, not horizontally, as Naismith's peach basket hoop was, but given the popularity of the writings about the Maya in the last half of the century—especially those by John Lloyd Stevens that included drawings by Frederick Catherwood—one might at least speculate that Naismith gained some inspiration for this new American game from a very old one.

American football, on the other hand, can unequivocally be traced to sources beyond the American continent, specifically to early versions of rugby and soccer, with the points of origin for both of them in the United Kingdom in the mid-nineteenth century. American football diverged from rugby through rule changes instituted by Walter Camp, who is considered the "father of American football." Thus, the introduction of the line of scrimmage and of a prescribed number of downs (four) in which to proceed a prescribed minimal distance (ten yards) was part of that transformation.

The popularity of the sport was first apparent at the college level, where the first crop of renowned coaches like Knute Rockne and Glenn "Pop" Warner left their indelible marks. The beginning of a professional form of the sport may be traced to 1892—by coincidence, the same year in which the first basketball game was played—when William "Pudge" Heffelfinger signed a contract for $500 to play in a game for the Allegheny Athletic Association against the Pittsburgh Athletic Club. By 1920, the American Professional Football Association was formed; the association changed its name to the National Football League two years later.

From the outset, the United States has perceived itself as a place of refuge to which individuals oppressed elsewhere in the world could look for succor. In a sense, the culmination of such a sensibility was symbolically expressed around the same time that baseball was beginning its journey as the national pastime and basketball and football were beginning their very existences. Therefore, during the early part of the period in which millions of immigrants were arriving into America, between the end of the 1870s and 1924, the United States proudly installed a magnificent gift from France—the Statue of Liberty—in the New York harbor, to which, by way of Ellis Island, so many immigrants and refugees were arriving onto these shores.

At the foot of that gigantic figure, with its upraised arm holding in its hand a shining beacon, is a sonnet that was written in 1883 and inscribed on a plaque at the statue's base in 1912. The poem was authored by Emma Lazarus, a Jew whose Portuguese Sephardic family had settled in New York in the Colonial period. Its title, "The New Colossus," refers less to the statue, its ostensive subject—viewed as an image that contrasts with the famous Colossus of Rhodes from Greco-Roman antiquity—than to the United States itself, for which the gigantic bronze image is merely a symbolic stand-in.[3] The last lines of the poem read:

> ...Give me your tired, your poor,
> Your huddled masses, yearning to breathe free,
> The wretched refuse of your teeming shore.
> Send these, the homeless, the tempest-tossed, to me,
> I lift my lamp beside the golden door!

Of course, the American view of incoming immigrants has a diverse history, one that is not always consistent with the words of Emma Lazarus' poem or the image of Lady Liberty that rises above those words. As early as the mid-nineteenth century there developed a group whose members called themselves the nativist movement.

Without a scintilla of a sense of irony, they viewed incoming "New Americans" as unassimilable foreigners whose presence upon our shores would endanger the freedoms established by the founding fathers a mere three or four generations earlier. Nativists made a case for their own national, ethnic, and religious superiority, arguing that it was their "stock" that gave them (and them alone) the right to continue to shape those democratic freedoms.[4] Thus, whereas the ancestors of the nativists had typically arrived from northwestern and north central Europe, and were mostly Protestant, the majority of those arriving in the last decades of the nineteenth century and the beginning of the twentieth were Irish and Italian Catholics and Jews from Russia and Poland—and to the west coast, Asians.

From the time when the Federal government took control of immigration policy and Ellis Island was established as the primary point of entry, in 1892, until the Johnson-Reed Act of 1924, which effectively slammed shut the door through which Lady Liberty had welcomed all to enter for nearly half a century, over 12 million people had legally entered the United States, including 4 million Italians and 2 million Jews.

Practically since the time of the birth of the United States, every ethnic group has faced its own brand of "Nativist" attitudes to one degree or another. Yet each has contributed to American culture in innumerable ways, even while facing discrimination, sometimes even from other immigrant groups. Add to this the experiences of a different sort of immigrant, people brought from Africa as slaves as well as the treatment of the earliest occupants, the Native Americans, and some of the complexity of the American tapestry becomes evident. It is clear that the inclusionary vision suggested by the Statue of Liberty and the poem that rests at its base has often fallen short of its promise.

Sports can be, and in many ways has been a particularized weaver together of diverse numbers of individuals whose success is a result of talent, sweat, discipline, and often cooperation, and not religion, race, ethnicity, or nationality. And like America itself, the world of sports—particularly the *national pastime* kinds of sports— has sometimes fallen short of this ideal.

The first openly paid professional baseball player in American baseball—in 1866—was a Jew by the name of Lipman Pike. Pike was one of the stars of the sport in its American nascence, renowned for his combination of power at the bat and speed on the base paths. His early arrival into a game that was and would remain self-conceived for decades as an arena of almost entirely White Anglo-Saxon Protestant participation was possible because of his skills. This pioneer's participation in the American pastime sport would, in retrospect, help pave the way half a century later for the emergence of Hank Greenberg, the first Jewish superstar in baseball as it emerged as the preeminent symbol of American sports by the 1920s.

But for the purposes of our discussion, Greenberg's various MVP accomplishments[5] with the Detroit Tigers *on* the playing field are less important than his decision to take himself *off* that field on a single day in 1934. And it is this act that leads our discussion back to the point where we left it, at the end of the chapter 10; the third in a trio of issues surrounding the rubric "Jews (or Judaism) and sports."

Greenberg chose not to play on the Day of Atonement—the holiest and most somber day of the Jewish year, a 24-hour-fast day[6]—although the holiday fell during the intense autumn stretch in that year in which the Detroit Tigers were neck-in-neck with the New York Yankees in the race for the American League pennant. This was Detroit's first chance to win a pennant since 1909. The decision was a shot heard round the world: he had, in effect, chosen his faith over his game—however narrow the confines of the decision; Greenberg played throughout the year on the Sabbath, and had played ten days earlier on the Jewish New Year.[7] But the symbolism of the gesture was profound.

And this was at a time not only when Hitler was in power and increasingly strangling Germany's Jews, but when the Fuehrer had an American acolyte in Henry Ford who, in the city in which Greenberg played and starred, had previously printed thousands of copies of the insidious anti-Semitic tract, *The Protocols of the Elders of Zion* in the mid-1920s, as a supplement to his newspaper, *The Dearborn Independent*, to distribute to his workers; and an echo in the form of Father Charles Coughlin, a Detroit-based Catholic priest who aired a popular radio program every Sunday morning in which he typically lambasted and excoriated the Jews in a manner quite consistent with the Füehrer's rhetoric.[8]

Greenberg would later write in his autobiography that "I came to feel that if I, as a Jew, hit a home run, I was hitting one against Hitler." Within the American Jewish community, Hammerin' Hank was already a messianic figure, particularly within the Hitler-Ford-Coughlin context, and the ultimate symbol of the possibility to become fully integrated into the American world of which sports in general and baseball in particular were such an essential element.[9] His decision not to play on Yom Kippur, to abide by a more solemn Jewish value rather than a "win at all costs" American value, was embraced.

When he entered his synagogue on that day, the congregation, led by the rabbi, completely broke with the sober norm of intense introspection and prayer: they applauded. The response of the non-Jewish American world was—with the obvious exception of the sort of groups who were fans of Father Coughlin—largely positive. Detroit poet Edgard Guest immortalized both Greenberg and himself with a poem that concludes with the lines

> ...Said Murphy to Mulrooney, "We shall lose the game today!
> We shall miss him in the infield and shall miss him at the bat,
> But he's true to his religion—and I honor him for that!"[10]

It might be noted that, four years later, as Greenberg was closing in on Babe Ruth's single-season home-run record, a number of pitchers whom he faced in the last week of the season intentionally walked him. While he himself gave little credence to the idea, many observers asserted that he got very few good pitches to hit because Major League Baseball did not want a Jew breaking that record. It is, of course, impossible to know that, but the ambiguities of the American majority's attitude toward representatives of any number of minorities—be they a minority of religion, race, or ethnicity—cannot simply be glossed over as if such bigotry did not and does not exist.

Indeed, within the larger context of sports and politics—the politics of race as well as of religion—one might wonder whether race had been an issue some two decades earlier in the matter of the skilled baseball play of Jim Thorpe, the brilliant Native American athlete who won both the pentathlon and decathlon events at the 1912 summer Olympics. In 1950, 400 writers for the Associated Press voted Thorpe the greatest athlete of the first half of the century, and he was honored by the U.S. Congress in 1999 as America's athlete of the century. His Olympic medals, however, had been taken from him a year after the Olympics 38 years before the AP writers' vote, when it emerged that he had played baseball for two summers for pay—for about $2 a game—back in 1909 and 1910. The fact that college athletes typically did that at the time, but used aliases, whereas Thorpe, as he would write to the authorities, did not, because "I was simply an Indian school boy and did not know all about such things" did not exonerate him.

Nor did the fact that the very rules of the Amateur Athletic Union and International Olympic Committee required that any protests that might lead to disqualification needed to be filed within 30 days, and the case against Thorpe was made more than six months after his triumphs. I am not suggesting unequivocally that the AAU and IOC operated as they did because Thorpe was a Native American and not a Euro-American, but one must at least entertain the possibility, particularly in the context of other issues— such as the fact that Native Americans were not even considered American citizens until 1924—that, had he been a "white man," the issue would not have been raised or, at the very least, would have been resolved differently. [11]

More than two decades later—after the world had moved through a World War, a Great Depression, and Hank Greenberg's heroics on and off the field—the 1936 Olympics in Berlin, as we have seen, would put race and religion front and center. As we have noted in chapter 10, among the key figures in the ugly side of that Hitler-hosted narrative would be Jim Thorpe's teammate from the 1912 American Pentathlon team, Avery Brundage, as well as Jewish sprinter Marty Glickman and African American athlete Jesse Owens.[12]

But the matter of Jesse Owens raises the question of how *race* was regarded in the national pastime sport of baseball. It may be true, as opined later on by Tiger catcher Birdie Tebbetts regarding his teammate, that "...Hank on the ball field was more abused than any other white ballplayer or any other ethnic player except Jackie Robinson." And although a small number of African Americans played in the nascent game in the 1880s, by the 1890s a color line had taken shape in baseball that effectively prevented African American athletes from playing either in the major leagues or in their affiliated minor leagues. That line would not be crossed and broken *until* Jackie Robinson came to play for the Brooklyn Dodgers' minor league team in Montreal in 1946, and then made his debut with the Dodgers themselves the following year—the year in which Hank Greenberg retired.

For half a century, black baseball players played on their own teams in their own leagues—the so-called Negro Leagues—in spite of there being no formal restrictions preventing integration within Major League baseball. It simply took someone willing to break with an unhappy tradition. My point, of course, is that, whereas sports at its best is the stunning tapestry of effort and accomplishment, it can be—and has been—part of an America in constant historical (often, unacknowledged) debate between the ideals for which the republic stands and the reality of how varied Americans diversely feel and act with regard to race, ethnicity, nationality and religion.

Where baseball and the specifics and practices of religion are concerned, the Jewish question raised by Greenberg would be rephrased 31 years later, when Sandy Koufax, star pitcher for the Los Angeles Dodgers, (lineal descendants of the Brooklyn Dodgers for whom Jackie Robinson played), elected to sit out a game that fell on Yom Kippur. One might say that the context of Koufax's decision upped the ante from the pennant-chasing context of Greenberg's decision: the 1963 game in which Koufax did not pitch was *the first game of the World Series*. On the other hand, Koufax was shocked, responding with disgust when a journalist for the *St. Paul Pioneer*

Press wrote ugly words regarding that decision not to pitch, and the star received piles of positive mail applauding his decision from players and journalists as well as fans.[13]

The lines of both religion and race have been crossed and criss-crossed by changes in attitude and involvement in the century between Jim Thorpe's astonishing Olympic performance and our own time. For one thing, the other "national" sports of football and basketball have also had their Jewish stars, from Dolph Schayes, the first big man in basketball who could also shoot, dribble, and pass; to Sid Luckman, greatest quarterback ever to play out of the T-formation in football. For another, the sort of questions that such athletes have confronted with regard to matching their commitments to their Judaism with the demands of their sport and to their desire to be, simply, *Americans*, have been paralleled by Muslim athletes in American sports, as we have seen, particularly with the rise in participation in these sports by Africans and African Americans, who include among their numbers some noteworthy Muslim athletes.[14]

We have noted the issue of how an NBA star such as Hakeem Olajuwon, originally from Nigeria, managed the maintenance of the fast of Ramadan with his playing schedule.[15] We should recall that the emphasis during Ramadan is on the act of not eating, whereas the emphasis during Yom Kippur is in large part on participating in the day-long prayers that accompany the fast—so these are parallel, rather than identical issues. We might ask other, related questions, such as how simple or difficult it would be for a Jewish athlete to observe the Sabbath or for a Muslim athlete to pray five times daily—or for a Jewish athlete to find kosher food or a Muslim athlete to find hallal food as their teams move about the country.[16]

The ongoing interest in this sort of issue continues to pepper the sports pages from time to time. Ben Strauss's *New York Times* article (D4) of January 28, 2013 offers the headline "Studying X's, O's and the Torah." The article highlights Aaron Liberman, a redshirt freshman basketball player for Northwestern—perhaps the third practicing Orthodox Jew in history to play for a Division

I school.[17] Liberman maintained a strict regimen of thrice-daily prayers, eating only kosher food, and travelling only by foot on the Sabbath—from sundown on Friday to shortly after sundown on Saturday. Interestingly, however, he chose (after much reflection and discussion with rabbis) to play on the Sabbath—once walking eight miles to get to practice.

For Saturday away games, Northwestern made arrangements that allowed Liberman to travel separately from the team if the flight time interfered with the Sabbath. "Actually, playing basketball is not breaking any of the 39 laws [that pertain specifically to] the Sabbath," he said. "But I'll only be taking cold showers afterward because you can't use hot water [which would require 'kindling a fire']." We are reminded how the double basis for religious sensibility is revelation—as, in this case, it is recorded in the Torah—and interpretation.

This sort of issue isn't limited to Jewish athletes, of course. An article in the November 14, 2011 issue of *Sports Illustrated* magazine highlights the questions facing Dewayne Dedmon, a 7-foot-tall Jehovah's Witness playing basketball at the time for USC.[18] A member of a religious denomination that numbers only several million across the world—about 1 million in over 10,000 congregations in the United States—for whom the Father, and not the Holy Trinity constitutes God, Dedmon abides by a set of restrictions derived from a defined literalist interpretation of the Bible. This ranges from nonparticipation in the political process to refusing blood transfusions. Sports is not inherently unacceptable, unless, of course, team-loyalty interferes with full-time God-focus. Dedmon's relationship to basketball was nonexistent until he was 18; then, this gangly, 6-foot, 8-inch kid was "discovered" by and started training with Dieter Horton, a coach with a stunning junior college record who gray-shirted Dedmon into Antelope Valley College while he learned the game. Horton eventually moved on to USC as an assistant basketball coach, shortly after shepherding Dedmon in that direction.

Dedmon developed basketball skills even more quickly than he continued to grow towards 7 feet. He also wrestled with the question of whether—as asserted by the two men who came from the Kingdom Hall to discourage him from playing, at his mother's behest—"basketball could take Dewayne away from his Christian upbringing. How it could corrupt him."[19] By the time he was committed to go to USC after his two years at AVC, his story had become known throughout the region. Whereas "most of the time we hear about wayward young men who one day find God[,] Dedmon... was the opposite. As [AVC] history professor Cynthia Lehman says, 'He just walked into the gym one day and found basketball.'"[20]

At USC, "[h]e remained torn between two worlds. He says he still accepts some of the religious doctrine he was raised to believe—he won't take a blood transfusion, for example—only now, 'I'm not so much into it,' he says.[21] His mother has been to some of his games, but focuses in their conversations on reminding him of his Christian upbringing—and he responds that he continues to think about it all the time. She won't stand in his way if he goes into the NBA, but hopes that he will return more fully to the fold." As of early 2014, Dedmon had been playing for the NBA D-league Santa Cruz warriors but had also played on two successive ten-day contracts for the Philadelphia 76ers. The question of his NBA future intersects, but is different from, the question of his religious practice: he seems to be able to continue to balance his love of God and his love of basketball with considerable equanimity and discipline.

We might also note situations almost the opposite of Dedmon's: the phenomenon of Muslim athletes born in this country and raised as Christians, who embraced Islam in their adulthood— at the peak of their athletic careers. For example, one might think of the great basketball player Kareem Abdul-Jabbar—previously known as Lew Alcindor—whose embrace of Islam may have, in part, reflected his sense that the Christian faith into which he had been born was historically involved with the process by which his ancestors arrived to America, as slaves from Africa.

Jabbar would comment in a magazine interview that his decision to become a Muslim derived from a wish to connect "to something that was part of my heritage, because many of the slaves who were brought here were Muslims. My family was brought to America by a French planter named Alcindor, who came here from Trinidad in the 18th century. My people were Yoruba, and their culture survived slavery [...]. My father found out about that when I was a kid, and it gave me all I needed to know that, hey, I was somebody, even if nobody else knew about it. When I was a kid, no one would believe anything positive that you could say about black people. And that's a terrible burden on black people, because they don't have an accurate idea of their history, which has been either suppressed or distorted."[22]

Kareem's sense of whether and how to maintain the tenets of his newfound faith while within the throes of his athletic career were informed by a combination of spiritual and socio-historical—religious and race-related—elements. That sense of religion interweaving with other issues in the context of sports was expressed in a very particularized manner by the NBA basketball player, Mahmoud Abdul-Rauf. Born as a Christian in 1969, Chris Jackson changed his name when he converted to Islam in 1991. He became best-known when, as a player for the Denver Nuggets in the early 1990s he refused to stand during the pre-game playing of "The Star-Spangled Banner," asserting that the American flag was a "symbol of oppression" and that the U.S. has had a "long history of tyranny." More to the point within the context of our discussion, he further maintained that standing for the national anthem, given these stated "facts," would conflict with his Muslim beliefs.

This stance offers a distinct intertwining of religious conviction with a political viewpoint. It might strike some as odd that one would continue to play and draw a paycheck from a system that is perceived in such negative terms, rather than leaving it—Abdul-Rauf would, in fact, upon his retirement from the NBA, play professional basketball in Europe and at the time of this writing plays for Al-Ittihad in the Saudi Arabian league. Interestingly, at the time of his sitting protest, he was suspended by the NBA (on March 12, 1996), but the suspension lasted for only one game, after which the league worked out a compromise with him, whereby he agreed to stand during the playing of the national anthem, but could close his eyes and look downward. Usually, according to his comments, he would recite Muslim prayers at that time.

The relationship between religion and politics within recent history is even more evident in the highly individualistic case of Muhammad Ali—originally known as Cassius Clay. Ali gained greater notoriety than Abdul-Jabbar or Abdul-Rauf with respect to his embrace of Islam for two main reasons. First is the path he took to mainstream Sunni Islam in 1975. That path carried him through Elijah Muhammad's Nation of Islam in the 1960s, when that movement was an object of suspicion for many Americans (both white and black) because its leaders preached that all white people were devils. More recently, he has been referred to as a Sufi—a Muslim mystic—whose views are universalistic and peace-driven.[23]

One might perhaps have expected Ali to give up boxing when he became a Muslim, given the traditional opposition to this sport.[24] That he did not may be a consequence of the different sort of path he took toward Islam's mainstream; or because, as always, in religion, there is a range of interpretive views regarding many issues; or perhaps due to his unusually important role as a public symbol of Islam, for which his skill as a boxer played such an important role.[25] That role expanded exponentially when he was forced to give up boxing for several years.

That circumstance leads our discussion toward the second aspect of Ali's relationship to his religion, which gained a great deal of media attention. This was his refusal to be inducted into the army during the period of the Vietnam War, asserting that that war was being fought contrary to the will of God and therefore of Islam—and that the only wars that a Muslim should fight are those prescribed directly by God or by the prophet Muhammad.

The impact of his stance was considerable. Aside from raising issues with regard to the relationship between religion and politics from a particular angle, it deprived Ali himself of the opportunity to pursue his sport at the time when he had reached the peak of his powers as a fighter; he was stripped of his heavyweight title by the New York State Athletic Commission (other boxing entities soon followed suit) as well as of the legal right to continue his career.

Eventually, the Supreme Court would reverse the second of these two decisions regarding Ali, and he would climb back into the ring to achieve the reversal of the first. Throughout the often spectacular and occasionally unhappy second stage of his career, Islam remained both a steadfast source of internal peace and an articulator of his identity that he shared eagerly with the world.

If the world of boxing gave Muhammad Ali a platform from which to declaim poetry and proclaim his understanding of the world as he floated within it—to be *political* in the full historical sense of that community-based term—we may also recognize him as someone who emerges as bigger than the sport he dominated as he came to place the concerns of religion rather than, simply, sports at the center of his life.

Indeed, however great he was as a boxer, the most significant parts of his legacy pertain to the decision that forced him out of the ring at the peak of his career and how he was able to articulate his reasons for that decision—and in turn the eventual growth in his stature as a cultural-political icon that that process yielded. His being awarded the Presidential Medal, and his being invited to kindle the Olympic flame at the 1996 games in Atlanta, offered consummate symbols of this status.

The discussion of Muhammad Ali following that of Mahmoud Abdul-Rauf leads further in time toward two signal moments. Abdul-Rauf's refusal to stand and Ali's refusal to enlist in the army offer conceptual connections to the protest of Tommie Smith and John Carlos in the aftermath of their respective gold-medal and bronze-medal finishes in the 200m race in the 1968 Olympics in Mexico City.

Formally the protesting gesture—raising a hand in a black-gloved fist—bore greater resemblance to Mahmoud Rauf's gesture, but the inspiration was derived particularly from Ali's refusal to enlist, because of the larger-than-life figure he had already become.[26]

In the cases of both Abdul-Rauf and Muhammad Ali, however, the grounds for their actions interwove race with religion (and, by definition, politics). In the protest gestures of Smith and Carlos, religion was not an issue, but exclusively the still-rampant racism in the United States to which they were responding. Racial tensions were at a height, and the Civil Rights movement had given way to the Black Power movement. African Americans such as Smith and Carlos were frustrated by what they perceived to be the passive nature of the Civil Rights movement. They sought out active forms of protests and advocated for racial pride, black nationalism and dramatic action rather than incremental, overly slow, change.[27]

As Black athletes representing and succeeding on behalf of a country where Blacks were still enduring second-class status in many, many different places and ways, both obvious and subtle, these two figures made a statement. The gloved fists were, in fact, intended to express solidarity with black people and oppressed people around the world. It was a statement, as one can imagine, that was jeered by many and cheered by many others. Indeed, as they raised their fists, the stadium hushed, then burst into racist sneers and angry insults. Smith and Carlos were rushed from the stadium, suspended from the U.S. team, and kicked out of the Olympic Village for turning their medal ceremony into a political statement. They went home to the United States, only to face serious backlash, including death threats. However, they were both gradually re-accepted into the Olympic fold, and went on to careers in professional football before retiring.[28]

More recently, this race-based narrative points most distinctly forward toward the story of Colin Kaepernick in the past several years—for whom, not surprisingly, both Smith and Carlos have publicly expressed support. Kaepernick was the quarterback for NFL football's San Francisco 49ers in 2011-16. He began out of college as the back-up quarterback for Alex Smith, replacing the starter after Smith sustained a concussion in the middle of the 2012 season; Kaepernick ended up leading the team that year to its first Super Bowl appearance since 1994.[29]

In 2013, his first full season as a starter, he led the team as far as the NFC championship game, but the team's overall level of play diminished over the next several years, and its failures were variously blamed and not blamed on him. In the 49ers' third pre-season game in 2016, Kaepernick sat during the playing of the U.S National Anthem before the game, rather than standing. He did this as a protest against racial injustice and systematic oppression in the country.[30] During a post-game interview, he explained his position, asserting that "I am not going to stand up to show pride in a flag for a country that oppresses black people and other people of color. To me, this is bigger than football and it would be selfish on my part to look the other way. There are bodies in the street and people getting paid leave and getting away with murder," referencing a series of African-American deaths caused by law enforcement in several different American cities in the aftermath of which the offending officers were merely placed on paid leave. This led to the shaping of the "Black Lives Matter" movement. Kaepernick added that he would continue to protest until he feels like "[the American flag] represents what it's supposed to represent."[31]

Having thought further about the most effective way to express his feelings on this subject, and after a long conversation with former NFL player and U.S. military veteran, Nate Boyer, Kaepernick knelt with one knee on the ground during the U.S. national anthem, before the 49ers' fourth and final preseason game, in order to show more respect to former and current U.S. military members while still offering a protest during the anthem. He continued to kneel that way during the national anthem throughout the season.

He also continued to be outspoken. Following the September 2016 police shootings of Terence Crutcher and Keith Lamont Scott,

Kaepernick commented publicly on the shootings, noting that "this is a perfect example of what this is all about."[32] Shortly thereafter, some photos surfaced of him wearing socks depicting police officers as pigs—which some members of the public interpreted as an incitement to violence. In a statement in which he acknowledged wearing them as a statement against "rogue cops," he asserted that he has friends/family in law enforcement and that there are cops with "good intentions" who protect and serve and that he was not targeting all police for criticism.[33] There are those who were satisfied with that comment and those who read it as a kind of cop out (pun intended).

Kaepernick's protests received highly polarized reactions, with some praising him and his stand against racism and others denouncing the protests as disrespectful to the armed forces. The actions resulted in a wider protest movement, which intensified in September 2017 after President Trump said that NFL owners should "fire" players who protest the national anthem.[34]

Inspired by Kaepernick, other NFL players and pro athletes conducted various forms of silent protests during the national anthem. There were also many players, both black and white, who were critical of his actions. His San Francisco teammates awarded him the team's Len Eshmont Award, as the player who best epitomized the inspirational and courageous play of former 49er Len Eshmont.[35] Then-49ers head coach Kelly later asserted that, contrary to what some people asserted, Kaepernick was a "zero distraction" for his team that season, although some of his teammates disagreed with that assessment.[36]

Meanwhile, Kaepernick pledged to donate $1 million to "organizations working in oppressed communities."[37] He donated $25,000 to the Mothers Against Police Brutality organization that was started by Collette Flanagan, whose son fell victim to police brutality.[38] In 2018, Kaepernick announced that he would make the final $100,000 donation of his "Million Dollar Pledge" in the form of $10,000 donations to charities that would be matched by celebrities.[39]

In 2018, Nike released an ad featuring Kaepernick with the text, "Believe in something. Even if it means sacrificing everything." NFL spokesperson Jocelyn Moore responded to the ad saying that Kaepernick's social justice campaign, "deserve(s) our attention and action."[40] If it seems clear that Kaepernick's NFL career has ended as a consequence of his stance, an entity like Nike may be seen to have stepped in, in practical terms, to fill the fiscal gap left by the athlete's unemployment. One might also assert, more cynically, that Nike saw—or at least gambled on—an opportunity to accrue fiscal points along with some moral points.

Indeed, Kaepernick became a free agent after the 2016 season, but went unsigned—and it will continue to be debated as to whether the reason was simply the insufficiency of his talent or the lack of a need for a fine quarterback anywhere in the league, or his front-and-center political stance. In November 2017, he filed a grievance against the NFL and its owners, accusing them of colluding to keep him out of the league. Kaepernick withdrew the grievance in February 2019 after reaching a confidential settlement with the NFL. In that same year, *GQ* named him the magazine's Citizen of the Year. Interestingly, he declined to be interviewed for the magazine, however, having decided to continue to represent the issue that led to his initial protests through the eloquence of silence.[41]

As of this writing, Kaepernick has remained unable to find a job as an NFL quarterback since that fateful year of quiet and dignified protest. The question that cannot be answered definitively is whether, had he not been a player of color—had he been a white quarterback of equal stature—the response by team-owners and coaches would have been the same. One might also ask whether, were he not a player of color, he would have been inspired in the first place to offer a protest gesture directed most particularly to racially-connected malfeasance on the part of American law enforcement. Just over a century after Jim Thorpe was stripped of his

Olympic medals, Colin Kaepernick was stripped of his career and it is difficult not to imagine that at least part of the reason behind this was race—not only the race issue about which he was commenting by kneeling, but his own race. But I cannot claim to be certain of this.

This entire mini-saga represents a distinctive continuation of the relationship between sports and politics of the kind that is particular to the 20th and 21st centuries—increasing in ubiquity in the last 15 years or so—in which some athletes willingly use their positions as public figures to engage as socio-political activists. Further, it reflects the willingness of some athletes to risk and even sacrifice their careers in sports in order to be consistent with their socio-political—or in Abdul-Rauf's and Muhammad Ali's cases, religious and socio-political—convictions. Kaepernick's kneeling gesture recalls Abdul-Rauf and his words recall those of Muhammad Ali. As we have noted, Abdul-Rauf was able to work out a compromise with NBA authorities; Muhammad Ali lost the best years of his prime as a boxer—although his career both as a boxer and as a public figure continued along a remarkable arc, nonetheless. Kaepernick's career as an athlete is likely over.

Needless to say, the issue of race is not limited to the United States or its sports world. Our country is in a somewhat unique position on this matter, thanks to the particulars of its history of enslaving people of color on the one hand, and its wonderfully articulated principles of freedom and equality on the other: the tension between these two realities is far from resolved at the beginning of the third decade of this millennium. That said, there are other countries in, for instance, Europe, where race can emerge and has emerged as an ugly issue. Thus the Turkish-originated German soccer player Mezut Ozil—he was a key part of Germany's World Cup-winning team in 2014 and a star midfielder for Arsenal—"quit Germany's national soccer team after receiving intense criticism over his decision to pose for a picture with President Recep Tayyip Erdogan of Turkey... He attacked the German federation...

its president, fans and the news media, criticizing them for what he described as racism..."[42] Interestingly, the criticism of Ozil by Reinhard Grindel, head of Germany's soccer federation, accused him—and his Turkish-originated German teammate, Ilkay Gundogan—of "allowing themselves to be 'exploited' by Erdogan for political purposes," reminding us of how various issues interweave in the sports world.

It might be further noted that Ozil, in his retort to Grindel, pointed out that there had been "little criticism of former German captain Lother Matthaeus regarding "his recent meeting with President Vladimir P. Putin of Russia." A further interesting element in this dust-up is that what Ozil interpreted as racial prejudice may either have been religious (anti-Muslim) prejudice or nationalism. In any case, it is fair to say that politics, religion, and race are all part of this particular knot—and what in the German, Turkish, and European contexts is understood to pertain to race would, most likely in the United States, be referred, rather, to religion or nationality.

If sports has been an imperfect microcosm of an imperfect America—one is not always and only judged by one's talent and effort—yet sports has generally offered a more reasonable range of possibilities for achieving success and recognition regardless of one's race or religion than in many other areas of American enterprise. And one can see this not only by looking forward but by looking backward from the time-frame perspective of Muhammad Ali.

Ali famously began his fighting career as a street kid in the Louisville inner city, who was drawn into the gym to learn to fight after enduring the frustration of having his bicycle stolen. So, too, many of the great fighters in twentieth-century America started in the tougher corners of American cities. An important sub-story of that narrative is that the inhabitants of those corners, who were able to rise to boxing stardom, were either disenfranchised because they were African American or because they were immigrants to America. If we follow the line of boxers back through Rocky Marciano and Joe Louis to the 1930s and 1920s—the heyday of Hank Green-berg and Babe Ruth, respectively—we come to a period in which the various weight classes were dominated by Jews. Mostly, these were the children of immigrants for whom boxing skills proved to be one way both of asserting themselves against gangs who as-sailed them as Jews and also of finding their way up and out of the inner cities into socio-economically more advantaged parts of America and its mainstream Dream.

Among the most renowned of these Jewish descendants of Battling Mendoza in England and the stylistic anticipators of Mu-hammad Ali was Benny Leonard—born Benjamin Lerner—known as the "Ghetto Wizard." Leonard won 204 fights and lost 5 in a career that included defending the light-heavyweight boxing title that he held 80 times, from 1917 to 1924. He was certainly the most renowned of an extraordinary array of Jewish fighters, but there were many others. Barney Ross—who fought 329 bouts, 82 of them as a professional, in a career that extended from the mid-1920s to 1938—was inspired to start his career out of anger and frustration resulting from a crime in a manner anticipating the beginning of Muhammad Ali's boxing path four decades later. In Ross's case, the event that changed his life was when his beloved father, a rabbi, died in his arms from a gunshot wound administered in late De-cember 1923 by a man trying to rob the small grocery run by the Rasofskys (their Russian family name) in the Maxwell Street area of Chicago—that city's equivalent of New York's Lower East Side.

The young Rasofsky had been a rabbinical student who had expected to follow in his father's footsteps. But his father's murder caused him to lose his faith in God and to abandon his studies. His mother suffered a nervous breakdown in the aftermath of her husband's death and his three younger siblings were farmed out to other members of the extended family or placed in an orphanage, and 14-year-old Dov-Ber, as he was originally named, and his older brother, were left largely to fend for themselves. His anger caused him to turn his back on the notion that his father had tried to instill in him that Jews do not fight back physically[43] — and he became a street brawler, together with his buddy Jack Ruby[44] and other Jewish toughs. He also began training to box, and as he began to fight and win bouts, he would pawn the awards he garnered and set the money aside for the family that he hoped eventually to reunite.

He changed his name so as not to soil the real family name with such "improper" labor; and, perhaps, so that his mother would not realize that he was fighting. Perhaps, too, he was following the tendency of immigrant Jews, in particular, to Americanize their names in the hope of more complete assimilation in their adoptive homeland. Ross became a Golden Gloves Champ and, eventually, in the course of his career he would hold titles in three different weight classes. After his retirement, he volunteered for the Marines, insisting that he be sent to the action (most star athletes played a more ceremonial role in the military). At Guadalcanal in the South Pacific, he and three fellow Marines were trapped and seriously outnumbered by the enemy. The other three were wounded — two of them died — and Ross singlehandedly continued to fight off the Japanese, killing 22 of them and then carried his surviving comrade (who outweighed him by 90 pounds) to safety.

But from the perspective of our particular focus there were two aspects of his career that were most noteworthy. One echoes the sentiments expressed by Hank Greenberg as he played baseball during the era of Hitler's rise to power. Ross, like Greenberg, was seen by American Jews as one of their most important instruments in the struggle against anti-Semitism. He represented the quintessence of the Jew who was able to thrive in the country to which so many had managed to immigrate, and who didn't back down but fought back. His ideology echoed that of "muscular Judaism" as it had been articulated in Europe in the early part of the century. For Ross, this was true in the boxing ring (most stunningly in his last fight, when he was being pounded by his much younger opponent, Henry Armstrong, but refused to go down) and on the battlefield at Guadalcanal.

Ross embraced this role, regardless of what had evolved for him with regard to his faith in God. When he fought Jimmy McLarnin for the welterweight title for the first time in New York in May 1934, there were pro-Nazi rallies going on in the city at virtually the same time. Barney said that he felt like he was fighting for the entire Jewish people. The second point of great interest to us was his decision to respect aspects of Jewish religious conduct, based on a promise that he made to his mother. So, for instance, the rematch that he gave to McLarnin was postponed four times in 11 days, and one of those times was due to the Jewish New Year, Rosh Hashanah.

However, the night he won the lightweight championship (defeating Tony Canzoneri), his mother was there, although it was a Friday night: Sabbath eve. She had by then accepted and even embraced the pugilistic medium that had enabled her son to reunite the family. But as a religious Jew, while she was willing to compromise as far as seeing Barney fight, she would not ride on the Sabbath, so Barney always walked her home from the stadium. Before the rematch that Ross gave to Canzoneri, he pulled out his long-ignored phylacteries and prayed in the Orthodox Jewish manner for the first time in years.[45] Some aspects of his faith seem to have returned to him as his life progressed.

So, too, the issue of religious observance of various sorts might affect—and in recent years has affected—entire basketball teams, and not just individual players, particularly at the high school level. What of a school of, say, Orthodox Jews with a basketball team that plays in a league that ordinarily has games on Friday night or Saturday in the late afternoon? That hypothetical question has at least twice affected such schools in Texas fairly recently: Beren Academy in March 2012; and the Texas Torah Institute of Dallas in 2011.

In each case, the school in question was in the playoffs of its respective league. When the Texas Association of Private and Parochial Schools—not inherently affected by the same strictures that would affect public schools—initially refused to reschedule the semi-final game between Beren Academy and Dallas Covenant that was scheduled for a Friday evening, a group of parents (*not* the school administration) sued. TAPPS reversed itself within a few hours of the filing, shifting the time of the game to 2:00 p.m. on Friday—and agreeing, were Beren to win, that the finals would begin at 8:00 p.m. on Saturday evening, after the end of the Jewish Sabbath.

Similarly, although without any legal action, the finals between Texas Torah and Allen Academy of Bryan was shifted, by agreement between the schools and the Texas Christian Athletic Association (the league in which the two schools were competing), to a post-Sabbath hour. Allen's coach Dave Bliss commented that accommodating Texas Torah's spiritual need was a no-brainer: "I didn't even think of doing anything different," he said.[46]

What is to be done when a high school team has a majority of members who are Muslim—and Ramadan falls during the season? That very situation was discussed in a *New York Times* article by Jere Longman, "Tackling by Moonlight."[47] The article focused on Dearborn, Michigan's Fordson High School, in which 90 percent of the students are Muslim, in a year when, for the second consecutive season, Ramadan and football coincided. Coach Fouad Zaban shifted his initial week of two-a-day practices to a late-night schedule—from 11:00 p.m. to 4:00 a.m. The issue was a matter of both religion and health: "If kids were going to fast, and the majority are, [said Zaban], it was much safer not to be outside in daylight in 90-degree weather for hours each day." Rival Dearborn High School, where a third of the players were fasting during Ramadan, held practices between 6:00 and 11:00 p.m.

Late in his article, Longman quotes "Rashid Ghazi, a filmmaker whose documentary *Fordson, Faith, Fasting, Football* [was] set for theatrical release [the] next month, [and who] said he encountered a variation of the classic immigrant story in Dearborn. 'The school means everything to the community, and the team is the embodiment of the school,' Ghazi said. 'There is nothing more American than high school football.' It just so happens, he said, that 'this all-American story is set in an area with hijabs, mosques and baklava rather than baseball caps, churches and apple pie.'"

The turn to sports in America yields an interesting array of perspectives with which to view the weaving together of religion and athletic competition, from games played by the First Americans hundreds and thousands of years ago to those played by Jewish immigrants making a transition from the Old World to the New, and from Ellis Island to the suburbs decades ago. The American sports melting pot has encompassed Muslims recruited from Africa to become stars in collegiate and professional leagues—that conscription accomplished with no sense of the irony that, over the centuries, so many tens of thousands of Africans were kidnapped and/or purchased from their native lands and brought to America under the most oppressive of circumstances—and Christian athletes born in America who have turned to Islam during their careers.

We might turn the screw of this part of our discussion one further twist by observing the intersection of sports and religion in America in terms of the engagement by a contemporary cadre of athletes with a centuries'-old Native American sacred site. In an article in the *New York Times* entitled, "A Boulder-Climbing Paradise, Where the Sacred Meets Sport," reporter Michael Brick writes about an 860-acre stretch of land northeast of El Paso, Texas, known as Hueco Tanks—a site covered with scores of large boulders.[48] What "[t]o certain American Indian tribes, ... marks the sacred place of emergence from a prior world" is to "far-flung devotees of the intensely physical rock-climbing style known as bouldering ... the Colosseum." Boulder climbers "have identified more than 1,600 bouldering routes, or problems, ranked on a scale of difficulty" across the stunning Hueco Tanks landscape.

The issue that has emerged for this unparalleled site, where in the twelfth century the Jornada Mogollon people began farming, and left an array of pictographs; and where the Kiowa, Mescalero Apache, and Tigua tribes also left their imprint—and to which "we made our pilgrimages and offerings to our grandfathers of the mountains"—is twofold. First, that by 1991 it was receiving some 150,000 visitors a year, leaving behind litter, human waste, and damage from climbing bolts and graffiti, so that the site was being continually desecrated. One could see "Yo" inscribed with a recent scrawl barely inches from a centuries'-old drawing of the rain god, Tlaloc.

In order to regulate Hueco Tanks' use in order to cut down on such forms of desecration, the state took control of it as a historic site. The Tigua tribe tried unsuccessfully to purchase it, and the state applied access restrictions in 1998—which means that the 1,600 members of the tribe who live on the nearby reservation of Ysleta del Sur also have to pay admission fees in order to enter the site for religious ceremonies. Thus, restrictions on their primary ancestral site and "the commercialization of the Huecos [are viewed by the Tigua] as a desecration" of a second sort that has taken place, in addition to that committed by insensitive visitors—as expressed by Javier Loera, whose elected tribal position puts him in charge of stewarding tribal customs. In this case, then, sports and religion collide through a meeting of ancient spiritual needs with modern secular desires.

The focus on sports in America has not only offered diverse angles from which to address the rubric of "religion and sports" but to recognize that the rubric is ultimately a much larger one, encompassing ethnicity and race—and, in turn, including politics within its ambit. If a central element in this multivalent discussion pertains to the tension between an ideal America and a real America, then we may be said to be approaching the end zone and home plate of our discussion. That is to say that we are approaching the completion of a circle back to the point of our departure: the various ways in which religion and religious expression have asserted themselves in the world of contemporary sports, and how that reflects and refracts a long and diverse history. This is the point—the world of today—to which we direct ourselves in the next chapter of our narrative.

Notes

1. The Nine defeated the Knickerbockers, 23-1, in four innings!

2. At that time, the school was known as the YMCA Training School.

3. The statue, designed by Frederic-Auguste Bartholdi, was built with the assistance of the architect/engineer, Gustave Eiffel. While the original idea had been to have it in place by 1876 for the American centennial, it was not actually erected in the harbor until 1886, a few years after Lazarus's poem was penned.

4. When I refer to a lack of a sense of irony, I mean the obvious: that the nativists were not natives of these shores, but immigrants of an earlier generation; and that their attitude to Native Americans/First Americans was as ungenerous as it was to immigrants from southern and eastern Europe. The *forced* immigrants from Africa of the previous several centuries were altogether a nonfactor in nativist thinking.

5. He was the American League MVP in 1935 as a first baseman and again in 1940 as a left fielder; he drove in 183 runs in 1937, and most famously, 58 home runs in 1938—the very year in which, two months after the end of the baseball season, Nazi violence against German Jews would reach its first crescendo with *kristallnacht.*

6. The Yom Kippur fast is traditionally carried out from sundown to sundown—it is actually a 25-hour fast, the added hour included lest one perchance inadvertently fast less than an entire day. Thus, it is different from (but parallel to) the Muslim fast of Ramadan, which takes place from dawn to dusk, but for an entire month. It might be noted in passing that both holidays shift year-by-year vis-à-vis the Gregorian calendar, due to the fact that the Muslim and Jewish calendars are lunar and lunar/solar respectively.

7. To be precise, after a lengthy consultation with his rabbi and with his conscience, he went to the synagogue to pray in the morning of the Jewish New Year and to the stadium to play (but without taking batting practice) in the afternoon. He hit two home runs that day, leading Detroit to a 2-1 victory over the Boston Red Sox.

8. To be fair, Henry Ford had reformed and even apologized for his outspoken anti-Semitic style by the time Greenberg was in his prime. Father Coughlin picked up that style in spades.

9. For a more detailed discussion of this and of the relationship between American Jews and baseball in general, see Soltes: "Centerfield of Dreams and

Questions: Baseball and Judaism," in Raphael and Abrams's *What Is Jewish About American's "Favorite Pastime"?*.

10. In fact, the Tigers did lose that day to the Yankees, but Greenberg returned the following day and hit a home run that clinched the pennant. The Tigers went on to lose the World Series to the St. Louis Cardinals in seven games, but came back the next year to win it all; Greenberg won the first of his MVP awards that year. Six years later, after Pearl Harbor, he was the first Major Leaguer to voluntarily enlist in the army. When the war ended in 1945, he returned to the Tigers' lineup in midsummer and hit a home run in his first game back—and led the Detroit Tigers to another World Series title that year, bringing his team the pennant with a grand-slam home run on the final day of the season.

11. Jim Thorpe's medals were posthumously re-awarded to him in 1983, after a long campaign to right what most historians view as a wrong derived from the racial prejudices that I am suggesting were distinctly operative in 1912.

12. See above, 187-8. To be more precise: Together with the replacement of Jesse Owens for Marty Glickman, a second Jewish runner, Sam Stoller, was also replaced by a second African American runner, Ralph Metcalfe, Glickman subsequently achieved fame as a sportscaster and he was more emphatic in the following years about the antisemitic basis for the decision and that it was Brundage who was behind it, albeit there has been some controversy about this datum over the years. I see little cause to doubt Brundage's role. I had an opportunity to chat briefly with Glickman in 1992, in the context of discussing the now-defunct National Jewish American Sports Hall of Fame that I was developing at the (also now-defunct) B'nai B'rith Klutznick National Jewish Museum. The most affecting and effective discussion of this story is found in Peter Levine's *Ellis Island to Ebbets Field,* (chapter 11: 216-234).

13. Like other minorities, Jews tend toward a particular interest in knowing which athletes are Jewish. The Greenberg-Koufax beat continued on when former Boston Red Sox standout first (and sometimes third) baseman Kevin Youkilis become a Yankee in 2012. (After a season-ending back surgery, he was not re-signed by the Yankees and will apparently be playing in Japan when the 2014 season begins). In Richard Sandomir's December 13, 2012 *New York Times* article, (in section B13), headlined, "Fascination with a New Yankee's Jewish Roots," that fascination is described as shared. When the comedian, Denis Leary, visited the Red Sox television booth one night in 2006 and was told that Youkilis was not Greek, but Jewish, his response was: "That's one bottle of whiskey away from being Irish Catholic. They got the Manischewitz, we got the Jameson's. It's the same guilt, the same bad food. That's fantastic…" On the same page of the *Times* sports section, an article by Ken Belson, "For New York Fans Accustomed to Letdowns, A New Reason to Kvell," offered a somewhat tongue-in-cheek overview of all kinds

of Jewish ballplayers—40 or so of them by Belson's count—who have played in the professional leagues over the many decades from Lipman Pike to Youkilis.

14. Oddly enough, there seem to be fewer Muslims in baseball than in football or basketball. A poignant article by Paul Brownfield on the front page of the Sports section of the January 2, 2013 *New York Times,* "Briefly a Rising Star, Forever a Mourning Son," profiled Sam Khalifa, born in America, and raised in Egypt, Libya, and Tucson, Arizona. The article, which appeared three decades after his brief stint as a shortstop for the Pittsburgh Pirates and for their minor-league affiliate, back in 1982-89, was prompted by the capture, trial, and guilty verdict of the man who had murdered Sam's father in January, 1990. Sam's father, Rashad, had become the center of a small Muslim movement and mosque in Tucson—but other than the fact of being a Muslim who recognizes God as more important than baseball, Sam's profile in the article is more about the fact of his being, at that time, a rarity in Major League Baseball and the resolution regarding the murder, rather than about how he practiced his faith while an active professional athlete.

15. See above, 146-7.

16. These are not identical, incidentally. Both traditions eschew products derived from pigs, so that both kosher and hallal food will be devoid of bacon, ham, pork, etc. But kosher food also excludes seafood whereas hallal does not, and kosher meat also needs to be slaughtered and prepared for the table in a particular manner, which hallal meat does not. Hallal also excludes alcoholic beverages from one's gastronomy, whereas kashrut does not.

17. The first was Tamir Goodman, who was expecting to play for University of Maryland but opted for Towson since they were willing to work with his decision not to play on the Sabbath, whereas Maryland was not. Goodman was also discouraged from coming to Maryland when it became clear that he really was not the "Jewish Jordan," after all. Na'ama Shafir, playing for University of Toledo, was the second—and the first practicing Orthodox Jewish woman to play in Division I. Wearing a short-sleeve shirt under her sleeveless basketball jersey to conform to Orthodox modesty sensibilities, she scored 40 points in the NIT championship game in 2011.

18. Chris Ballard, "Dewayne Dedmon's Leap of Faith," *Sports Illustrated* magazine, November 14, 2011, 98-110. The headline beneath the title states that "Discouraged for religious reasons from playing basketball, a young Jehovah's Witness who would soon be 7 feet tall had to decide whether to follow his mother's ardent beliefs or his own heart"—words that resonate from the Barney Ross boxing story of 80 years earlier. (See below, 232-4).

19. Ibid, 105, right column.

20. Ibid, 108, left column.

21. Ibid, 110, left column.

22. See the interview in the June 1986 issue of *Playboy* magazine.

23. In a 2004 interview on *Beliefnet* with Executive Editor, Deborah Caldwell, the boxing legend's daughter, Hana Yasmeen Ali (said to be the closest of his children to him), asserted this, specifically referencing his connection to the writings of Hazrat Inayat Khan, leader of the Western Sufis (Regarding Khan, see Soltes: *Searching for Oneness: Mysticism in Judaism, Christianity and Islam*, 257-60).

24. See above, chapter 7, 129.

25. It turned out that, approaching the podium, Carlos had realized that he had forgotten his gloves. The Australian silver medalist, Peter Norman, suggested that the two of them share Smith's pair, which is why each raised a different fist. They also stood on the podium in black-socked feet without shoes to bring attention to black poverty, and wore beads to protest lynchings. Norman also asked how he could support his fellow medalists. They suggested he wear a badge for the Olympic Project for Human Rights. Norman didn't raise his fist, but by wearing the badge he made his stance clear.

26. Leading up to the Olympics, Smith and Carlos helped organize the Olympic Project for Human Rights, a group that reflected their black pride and social consciousness. The Games were perceived as an opportunity to agitate for better treatment of black athletes and black people around the world. Demands included hiring more black coaches and rescinding Olympic invitations to Rhodesia and South Africa, both of which practiced apartheid. Though the project initially proposed boycotting the Olympics altogether, Smith and Carlos decided to compete with the hope that they could use their anticipated success as a platform for broader change.

27. By contrast, Norman was punished severely by the Australian sports establishment. Though he qualified for the Olympic team over and over again, posting the fastest times by far in Australia, he was snubbed by the team in 1972. Rather than allow Norman to compete, the Australians did not send a sprinter at all. He was regularly excluded from events related to the sport. Even when the Olympics came to Sydney in 2000, he was not recognized. When Norman died in 2006, Carlos and Smith were pallbearers at the Australian's funeral. It took until 2012 for the Australian government to apologize for the treatment Norman received in his home country.

28. Kaepernick had a stunning game in a losing effort against the Baltimore Ravens. He threw for 302 yards, one passing touchdown, and ran for a touchdown, but the 49ers fell behind early and could not come back, losing by the very close score of 31–34.

29. Steven Wyche, "Colin Kaepernick explains why he sat during national anthem" NFL.com Archive, August 20, 2017. See also Cindy Boren, "Colin Kaepernick reportedly will now stand during the national anthem," Chicago Tribune, August 20, 2017.

30. Steve Wyche, Ibid. See also David Fucillo, "NFL issues statement on Colin Kaepernick not standing during National Anthem," August 27, 2016; and "Colin Kaepernick Takes The field in Socks that Depict Cops as Pigs," September 4, 2016.

31. "This Time, Colin Kaepernick Takes a Stand by Kneeling," September 1, 2016.

32. "US: Colin Kaepernick says he has received death threats," Al Jazeera English, September 22, 2016.

33. Will Brinson, "Colin Kaepernick explains why he wore socks with police pigs on them: He was making a statement, CBS Sports, September 1, 2016.

34. "Trump says NFL should fire players who kneel during national anthem," L.A. Times, September 22, 2017. See also "Pence leaves Colts game after protest during anthem." October 9, 2017.

35. Payne, Marissa, "Colin Kaepernick's 49ers teammates vote to give him prestigious award," The Washington Post., Devember 31, 2016.

36. Gleeson, Scott (June 29, 2017). "Chip Kelly defends Colin Kaepernick, says former 49ers QB was 'zero distraction' in 2016". USA Today. Retrieved November 15, 2019.

37. Josh Peter, "Colin Kaepernick: I'm not anti-American, will donate $1 million," USA Today. September 1, 2016. See also "Million Dollar Pledge" kaepernick7.com.November 14, 2017.

38. Greg Bishop, "The KAP EFFECT". Vault. Retrieved April 25, 2019.

39. "Kaepernick announces celebrity friends to match 10 $10G donations". NY Daily News. Archived from the original on January 17, 2018. Retrieved January 17, 2018.

40. Romero, Dennis. NFL says issues raised by Colin Kaepernick 'deserve our attention and action'. NBC News. 4 September 2018.

41. For more detail regarding this last point, see Benjamin Hoffman and Talya Minsberg, "Kaepernick's Eloquent Silence," The New York Times, Wednesday, September 5, 2018, B8 (SportsWednesday).

42. AP (no credited author), "Citing Racism, Ozil Quits Germany's National Team," The New York Times, Monday, July 23, 2018, B5 (SportsMonday).

43. His decision to continue boxing might be compared to Hank Greenberg's decision to play on *Rosh HaShanah*, or Barney Ross's decision to box on Friday nights.

44. "Let the atheists be the fighters, the murderers," Ross would later recall his father having repeated to him, "... we are the scholars."

45. This is the same Jack Ruby who, nearly three decades later, would achieve notoriety by killing Lee Harvey Oswald, alleged assassin of John F. Kennedy.

46. Phylacteries are two small leather-covered boxes with parchment scroll inside on which fundamental verses from the books of Exodus and Deuteronomy in the Torah are written, with a pair of leather straps attached to each box. A traditional Jew places one on his forehead and another on his left arm when he offers his morning prayers, except on the Sabbath and festivals. This is understood to fulfill a commandment to "bind it for a sign upon thy hand and put it as frontlets between thine eyes" — which is, in fact, part of the verses written on the phylactery parchment.

47. The story of both these moments was told in a March 1, 2012, unsigned *Sporting News* story, "Jewish school back in Texas tourney semifinals."

48. The article appeared on the first sports page of the Thursday, August 11, 2011 issue.

49. Michael Brick, "A Boulder-Climbing Paradise, Where the Sacred Meets Sport," the *New York Times*, Tuesday, April 14, 2009; B1, B15.

CHAPTER THIRTEEN
God on the Gridiron and Elsewhere:
From Locker Room to Finish Line

When the Frenchman Alexis de Tocqueville (1805-59) visited the United States in 1831, he made a number of observations regarding the young republic. One of these was that, in spite of the rigorous separation articulated in the U.S. Constitution between church and state, so that the United States could be regarded as a fully secular nation with regard to the *working* of the state—at least in theory and enshrined in law, no particular faith could hold sway, and religion could not be a criterion for public service—nonetheless, it was a very religious country. In fact, Tocqueville wrote, "the religious atmosphere of the country was the first thing that struck me on arrival in the United States."[1]

The paradox of a secular and yet profoundly religious America—one of the things that astonished Tocqueville was the endless range and variety of *types* of religious denominations— is nowhere better expressed than in the building that sits atop a high hill overlooking northwest Washington, DC known as the National Cathedral. Can a country without a state religion have a national cathedral? Apparently, it can and does. While it is true that it is not "national" in the government-sponsored sense—not

245

246 God and the Goalposts

a single tax dollar has gone into the century-long process of designing (in the late medieval Gothic style) and building it—yet it is called *the* national cathedral. And it is not to be confused, of course, with the Catholic Cathedral of St. Matthew that, in serving Catholic residents of Washington, DC, is an altogether different—sectarian—entity.

Indeed, while it is also true that, in one fundamental, functional sense, the National Cathedral is open to all denominations—so that it can be understood to be both omnidenominational and therefore nondenominational—it is, in another fundamental, functional sense, clearly denominational. Specifically, it is an Episcopal cathedral; its bishop is, always has been, and is likely always to be an Episcopal bishop. So, while other Christian and non-Christian denominations may pray there—and have done so, particularly on special occasions with a national connotation—they can hardly feel that it is *theirs* in the way that an Episcopalian might.

One might also note that, in 2009, for example—a year in which a new president (Barack Obama) was inaugurated in a ceremony that was suffused with general religious sentiment and specific allusions to the Bible—the new president's first official public role (as it was referred to by the media) was to lead a national prayer the following day within that very cathedral. There is certainly nothing wrong with that (any more than there is anything inherently wrong with religious sentiment or biblical allusions during the inauguration ceremony), but it is more than a little bit odd that the nation be led in a prayer—however interdenominational—by the chief executive of a polity that proclaims its administrative leadership to be completely secular in how it functions![2]

With this double paradox in mind, (of a National Cathedral and, in effect, a National Prayer Day), it is hardly so surprising that religion has an intimate relationship with all kinds of enterprises across the American historical and geographic landscape, and that while church and state remain separate mechanisms, non-church issues frequently infiltrate church just as church penetrates realms that are not church-related. Thus, while religious denomination has remained theoretically separate from political participation,[3] and while various studies by the Pew Forum on Religion and Public Life have shown Americans to be uncomfortable with "churches and other houses of worship speaking out in favor of one candidate over another;" yet Americans are shown in those same studies to assert overwhelmingly that they could not support a political candidate who did not express himself or herself as a person of faith—a believer in God—on the alleged grounds that without belief in God, an individual would lack a moral compass.[4]

Indeed, as in history in general, so in American history in particular, religion and politics have rarely lacked a linkage, even if the nature and intensity of that linkage has varied. The line between pulpit preaching and platform speech-making has often been thin, as has the line between the spiritual subject matter expected within sermons delivered in a house of worship and the way the content of those sermons may take the shape of directives to support or oppose a given candidate for office—presumably based on the preacher's perception of that candidate's spiritual and moral stance. Any number of books in the past decade has considered the phenomenon of religion's infiltration of American politics, from both broad and more focused perspectives.

Randall Balmer's book, *God in the White House*, considers the role of religious faith in shaping the presidency from John F. Kennedy to George W. Bush—and in particular, the role of Christian Evangelicals in the successes or failures of specific presidential candidates.[5] Another book, *The Preacher and the Presidents* by Nancy Gibbs and Michael Duffy, discusses the relationship between the evangelist Reverend Billy Graham and nearly every president since Harry S. Truman, and Graham's influence on nearly all of them.[6] A third book, *Thumpin' It* by Jacques Berlinerblau, analyzes the bible-laced rhetoric found in general presidential speech-making over history and in particular in the speeches of presidents and presidential candidates from Bill Clinton and George W. Bush to Barack

Obama and Hillary Clinton.[7] There are many more such volumes crowding the bookstore and library shelves these days.

An obsession with sports is also endemic to American history, particularly since the escapist frenzy of the post-World War I "Roaring Twenties."[8] In recent decades, moreover, we can recognize the graduation of that obsession into the increasing ability of superstar athletes to get elected to political positions of prominence. Thus, Bill Bradley would leverage his basketball fame to a seat in the Senate and almost as far as a presidential nomination; and Jack Kemp would use his football fame to become a member of Congress and to seek a vice-presidential candidacy; more recently, pro wrestler Jesse Ventura became governor of Minnesota; and Austrian-born Arnold Schwarzenegger continued his transformation from being the consummate weightlifter and body-builder to the ultimate action-movie-hero (and occasionally, villain) to being the governor of California.[9] The interesting thing is that, as often as not, the skills—the discipline and ability to think quickly and outside the box—that served them as athletes, were eminently translatable into enviable accomplishment on the political front.

Given the longer historical continuum that we have been discussing in previous chapters, it should really be no surprise, therefore, that sports and religion should have become intimately interwoven in general—and in America in particular—over these same decades in which sports and politics have been increasingly interwoven. And at the same time, as with religion and politics, the nature and intensity of the linkage between sports and religion has been varied in mode.

As we have already noted, where Jews and Muslims are concerned, a primary issue of interest as we move through the twentieth century and into the twenty-first has been how to retain and/ or assert their respectively Jewish or Muslim identities in a sports world designed to accommodate either secular or secular Christian sensibilities. Where Jews are concerned, we have also observed two particular historical flash points—the 1936 and 1972 Olympic

Games—where either the politics of overt anti-Semitism or the politics of anti-Zionism[10] have entered the sports arena with profound and, in 1972, particularly tragic consequences.

The 1972 flashpoint has also offered an intersection of Jewish and Muslim (or Christian) issues (and thus religion), in that the perpetrators were specifically Muslim (or Christian; there are Palestinian Arab Christians and at least one significant Christian Palestinian Arab anti-Israel terrorist organization) and the victims Jewish, within the intersection of sports and politics that it demonstrated.[11] Conversely, we have noted that, ideally, sports can be—whether on the international scene or the American scene—a functioning melting pot or tapestry where individuals meet and meld and interweave, based on their talents and efforts and individual tastes that leave national, religious, ethnic, and racial politics behind.

So, within the specific realm of Jewish-Muslim interface one might note the happy phenomenon of the success of a Muslim/Christian/Jewish Arab soccer team in Israel. The Arab Israeli Bnei Sakhnin team was victorious in the Israeli State Cup soccer championships in June 2004 and therefore represented Israel in the European UEFA Cup Tournament. More to the point, as noted on the Web site Jewish Toronto, "'this is what's called the New Middle East and this shows the Arabs are here and they are an integral part of Israeli society,' said Bnei Sakhnin's Arab Chairman Mazin Ghanim after his team beat HaPoel Haifa 4-1 in Ramat Gan Stadium before 30,000 cheering fans."[12]

The same article goes on to observe that "Bnei Sakhnin is seen as a model of co-existence with six Jewish players mixed among the Arab players—joined by four players from four different countries." Moreover, "for most Israelis, Sakhnin is known as the town [that] hosts annual 'Land Day' commemorations for six Arab Israeli demonstrators killed by the police during protests against land confiscations in 1976. It was also in this town of 23,000 that 13 Arabs were killed by the Israeli police during demonstrations of support to the Palestinians in the early days of the *intifada*, three-and-a-half years ago. But with last week's game these incidents have faded to the back burner."[13]

A later *New York Times* sports-section article would observe how the team "captain, Abbas Suas, Muslim and outspoken on Palestinian rights, briefly united Israelis of all backgrounds when he scored a last-minute goal for the Israeli national team that tied Ireland in a World Cup qualification match in 2006."[14] In the late night celebrations in 2004 and again in 2006, Jews and Arabs were joined together, their sports heroes common property. In an oblique manner, the success of the Bnei Sakhnin team might recall the success of the all-Jewish (and therefore, minority, non-Christian) soccer team in Austro-Hungary in the early twentieth century.[15]

Alas, the other side of the coin of sports and religion in Israel can also be seen. In 2013, members of a virulent, right-wing group that calls itself *La Familia* (intending to connote the *Casa Nostra*, but in its mentality, recalling the Nazis), protested vehemently and violently at a decision of the recent owner of the Beitar Jerusalem soccer team patronized by *La Familia*. The Russian-Jewish billionaire had signed two Muslim players from Chechnya. Beitar Jerusalem remained—and remains—the only team in the league to be "pure" in excluding non-Jewish players. *La Familia* fans burned down the Beitar clubhouse in their fury—and not long thereafter the owner relented and sent the two new players back whence they had come.

Within the United States, gestures such as Sandy Koufax's decision not to pitch on Yom Kippur when that solemn 24-hour Jewish fast-day coincided with a baseball game, even a World Series games, or Hakeem Olajuwon's decision to observe the sunrise-to-sunset Muslim Fast of Ramadan even if that month coincided with the NBA play-offs, are private decisions with varied public consequences. Olajuwon's teammates may or may not have been aware that he was not eating in the daytime during that month; the public would not likely have been aware at all, unless and until the press somehow heard and publicized the fact. Koufax's gesture could not help but call attention to itself, whether the famously private pitcher liked it or not, since the game was such an important one.

But nobody was likely to know whether or not Koufax was choosing to exert himself "Jewishly" beyond that one-time decision—to attend synagogue weekly, say, or to find only kosher food when playing away games—or if Olajuwon was doing the same with regard to praying five times daily or finding hallal food while playing on the road. Players such as these may or may not choose to make the religious issue that they are upholding a loud, public one—most have usually chosen not to. And the issues, to repeat, arise for them *because* they are part of a minority faith within the world of sports.

But what marks the relationship between sports and religion as it applies to Christian athletes (who are, by definition, members of a religious majority, certainly in the United States) are all the emphatically *public* expressions of it that inspired this narrative in the first place. Or perhaps I should put it differently: Sports, in the modern era, has been largely defined not only as offering an ideological melting pot, so that its backdrop has been largely secular. In that case *non*-secular Christians have been as much of a minority as have Muslims and Jews within its arenas. But as with Evangelical and other Christians in the political arena,[16] non-secular Christians have been increasingly vocal and/or visible with regard to their faith in the past few decades compared with their counterparts in the generations preceding.

It may be the case that there are more non-secular Christians who feel comfortable being assertive about their faith—in part, perhaps because they *are*, as Christians, a comfortable part of the majority, however secularized the Christianity of that majority may be—than there are Muslims (in the United States, where they are a minority). Or than there are Jews (virtually regardless of the location of the playing field, since they will be a minority everywhere—except in the Maccabiah Games in Israel, where events are not going to be staged on Saturdays and kosher food is easy to come by).

But there may be diverse reasons as to why a given athlete does or does not publicly assert this or that aspect of his or her religion in the context of playing sports, ultimately having more to do with the individual athlete's particular sensibilities than with anything else.

One of the more interesting and more recent instances of public expression of a somewhat oblique sort was during the 2012 women's Olympic gymnastics competition. The captain of the gold-medal-winning U.S. team, Aly Raisman, also won an individual bronze medal on the balance beam and an individual gold for her floor routine. In the latter event, the music that she performed to was an old Israeli classic, *Hava Nagila* ("Let Us Rejoice"), and she said she chose this "Jewish music," as she put it, as a tribute to the eleven Israeli athletes murdered at the 1972 Munich Olympics in this fortieth anniversary year.

The mention of Aly Raisman and her role as captain of the US Olympic women's gymnastics team in both 2012—she was captain of the gold-medal team popularly known as the "Fierce Five," and was also an individual gold-medal winner in the floor competition, as well as the bronze-medal winner on the balance beam, making her the most decorated American gymnast at those games[17]— brings this narrative directly into the issue of gender, which has, along with religion and race, played a number of important roles in the complex world of sports, particularly in the modern era.

Gender has offered itself as an issue in several different ways, particularly over the last 125 years or so—since, give-or-take, the outset of the modern Olympics. The first has pertained to competition: who is included and excluded and under what circumstances. Thus the story of women in basketball, for instance, as we have seen, (above, 212), has run on a parallel track to the narrative of men in basketball; the nature of the game's specifics, including attire, has had different sorts of histories for the two genders. The same may be said for a range of athletic events that have been included in the modern Olympic games.

The question of attire attaches itself to two parallel consider-

ations. We have noted above (144-46) that female competitors in
the Olympics from Muslim countries in the last few decades have
had a range of experiences depending upon the sport and its sartorial norms—with some instances—e.g., shooting competitions—offering no complications at all, and others, such as sprinting, with
potential deadly consequences in at least one case. We must also
recognize, however, that suppositions pertaining to modesty or to
how women should be attired under whatever the given circumstances, has its own male-mandated history in the West, as well.
Hence the aforementioned early female attire for basketball or that
for swimming, which required some time to be abandoned so that
women, offered the chance to compete, could play whatever the
particular game in a reasonable and unhampered manner. So, too,
it is a series of male overlords—who confuse their own lusts, for
power in general and for control over women in particular, with
God's notions about such matters as "women's modesty"—who
decree how women need to be attired, both on and off the playing
field in, say, Muslim Iran or Algeria.

This last issue intersects the evolving question regarding what
might be called "men's sports" and "women's sports." This question attaches itself not only to the Olympics, and the sorts of competitions that involve both genders and those that are exclusive to
the one or the other, but, in the United States at least, this question
emerges virtually as soon as children begin to attend school. Thus,
on the one hand, Olympic competition did not even involve women
athletes until 1900, in Paris—when 22 women competed, out of 997
athletes all told—and in 1904 archery was open to women for the
first time; aquatic events were open to female competitors only by
1912. By 1928 women competed in gymnastic events (and nearly 10
per cent of the competitors overall were women that year); skiing
was open to women in 1936; not until 1976 did basketball, together
with rowing and handball, include female athletes.[18]

Other related developments have included the 1991 decision
made by the IOC that any new sport that might be included in the

Olympic program would have to offer both men's and women's versions. Analogous to this issue, in pertaining to the decision-making rather than athletic-competing aspect of women in sports, the Second IOC Conference on Women in Sport, held in 2000, offered an adopted resolution that "[t]he Olympic Movement must reserve at least 20 per cent of decision-making positions for women within their structures by the end of 2005."

Among the more recent changes have been the inclusion of women's boxing in 2012—the same year in which Ms. Nawal El Moutawakal was elected as IOC Vice-President and also became the first woman to chair an IOC Evaluation Commission. In 2016, in Rio de Janeiro, 5,176 female athletes constituted 45 per cent of the 11,444 athletes who competed overall. By 2019, one-third of the IOC members were women. One might note, also, that there is the occasional situation that presents an opposite angle of approach to gender. Thus the incredibly challenging sport of synchronized swimming has almost entirely been a women's event—it entered the summer Olympic programme in 1984—although FINA added a mixed duet competition in the 2015 World Aquatics Championships and men have occasionally been permitted to compete in diverse other competitions.[19]

On the other hand, the gender question as it is found in schools resolved itself in a distinct manner as Title IX—an idea signed into law by President Richard Nixon, in 1972. The law stipulated that "[n]o person in the United States shall, on the basis of sex, be excluded from participation in, be denied the benefits of, or be subjected to discrimination under any education program or activity receiving Federal financial assistance."

Title IX was a follow-up to passage of the Civil Rights Act of 1964, which had been designed to end discrimination with regard to employment and public accommodation based on race, color, religion, gender, or national origin—but which failed to prohibit gender-based discrimination in the context of educational institutions—so Title IX was designed to fill that gap. While the original statute made no explicit mention of sports, that is the area, in high schools and universities in particular, where it has offered the most distinct impact. At a practical, ground level, the new legislation opened up an array of new possibilities for the participation of women in sports, trickling down to elementary schools and up into the realm of professional sports. This has not been without controversy, as there are those who have asserted that the increasing athletic opportunity—specifically in high schools—for girls has come at the expense of boys' athletics. They cite programs that have been discontinued or significantly diminished during the past several decades as evidence.[20]

There is yet more to the issue: subsequent to the original legislation, the Supreme Court issued several decisions in the 1980s and 1990s that made clear that sexual harassment and assault is regarded by law as a form of gender discrimination. A further articulation of Title IX protections came with President Obama's statements between 2009 and 2015 that folded in LGBT students into the same focal arena.

All of this has led, in recent years, in at least four related directions. One is the manner in which race has intersected gender in the matter of failed (and achieved) recognition rather than overt discrimination, as specifically exemplified with regard to the African American tennis great, Althea Gibson, who in 1956 won the French Open, and in 1957 as well as 1958 both Wimbledon and the US Open—and was voted female athlete of the year in 1958.[21] Gibson may certainly be viewed as the equivalent, in tennis, of Jackie Robinson in baseball. Perhaps Gibson's pathbreaking role in tennis was facilitated because of the color line that Robinson was able to cross in 1946 in a sport where a team owner (in Robinson's case, Branch Rickey) and the team manager were necessary elements of enabling that possibility—and where acceptance by a host of fellow-players would be needed for a player to feel accepted on his team (by no means the case with everyone playing with Robinson). In turn, her breakthrough helped facilitate the success of the first African-

American male tennis player, Arthur Ashe, to rise to prominence, winning the US Open in 1968—and the Australian Open in 1970 as well as Wimbledon in 1975.[22]

By the time of her retirement, in an era when both race and gender had eventuated as part of the national sports conversation in the United States, Althea Gibson was voted into the International Women's Sports Hall of Fame, in 1980. It took much longer for other, more—literally—tangible attestations to her unique role in the history of the game to appear. As noted in part of the headline of the front page of *The New York Times*, in the *SportsMonday* section of August 26, 2019, "She's getting her due at last." The headline and the article beneath it refer to the unveiling of a portrait statue of Gibson by the US Tennis Association at the National Tennis Center in Queens, New York: ground zero of US tennis, where Arthur Ashe had already been honored with a statue.

The second direction toward which the Title IX discussion points interweaves gender with religion—returning this discussion to the earlier-noted references to the specific issue of Muslim women and both the general matter of modest attire and also the specific and most obvious symbol of that concept: the head scarf (also referred to as a *hijab*). One might well criticize the rejection of the legitimacy of the head scarf in the context of competition—reflected in a sudden refusal in the midst of the play-offs to allow a Muslim woman to compete on the basketball court wearing her *hijab*—but a powerful antithesis to this prejudice-induced ruling resonates from the 2019 NBA champion Toronto Raptors.[23]

The team introduced "a new line of team-branded hijabs in an effort to be more inclusive to fans of all cultures."[24] Partnering with *Nike* to design the headgear, the unveiling on Twitter noted that this particular athletic garment was "inspired by those brave enough to change the game"—specifically, the Hijabi Ballers, a local organization that promotes Muslim women in sports.[25] Interestingly, Professor Norm O'Reilly, Director of the International Institute for Sport Business and Leadership at the University of Guelph (near

Toronto) compared this move with the recent effort (noted above, 229) by *Nike* to use Colin Kaepernick as the face of its marketing campaign.[26]

If the *ultimate* marketing campaign is to change prejudicial views regarding gender or religion or race, and if sports—the potentially magnificent melting pot, as we have noted much earlier in this narrative—can and should be a vehicle for such change, it must happen both at the upper reaches of the professional level and at the point when, as school-kids, we are beginning to hone skills as athletes and sowing seeds for life-long careers as fans. The front page of the *SportsMonday* section of *The New York Times* of July 30, 2018 focusses on a Muslim Canadian family (from the Toronto area) from which all six sisters play ball hockey in the summer league of the Toronto Women's Ball Hockey Association. The Azmi sisters use the standard equipment—helmets and hockey sticks—but also wear hijabs.

On the one hand, "'[p]eople are really embracing them,' said Judy Helo, who founded the women's league in 1983. 'This is truly the next evolution of who we've become in ball hockey.'"[27] "'A lot of people see religious Muslims who observe, so a lot of them are surprised when they see that you're actually like everyone else,' Husnah Azmi said."[28]

> Moreover, the league made a special accommodation for them early in the season, moving their games a couple of hours later during … Ramadan, [so that] the sisters could drink water and snack on home-cooked samosas to keep their energy and prevent dehydration.

> The girls asked and I didn't think twice about doing it," Beth Brotherstone, the league president, said. They love to play the game, they have a great attitude, they're awesome people and represent the community very well.[29]

On the other hand, prejudice and small mindedness can rear and has reared their ugly heads at times. Where their fellow players, including those on opposite teams, are embracing, social media occasionally has "'told us to go back to where we came from,' Nuha Azmisaid [reports, as an example.] 'But we're not immigrants. We were born here. But we're not angry. It's coming from a place where they don't know better.'"[30]

If the prejudices expressed in such tweets reflect anti-Muslim sentiment, gender-based prejudice *within* particular places and contexts within the Muslim world also remain unresolved—but perhaps tilt slowly toward resolution. As earlier noted, Iranian women have both competed and been extremely successful in Olympic events such as riflery, where participation is neither governed nor effected by attire such as the wearing of a hijab. Since shortly after the Revolution of 1979, however, when Iran became a self-shaped Islamic Republic, women have been forbidden to attend men's soccer games (and vice versa)—a particularly frustrating prohibition, since the national soccer team, popularly known as Team Melli, not only has millions of fans on both sides of the gender line, but is the highest-ranked soccer team in Asia, playing in the World Cup in Brazil in 2014 in Russia in 2018 and currently positioned as a favorite to qualify from Asia for the 2022 World Cup to be held in Qatar.

The irony is that, in those international venues, Iranian women have been welcomed into the stadia to cheer their team on, but they may not view any of the qualifying matches taking place in their own country. A campaign to change this is getting louder and louder. That campaign—that is asking FIFA to ban Iran from World Cup competition unless it removes the ban that explicitly contradicts FIFA's presumed "most basic" inclusionary principles—includes among its leaders, Maryam Shojael, sister of Iran's soccer team captain and star, Hamoud Shojael. FIFA has not shown a willingness to penalize Iran, however—at a time when "the Women's World Cup has given soccer a worldwide spotlight for players, fans, and others to speak out about several gender issues, including pay equity and investments in women's teams by national federations."[31]

The plot had thickened interestingly when Gianni Infantino, president of FIFA, attended a game in Tehran in November, 2018 with senior Iranian officials—for which game the prohibition against women viewers was lifted, so that a few hundred women (out of an audience of nearly 80,000) were in the stands, allowing Infantino to participate in the pretense of gender-equality progress. What is interesting for our narrative is the echo of the Nazi regime's pretense of allowing Jews to compete for Germany in the 1936 Berlin Olympics and the readiness with which the leadership of the IOC played along.[32]

The plot thickened tragically when, nearly 10 months later, 29-year-old Sahar Khodayari sneaked into Asadi Stadium to fulfill her life-long dream of watching a soccer match in Iran—in this case, her favorite team was playing a team from the UAE—but was arrested and sentenced to six months in prison. On September 2, she set herself on fire in front of the courthouse and died from the burns that covered 90% of her body. Her death sparked an outcry from both Iranian and international soccer players—and many players, including a former captain of the national team, began calling for a boycott of soccer games until the ban on women attending matches is lifted.[33]

A month later, a few thousand women were allowed to purchase tickets to watch the game—cordoned off by wire fencing from the rest of the 78,000-seat stadium, which was largely empty, in any case—in which Iran pummeled Cambodia,14-0, in an Asian qualifying match. The soccer team, however, led by captain Masoud Shojaei, streamed across the field after the game to salute and applaud their female fans. The question still remains unanswered as to whether women will be permitted to watch domestic games in Iran—or whether in other sports that have started to become popular in Iran in recent years, to which audience bans have been added, there will be progress with respect to bi-gender audience-participation.

If every step forward encounters half a step backward, and if whatever distance we move in completing the transformation of sports into an ideal playing field in which religion, gender, race, and politics are functionally irrelevant, there is still always more distance to cover. Indeed, the third direction toward which the Title IX discussion points—specifically the language derived from the aforementioned Supreme Court decisions in the 1980s and 1990s that refer to sexual harassment and assault—also carries us full circle back to the religion-based reference to gymnast Aly Raisman that provided the beginning point for this brief discussion of gender. Raisman is one of the American Olympic gymnasts who has spoken out regarding the sexual abuse of girls in that field of endeavor the discussion of which has reached gigantic proportions in the past several years, in the wake of an array of scandalous revelations.

Lawrence G. Nassar, former national gymnastics team doctor was accused and found guilty of molesting scores of girls and women over the course of 14 years, always under the pretense of providing medical treatment. As the scandal unfolded, other connected issues emerged. The first is that Dr. Nassar had served in a capacity as team doctor for the University of Michigan's sports program for years, which means that his predations were not limited to his encounters with Olympians—and it also means that the University was as guilty of mismanaging the cases brought before it as was Steve Penny, who was forced to resign as USA Gymnastics president in March, 2017 under pressure from the US Olympic Committee for his mismanagement of hundreds of sexual abuse cases—368 of them, including but not limited to those involving Dr. Nassar, but involving an array of "gym owners, coaches, and staff working for gymnastics programs across the country."[34]

Penny's successor, Kerry Perry, was forced to resign only nine weeks into her tenure, accused of a spectacular degree of insensitivity to the matter at hand. "Perry demonstrated nothing but a willful and heartless blindness to the concerns of survivors who were abused by Larry Nassar" from her "stunning and utterly shameful appearance before Congress in July [2018]" to her extremely limited appearance at Nassar's days-long sentencing hearings in March, 2018,[35] to her failure to reach out to high-profile abuse victims, such as Aly Raisman or Simone Biles, for discussions that might lead to change.[36] What makes this last issue so important—and disturbing—is that it underscores that sports-related gender abuses are not exclusively the province of males abusing females, even as it also underscores that there are very different kinds of abuse: Nassar's behavior is of an entirely different order from that of Perry.

In fact, the other major scandal involving sexual abuse in the sports world emerged slightly earlier from Penn State University, in November, 2011, and involved preying on boys, not girls: the scandal concerned allegations and subsequent convictions of abuse committed by Jerry Sandusky, an assistant coach for the Nittany Lions football team. His predatory actions had taken place over a period of at least 15 years, between 1994 and 2009. Sandusky was indicted on 52 counts of child molestation and ultimately convicted on 45 counts of child sexual abuse, in 2012, and was sentenced to a minimum of 30 years and a maximum of 60 years in prison.

In addition, three Penn State officials were charged with perjury, obstruction of justice, failure to report suspected child abuse, and related charges.[37] The Penn State Board of Trustees ended up commissioning an independent investigation from former FBI Director, Louis Freeh, that concluded that not only these three, but renowned head football coach, Joe Paterno, had known about Sandusky's behavior as early as 1998, and had turned a blind eye to it, thereby facilitating Sandusky's ongoing abuse of young players. Spanier resigned shortly thereafter, and the contracts of Curley and Paterno were both terminated; the NCAA imposed sanctions on Penn State.[38] It might be noted that he Paterno family then retained former Attorney General Richard Thornburgh (1988-91, under President George Bush, Sr.) to conduct a review of the Freeh report. The Thornburgh study concluded that the Freeh report had been rushed and had arrived at erroneous conclusions. That allegation was corroborated in a lawsuit against the NCAA by State Senator Jake Corman and State Treasurer Rob McCord that led to a judgment on January 16, 2015 that restored the 111 wins stripped from Paterno's record. The overall investigation was not concluded until March 25, 2017, when Spanier, Schults, and Curley were found guilty of misdemeanor charges of child endangerment. By that time, in any case, Joe Paterno had died.

What the University of Michigan/Olympics gymnastics and Penn State football team scandals have most obviously in common is that the victims were young, aspiring athletes, placed in the hands of adults who were both, to some extent, parental figures but also in a unique position to influence the aspiring athletes' abilities to participate in and thus potentially to succeed in their respective sports. So the victims were doubly positioned to be victimized. The scandals recall—albeit on a different level and from a different series of angles—the account of Kisik Lee and his archery proteges who were being victimized by his religious proselytization (see below, 275-76).

We might turn the screw inspired by the discussion of Title IX in a fourth direction—in reference to transgender athletes who saw their protections expanded by the legislation as this issue was articulated by the Obama Administration—the issue of gender *definition*. From the very public transformation of star athlete Bruce Jenner, winner of the Olympic Decathlon in 1976, as Caitlyn Jenner—in other words, he transitioned completely from male to female (albeit well after his athletic competition days were over)—to the issue that has been raised regarding several athletes, perhaps most famously, Caster Semenya, as to whether their testosterone levels should prohibit them from competing as women; the issue of gender definition has entered into the sports world with considerable impact in the last several years. Whereas as recently as two generations ago, gender seemed a simple matter—at least in the everyday public eye—it has become recognized as a far more complex and nuanced issue and one that has interwoven religion, ethnicity, and also race, and certainly politics, on an increasingly significant scale.

Bruce Jenner—thrice married, (last, for twenty-three years, to Kris Kardashian), with six children—began his public transition in 2015, culminating with re-assignment surgery in 2017. While an athlete like Jenner underwent a complete physical transformation after his competitive career had ended, Chris Mosier—a physiological female at birth—in 2015 became the first transgender athlete to compete, joining the US men's team. Mosier began his athletic career before transitioning—competing in a triathlon as a female in 2009. The following year he publicly identified as a transgender male and in 2015 earned a spot on the Team USA duathlon men's team for the 2016 World Championship—making him the first known athlete to join a US national team with a gender that was different from his gender at birth.

Mosier was uncertain, however, about his eligibility to compete in the Duathlon Age Group World Championship Race in Spain in June, 2016, due to the IOC policy regarding participation of transgender athletes. He challenged the policy, which resulted in the shaping and adoption of new IOC guidelines for the participation of transgender athletes. As a result, Mosier was indeed allowed to compete in the duathlon race in Aviles, Spain, making him the first trans athlete to actually compete in the World Championships.

In the same year in which Mosier was last competing as a female in a triathlon, world champion 800m runner, Caster Semenya, was the subject of a large media and public backlash after rumors emerged that she had failed a gender test—the Barr body test (that analyzes male [y] and female [x] chromosome levels). One of her competitors in that race, Elisa Cusma, complained that "these kinds of people should not run with us. For me, she's not a woman. She's a man."

The IOC began to develop new guidelines keyed to the level of testosterone in their bodies: this is not about getting injections under the table and trying to cover it up; these potential rules would affect women who are simply born that way. And some experts—such as Rebecca Jordan-Young and Katrina Karkazis—have argued that

"Testosterone is one of the most slippery markers that sports authorities have come up with yet. Yes, average testosterone levels are markedly different for men and women. But levels vary widely depending on time of day, time of life, social status and—crucially—one's history of athletic training... There is just too much variation in how bodies make and respond to testosterone—and testosterone is but one element of an athlete's physiology." In any case, it might be asked whether an athlete like Semenya should be disqualified because she happens to be a female gifted with an unusually high level of testosterone—any more than Wilt Chamberlin should have been disqualified from playing in the NBA because he was gifted with several more inches of height than those against whom he competed. This is certainly a different question from that of applying strictures—or not—to transgendered athletes.

Perhaps no case of a transgender athlete was more renowned in the emergence of this discussion than that of ophthalmologist and professional tennis player, the former Dr Richard Raskind, who transitioned in 1975 as Renee Richards and continued to play as a female, creating a huge stir when she sought to play in the 1976 US Open—at virtually the same time when Bruce Jenner was winning the Olympic Decathlon. While part of the controversy regarding her participation in tennis tournaments as a female may be ascribed to her being well ahead of the chronological curve—by the time Jenner and still later, Mosier, underwent their respective transitions, the public had become more acclimated to the idea—it may also be fair to suggest that there is a greater degree of prejudice against the competition of an athlete who has transitioned from male to female than from female to male.[39] The presumption seems to be that one is gaining an advantage in going in one direction but accepting a disadvantage in going in the other direction.

This issue interweaves, somewhat ironically, the entire matter originally encompassed by the Title IX legislation. For there is indeed irony to the notion that, after years of struggle—paralleling the Civil Rights movement and resonating from the Feminist Movement—to offer women the chance to compete as they choose on the athletic field—with men, or with women but in sports events formally reserved only for men—women now might find themselves disadvantaged by including among them former men who bring to the field all of the developmentally male attributes (and not only testosterone). If on the one hand, it is clear that the issue is not and should not be oversimplified by reference to testosterone levels, on the other, it is arguable that by puberty a male has gained all of the physiological features that make him male and not female, so that a subsequent gender change—whether at 20 or 30 or whatever the age—will not strip a male of developments in musculature, speed and other features that define an athlete's skill.

Recently this issue has offered a focal point through a law suit pressed by three high school runners in Connecticut. Sixteen-year-old Alanna Smith and two of her fellow runners, Selina Soule and Chelsea Mitchell, aided by lawyers from the *Alliance Defending Freedom*, are seeking to prevent transgender athletes from competing in their sport. The suit asserts that the Connecticut Interscholastic Athletic Conference's policy allowing transgender athletes (former males) to compete (as females) is a violation of the Title IX act, which bars discrimination on the basis of gender.

Smith has commented that competing against transgender athletes makes her feel like she can only compete to get a personal record, rather than a medal. "It makes me realize that before I even run, I already lost and I won't be able to get a fair sport," she commented in an interview on February 20, 2020, on the YouTube channel of *The Daily Caller*. The implications are not only with regard to athletic events, but to the ability of a talented athlete to win athletic scholarships: if there are limited funds in a given school for such scholarships, is a born-female athlete disadvantaged relative to a transgender athlete with regard to even being able to attend that school and thus to compete in a race if that ability is contingent on scholarship funds? At the same time, the American Civil Liberties Union is joining the suit on the other side, to defend the interests of transgender student athletes. "Efforts to undermine Title IX by claiming it doesn't apply to a subset of girls will ultimately hurt all students and compromise the work of ending the long legacy of sex discrimination in sports," ACLU spokesperson, Chase Strangio, commented. As of this writing the case has not yet gone to trial.

Meanwhile, any number of transgender athletes are hoping for a chance to compete in the 2020 summer Olympics in Tokyo.[40] American volleyball player Tia Thompson is hoping to represent her country in the 2020 Summer Olympic Games. Approved to compete in USA Volleyball events, the Hawaiian woman is headed to a USA Volleyball national tournament in May to showcase her talents. Fellow volleyball player Tiffany Abreu, who plays professional women's volleyball in Brazil, is also hoping to make her country's national volleyball team. So is weightlifter Laurel Hubbard of New Zealand—she already has a silver medal in the World Championships, and will compete in the Commonwealth Games in April, despite the protests of rival Australia. One might ask in this last context where exactly political motivation underlies the protests? The IOC guidelines revolve around testosterone levels—for at least 12 months prior to the time of competition. The array of ways in which sports has come to intersect gender along with the varied intersections with religion, politics, race—and war and art— has continued to expand into the new millennium as it moves into its third decade.

Let's circle back to religion, however. The arrival of Tim Tebow, the son of missionaries, into football prominence, first as a very successful, double-threat (pass and run) college football quarterback and then as a controversial, occasionally successful NFL quarterback, brought emphatic and overt expressions of strong Christian faith into the sports arena from a new angle. Greg Bishop's *New York Times* article on the front sports page in November, 2011, when Tebow was playing for the Denver Broncos, features a close-up photograph of him with a reference to Ephesians 2:8-10 inscribed in the bootblack beneath his eyes—a practice since banned by the

NCAA—and a second photo of Tebow fans in the stands, wearing robes emblazoned with large crosses.[41]

Bishop writes that "at the intersection of faith and football, the fervor that surrounds both Tebow's beliefs and his struggles in his second season for the Denver Broncos has escalated into a full-blown national debate over religion and its place in sports." What is perhaps most interesting is that there was little controversy while he was winning two national championships at the University of Florida; things shifted to a "nastier, more personal, more intense" level as he struggled to adapt to the NFL. "In the past three weeks, he has become the most discussed and most polarizing figure in sports...Opponents mocked his celebration pose—kneeling in prayer, which became an Internet meme known as Tebowing—and his coach offered a lukewarm vote of confidence."

Bishop quotes an ESPN football analyst, who asserts that "[y]ou can't say it's just religion. At the same time, you hear a lot of things that sound like an attack on his beliefs." In the article, Bishop also includes a quote by Howell Scott, an evangelical blogger and pastor at a Baptist church in New Mexico, who claims that "[t]here's always a religious component there, and with Tebow, it's often an anti-Christian bias. People want him to fall flat on his face." Bishop himself notes that "Tebow elicits scorn in a way that, say [retired Muslim basketball super-star] Kareem Abdul-Jabbar, or [retired star Christian quarterback Kurt] Warner, or other religious athletes, did not." Is this because the times have changed, because Tebow has, as a professional, been so far less successful than these two players, or because of the extensive public display of his faith? It's clear that his detractors see his actions as a distasteful and inappropriate combination of religion and sports—while his supporters don't find them wrong, and, in fact, many feel that they're singularly appropriate and commendable.

In any case, who can say whether such demonstrations of religion in sports are due to growing public acceptance in the past few decades, or because of the ever-expanding media attention—and visual preservation and publication of any given moment in sports. A key baseball hit or football touchdown will be precisely the sort of moment that will be captured, instantaneously transmitted around the globe (often "going viral" online), and followed shortly after by a televised interview with the athlete. It's clear that religious assertion in a range of modes in sports, most obviously within the American sports scene, has become more *obvious* in the past few decades than in the century preceding.

An example occurred when Ryan Howard delivered that key hit—a three-run-scoring double—in a remarkable rally that brought the Philadelphia Phillies from eight runs down to a victory in the ninth inning over the New York Mets late in the 2008 baseball season. As he arrived at second base, he raised his eyes toward the heavens and gestured upward with both arms, his index fingers also pointing to the skies, as if acknowledging God for providing the extra assistance that led to his momentous blast. In the absence of an ability to hear whatever specifics it was that Howard said—out loud or in his mind—we might refer to his gesture as generically religious.

A more distinctly Christian gesture which one can see in any number of professional football games is that of a player who has carried or caught the ball in the end zone and then kneels and crosses himself—genuflects—with his head bowed, or does that and then lifts his eyes and his arms toward the skies. One player who consistently crossed himself before or after a play was Pittsburgh Steeler defensive star Troy Polamalu—the Steelers' MVP—during the 2009 Super Bowl game against the Arizona Cardinals.[42] The NY Yankees young player, Starlin Castro, crossed himself and gestures heavenward after key hits. This sort of a gesture can be seen in any number of contexts as one follows sports like football and baseball, in particular, where a single play—a hit, a catch, an interception, a tackle—of significance can occur any number of times during a given game.

Even more overt because we hear the words rather than merely observe a symbolic hand movement, is the comment in a TV interview of a key player on the winning side of an important game in any given sport. Any number of times one can hear the interviewee begin his response to the reporter's queries by saying, "First of all, I'd like to thank Jesus," or "I owe my success in this game to Jesus" — or some similar assertion that places God, in a specifically Christian format, at the center of the playing field.

One can follow the narrative of faith into other media and other specific contextual angles than television and the moments of victory and their aftermath. Thus, in one of the many lead-up newspaper articles to the 2008 Olympics, in the sports section of the August 4, 2008 issue of *USA Today*, there appeared a human-interest-weighted story focused on the boxer Gary Russell, Jr. Russell has been trained throughout his career by his father. At the end of the article, the reader is informed that "the 27th Psalm is tattooed over his [Russell, Jr.'s] heart. He brought his Bible to Beijing. 'You got to have a certain relationship with God,' he said. 'A little quiet space with my Bible, and I'm good.' "

Thus, both Russell's success and his hope for continued success — specifically, at the time of the article, Olympic success — is tied not only to his skill ("his hand speed, his balance, having a very good eye at seeing punches coming and not get hit..."), to his own dedication and work ethic, and to the self-sacrificing support of his family (and not only his father), all of which the article delineates, but to his strong sense of an ongoing relationship with God, mediated by prayer and the Bible. This is to say that he is among the latest in a long line of athletes going back to David and Samson *in* the Bible, who have hoped and believed in the certainty of victory, regardless of the power of the opponent, when the spirit of the Lord is drawn onto either the battlefield or the playing field.

Along similar lines, Edgar Sosa, who at the time was playing as a point guard on the highly regarded Louisville University basketball team, "prays every morning before he steps outside. He prays in the locker room before every game. He prays in silence, only for himself. Edgar Sosa always asks for the same thing: To win and to be protected. It reassures him, he said, because in faith he finds routine." And when he hit the winning shot in a tough 74-71 win over the University of Kentucky midway through the 2008-2009 season, he commented, "I ask God when we need to come out on top. God definitely answered that one for me."[43]

Similarly, in a short article in the *New York Times* sports section of October 13, 2008, with the headline, "Hoping to Return, Giant Keeps Faith," reporter Joe Lapointe begins with the observation that "[s]hortly after David Tyree of the Giants made his unforgettably acrobatic catch in the Super Bowl's final minutes last winter, he shopped for his own replica jersey because one of his *spiritual* advisers wanted one [emphasis added]."[43] The article depicts Tyree's knee-surgery-induced, non-playing condition at the time and refers to the "self-destructive behavior of a few years ago [that] led to a religious awakening that saved his career and, possibly, his life."

The article notes how Tyree's book, *More Than Just a Catch*, chronicles this spiritual transformation, before observing that, in the athlete's new God-centered life, "[h]e gathers with him about a dozen teammates on Wednesdays for Bible study after practice." Lapointe continues:

> One of tho[se players] is defensive end Renaldo Wynn, a 12-year veteran who joined the Giants this season. During the summer, they got acquainted while Wynn was a free agent. Wynn said Tyree kept telling him: "Hey man, I'm going to keep praying. God has a team for you."
>
> "What do you know?" Wynn said. "It turned out to be the New York Giants." Among the Bible-study group is George McGovern, a non-denominational Protestant minister who works as a chaplain for the Giants.
>
> Wynn and McGovern said Tyree was using his high

profile as a platform not to get rich, but to profess his faith.

Yet further, the article notes that "referring to Tyree's religious direction, [Giants General Manager Jerry] Reese said the catch in the Super Bowl might have been 'the favor of God' choosing a particular person for a particular purpose."

> "I'm a spiritual person, too," Reese said. "I'm a Christian. When you learn to obey God, things are much easier and better for you."
> Tyree said the turning point for him was to accept "a certain level of surrender" to forces stronger than football or its players.

There are several issues that are engaged by the contents of this article, aside from the report of strong religious—specifically, Christian, presumably Protestant—faith on the part of Tyree as well as Reese. One is the notion that God is active on the playing field, rooting for and even playing for those who have surrendered to Him. Another is the notion of shaping a spiritually directed group within the larger group that constitutes the team, which implicitly raises a question—or *should*: is this subgroup an "inner group" in ways other than the decision of its constituent members to study the Bible together once a week after practice? If there were (or are) non-Christian players on the team—Jews or Muslims, most obviously, but there could be others, at least in theory—would they be welcome to join the study group, and if not, how would that effect the overall chemistry of the team and its ability to perform?

Moreover, how does one understand the concept of a team chaplain in a professional sport that (in theory, at least) is an altogether secular enterprise? How does such a chaplain function: he is a "nondenominational Protestant"—meaning, in theory, that he can comfortably serve Protestants of all denominations. But what do Catholic or Orthodox—or Muslim or Jewish or Hindu (or secular)—

players do who require or desire spiritual counseling? To whom do
they turn? If, presumably, they would look to their own pastors, rabbis, imams, priests, why wouldn't or couldn't all of the Protestant
players do the same? Why is there a chaplain at all—who seems,
by the particulars of his faith designation, to be inherently useful to
some but only *some* of the players?

This, of course, leads our discussion in yet another direction.
Far more fascinating within the overall issue of *asserting* one's faith
on the playing field is the *imposition* of that faith on others who do
not share it. Though Hank Greenberg was subjected to all kinds
of anti-Semitic taunts from both fans and fellow-players, hopefully Sandy Koufax endured less in an era of arguably greater religious tolerance and awareness in America; and, again hopefully,
neither Kareem Abdul-Jabbar nor Hakeem Olajuwon experienced
an undue amount of ugly jabber at them because of their Muslim
faith. Whatever the circumstances, it's not likely—but it is certainly
possible—that these Jewish and Muslim players were ever asked
to kneel with their teammates to participate in a team prayer of
pre-game hope or post-game thanksgiving delivered in a distinctly
Christian manner, directed toward God.

But in the last decade or two there have been increasingly frequent references in the media to *enforced* team prayer sessions—
specifically Christian prayer, by which I mean that the name of
Jesus is specifically invoked—in both the collegiate and the professional as well as the high-school ranks. Moreover, rather than
merely offering an occasional public blog discussion, this sort of issue—of the role of religion and specific religious leadership within
and outside the locker room at various levels of play—has come to
the fore in a number of court cases and decisions over the past three
decades. Thus, a 1989 11th-circuit Texas court decision (in *Jager v.
Douglas County School District*) ruled that pre-game invocations by
coaches, officials, or students at high-school football games are unconstitutional. On the other hand, a 1995 decision that carried from
the small town of Santa Fe, Texas, to the fifth-circuit Texas Court of

Appeals ruled that *informal, student-initiated, student-led* prayers at sports events are constitutional.

The issue has continued to be approached through the courts as time has moved forward. In March 1999, another Texas case—again focused on the town of Santa Fe and again decided in the fifth-circuit Court of Appeals and, in effect, challenging the 1995 ruling by that court—was based on a lawsuit filed by Mormon and Roman Catholic players' families, who clearly did not find the prayers being offered at sporting events nonsectarian. The judgment affirmed (in a 2:1 decision by the three-judge panel) that the policy embraced by the 1995 decisions was indeed unconstitutional. The decision opined that football games could hardly be construed as "appropriately solemnized by prayer," which had been the assertion of school officials favoring "informal, student-led" prayer at sports events.

A legal and political trail has followed these discussions and decisions, from temporary restraining orders (September 1999) to prevent student-organized, student-led "messages"—that might include a "courteous, reverent... reference to a deity" as part of the message—to resolutions in Congress (by 13 Texas congressmen, on October 20, 1999) to allow schools to include a formal, student-organized, student-led prayer before games, to a discussion before the U.S. Supreme Court in March, 2000 that led to a 6-3 decision asserting that public school administrations may not allow students to conduct formal prayer sessions over the school's public address system before sports events, on the grounds that "school sponsorship of a religious message is impermissible because it sends a message to members of the audience who are non-adherents that they are not full members of the political community, and an accompanying message to adherents that they are insiders, favored members of the political community."[45]

Thus, the court found that including a prayer in the game schedules constituted a state-sponsored act involving religion in a manner that is unconstitutional; that formal prayer unconstitutionally coerced attendees into participating; that the state may not endorse an overtly religious message; but prayer that is truly initiated by an individual student constitutes an act of free speech, so a player can spontaneously call for a group- prayer huddle. It might be added that the names of the Mormon and Catholic families were kept out of the public eye out of fear of reprisals against them, and that the district court felt compelled to threaten the school district with "the harshest possible" penalties were they not to cease seeking the identities of those families.

In October 2007, the *Washington Post* profiled the case of Marcus Borden, a high-school football coach in East Brunswick, New Jersey, who "after leading his team in prayers for 23 years... is involved in a legal battle that is pushing the courts to decide the boundaries of acceptable religious activity for coaches and other educators in public schools"—a case that began in 1997 and was not resolved a decade later.[45] What distinguishes this story from the others that I have noted, is the content of some of the comments accumulated in the article. Thus, Brenda Fisher, mother of the East Brunswick team quarterback, asserts that "you have to understand what the team prayer is. When you call it prayer, *it doesn't have to necessarily have a religious connotation*. You are wanting and hoping for safety" [emphasis added].[46]

Jeremy Bloom, who was already a graduate by the time the article appeared, comments to the reporter, "I'm Jewish. But I was never offended or anything." And Warren Wolf, coach of another (Brick Township) high-school team, asserts that "of course I pray with my team," and goes on to note that "football is a violent game... When you pray, you pray that nobody gets hurt on either team. You pray that God looks after all the boys playing the game..." One wonders how frequently such prayers are for everyone's safety or are used to invoke God's help for the victory of one team—and at the same time, one asks how often the prayers are so nondenominational as to lack a religious connotation altogether, in which case why would they be called "prayers"?

In any case, the question of whether or not Coach Borden might bow his head and join his football team when they decide on their own to drop to one knee and pray as a team, reached its conclusion (so far, as of this writing), on March 2, 2009. On that day, the Supreme Court refused to hear the coach's appeal of a school district ban on employees joining student-led prayers that has been in place since 2005—as reported in a small article in *The New York Times* sports section of March 3, 2009.

The question of how and where the line might be drawn between sharing one's faith—or merely sharing a moment of prayer across faiths—and imposing one's faith on others has certainly entered the sports arena on diverse fronts as one reviews these stories and issues. Coach Borden sees his own case as one of sharing, not imposing, and so does David Tyree, although others might see either of their situations otherwise. But a more unequivocal instance of imposing one's faith on others—particularly under uneven circumstances in which that imposition has a greater chance of succeeding—is well-articulated in a second article that focused on the summer Olympic Games in the August 19, 2008 *New York Times*. What I mean by "uneven circumstances" is that it's a coach, and not a player, who's in a position of influencing or seeking to influence his players (which is *not* what Coach Borden seems to be about) in a particular spiritual—as opposed to merely athletic—direction.

This is precisely the condition highlighted in the article. The front-page (as opposed to sports pages) coverage—on the same page with articles about the Obama-McCain presidential campaign, the escalation of Taliban aggressiveness against U.S. troops in Afghanistan, and ethnic killings during the Russian-Georgian war—was part of the extended focus on the Beijing Olympics. The headline, "For Coach, God and Archery Are a Package Deal," profiled the head coach of the United States, Kisik Lee, a deeply believing Christian who is also a pioneer—perhaps the inventor—of scientifically based archery training.[47]

The accompanying front-page photograph shows Lee participating in the full-body baptism, in "a pool not far from the Olympic Training Center in Chula Vista, California" of one of his athletes, 19-year-old Brady Ellison. Lee "...has become a spiritual guide for Ellison, 19, and the larger group of athletes who train and live full-time at the Olympic Training Center. He has also served as a sponsor in the baptism of three other resident archers." The article continues:

> During the Olympics at least three of the five United States archers who qualified to compete in Beijing met every morning to sing hymns and read from the Bible, and to attend church together in the chapel at the Olympic village. Lee believes having a strong faith makes for better archers because it helps quiet their minds. To that end, he tailored Ellison's Olympic schedule to include spiritual and athletic objectives.
>
> "I give him six tasks a day, including reading the Bible and education," Lee said. "And he's doing it."

If we think our way back through the long and diverse history that we have considered in the course of this book, then we might suggest that Lee is not the first to make that sort of assumption. We have encountered the idea, going back for millennia, that one's success on the playing field—or the battlefield for which the playing field, particularly in a sport such as archery, has so often been a surrogate—is connected to and might even be dependent upon one's belief in and connection to a divinity. The sense of calm necessary to succeed might indeed be understood as deriving from one's faith.

But, as with the question of a moral compass in politics: is it not possible to derive that calm from sources other than religion? And even, let us suppose, for the sake of argument, that it is not possible: who is to say and how can one say *which* religion? Is it necessarily

Christian faith that provides that which "helps quiet their minds?" For the education to which Lee refers is a specifically Christian one, and he instructs his protégé to read the Bible (the Old and the New Testaments) through the lens of Protestant interpretation.

Lee points out that his zeal for Christianity came after "a personal encounter with Jesus in 1999 that transformed his life." The consequence of this is that he feels compelled "to encourage others to know God… 'I'm the witness of Jesus, not just an instructor. So I have to encourage them how, how we can change in Christ.'" Lee explains that "I don't want to have any favorites. I would love to be fair to everyone. But sooner or later, if they can see through me God, that's what I want to try to do. I'm not God, and I can't drive them to God, but I can pray for them."

Most astonishingly, from the perspective of sports as a secular activity on behalf of a nation that has spent two centuries continuously seeking to develop a distinctive separation between Church and participation in the varied functions of the State, the article notes that "Lee said coaching was more of a challenge for him when members of the team did not share his beliefs." This would seem to suggest a direct conflict of interests—in the moral as much as in the legal sense. How, one might ask, can an individual with such clearly stated prejudices—in this case, religious prejudices—coach a team derived from the American tapestry? One might also ask whether such prejudices would be tolerated for an instant if Lee were Jewish or Muslim or Hindu and expressed such sentiments, or if he were speaking of racial or ethnic differences instead of religious ones?

While Lee's defenders may assert that he is tolerant of other beliefs than his own or does not pressure his protégés to follow his path, his viewpoint is distinctly proselytic and prejudicial. His own words make this clear, when the reporter comments that Lee notes that "to be an effective archer…athletes must learn to clear their heads and focus. 'If you are Christian… then people can have that kind of empty mind.'" The obvious question that such a statement provokes is whether it is or is not possible to clear one's head and focus; to have "that kind of empty mind" through any medium, religious or otherwise, other than Christianity.

If it is possible that there are people—perhaps billions of them—who believe that their form of faith is the only legitimate one, the only one that can induce the sort of calm and focus that will truly get God's attention, is it reasonable to put an individual from those ranks in charge of a group of young people who represent the United States in international athletic competition?

Not surprisingly, Lee's convictions have raised both worries and objections, as noted in the same Katie Thomas article: "...Lee's advocacy has raised concerns in the United States Olympic Committee, and some in the elite archery community feel uncomfortable with his proselytizing."

It would seem that he has not merely taken young athletes so inclined under his wing, but has sought to turn all of them in the spiritual direction that he has found satisfying for his own spiritual needs. According to the *Times* article, Lee was warned by USOC officials a year ago "not to pressure athletes to participate in religious activities." So, it would also seem that his efforts, aside from the prejudices he expresses, are hardly benign from the perspective of those not inclined to follow his directional lead.

Some of the archers were already religious Christians who were apparently not disturbed at all by Lee's religious discourse, and there were others who were drawn in by the missionary aspect of his instruction, or at least did not express discomfort. There were certainly others, however—specifically a mother whose 16-year-old daughter was training at Chula Vista—who were made quite uncomfortable. Raquel Caldwell's family is Buddhist, and her mother, Susan, asked rhetorically whether "'the Olympic Training Center ...is the appropriate place to be pressing people to decide on their faith.' She was alarmed by the extent to which Lee pushed his faith on the athletes...[and] when she complained to Skinner, the assistant, [he] told her Lee had a right to practice his religion."[48]

Susan "did not take the issue to Lee or his bosses because she feared it might jeopardize her daughter's future in the sport."[49] In that case, not only have his efforts moved beyond benign or even aggressive attempts to impose his mode of spirituality on his athletic charges, but they have created an atmosphere which one might suppose offers exactly the opposite of what, in justification of those efforts, Lee claims that they will. Can it be comfortable and calm to be a young athlete trying to perform under intense conditions when you feel that the head coach is judging you not only by your physical performance but by your spiritual beliefs?

So, the fact that, according to John Ruger, the athlete ombudsman for the USOC, "no athlete had formally complained" can hardly be considered a satisfactory response: how many young athletes would volunteer to speak up against the head coach of the Olympic team—the once-in-a-lifetime *Olympic* team!—particularly if they have any serious hope of competing for that team? While the USOC is typically extremely vigilant with regard to the matter of respecting and protecting the sanctity of racial and general diversity, one wonders how clear the committee is regarding religious diversity.[50]

One might note that this issue has parallels in other realms— most noteworthy, in the U.S. military. In the past several years, there has been a number of controversial moments pertaining to the Protestant Evangelical proselytization of privates and junior officers by more senior officers not only in army camps but at the Air Force Academy in Colorado. Thus, in our ongoing theme of the connection between sports and warfare and the relationship between both of these enterprises and religion it should not surprise us, perhaps, that if in the current era the question of what is and what is not appropriate with regard to religious persuasion and Olympic athletic training has arisen, the same question should have arisen in a military context.

In fact, the beginning of the controversy was a flare-up regarding religious discrimination at the Air Force Academy back in 2005 that stemmed from the posting on the locker room wall of a banner for "Team Jesus" by the football coach. That moment, after which military officials asserted that they were working "to enforce tougher restrictions on proselytizing and religious bias," has apparently extended itself, four years later, into more recent events. A March 1, 2009 *New York Times* article referred to "continued friction over the issue" and to a "memorandum distributed last month at the Air Force Academy in response to several recent complaints about religious bias... The memorandum said cadets should not be made to feel that they would get better jobs by going to optional Bible study sessions."[51]

In spite of the memorandum, some military personnel "said they believed the problem had continued largely unabated.... 'The Army enforces policies against racism and sexism, but doesn't bat an eye at these kinds of religious discrimination,' said Specialist Dustin Chalker, an Army medic... who was raised in a Christian home but is now an atheist."[30] Chalker is part of the plaintiff side of a lawsuit against the Pentagon that accuses it of "ignoring laws and policies banning mandatory religious practices." So is David Horn, a former fighter pilot in the Air Force Reserve, who was so bothered, as Chalker had been, by "returning from tours of Iraq and Afghanistan and, like specialist Chalker, hearing prayers 'in Jesus's name' at homecoming ceremonies ...that he wrote a letter to his local newspaper.." which led to "a negative evaluation—after years of positive appraisals—and [to his losing] his flying certification and his post. With his flying career in jeopardy, he plans to join the lawsuit against the Pentagon."[52]

However, religious advocates are concerned that "overreaction" will lead to the elimination of the spiritual component altogether from the military, which would remove one of the bases for emotional support under the trying conditions presented by such tours as those in Iraq and Afghanistan. The issue has been debated from the halls of the Pentagon to those of academia.[53] The discussion has encompassed the matter of carrying stacks of Bibles translated into Pashto and Dari (languages in use in Afghanistan) by evangelizing American soldiers. U.S. military policy expressly forbids its members on active duty from trying to convert people to another religion. Like other issues raised throughout our narrative, this one has its own twists, turns, and sub-issues.

There is considerable irony in all of this. The founding fathers wrestled with the question of what should be the proper relationship between religion and the armed forces practically from the time of the Revolution against an England from which any number of American groups had fled due to religious persecution.[54] George Washington and those around him wondered whether or not there should be chaplains in the military. In the end, there were, but eventually, as the United States became increasingly pluralistic by the last third of the nineteenth century, the question arose as to whether there could and should be other than Protestant chaplains. That question has increased in nuance with the expanding diversity of religious groups that are represented in the American armed forces. What is the proper line between spiritually serving those who serve and oppressing them by seeking to impose a particular mode of spiritual service upon them?

These stories bring up rather interesting questions with respect to the overarching importance of religion in the world. In thinking back to the Pew Center study to which I referred previously regarding Americans' concerns about politicians who do not profess some form of faith—that they will accordingly lack a moral compass— we may recognize that a key purpose for religion is to offer such a compass. The need for the compass is, according to most traditions, twofold. One is so that we might live better lives in the here and now. The other is so that we might fare better than worse either in the world to come (as Christianity and Islam most emphatically teach with parallel intensity of conviction) or the next time we find ourselves in this reality (as Hinduism, for instance, teaches).

Ultimately, then, one might understand the focus of religion and the need for good, moral behavior—defined as behavior that is pleasing and not offensive to God—as based on a concern for survival. This brings us full circle back to our introductory discussion. Every form of religious belief has in common with every other form the conviction, the belief, the certain sense that the God (or gods) who has (or have) made us has (have) the concomitant power to destroy us—to help us or harm us, to further us or hinder us, to bless us or curse us. And thus, every religion has as its province and purpose to guide us in behaving in a manner that, in pleasing rather than displeasing God (the gods) will lead to blessing rather than to curse.

So, the concepts of good and evil and of moral and immoral or amoral behavior are rooted in what we believe to be God's (the gods') will and desire—God's goal and purpose—for us, individually and as a congregation or a community or a species. With that in mind, each particular religion translates this broad set of concerns into the particulars that define its understanding of divinity, and its sense of what texts articulate God's (the gods') word most effectively and which texts most accurately interpret that word—together with the body of customs and ceremonies, life-cycle events and annual or monthly or even weekly holidays, and weekly or even daily prayers that are prescribed by those texts. Across history and geography, as we have observed, the various disciplines that have intersected religion and its concerns have included sports.

But the question in the discussion of the past dozen paragraphs or so pertains to the moral legitimacy of *promoting* a particular form of religion (to the implicit or explicit exclusion of others) in the context of sports—specifically and/or particularly in a context when the one doing the pushing is a coach and the one being pushed is an athlete. Should such religious proselytism under such uneven conditions—coach to athlete, as opposed to coach to coach, or athlete to athlete, or for that matter, athlete to coach—be considered as a positive or a negative, a promotion of the moral good (i.e., the divinely approved) or its opposite? Should such promotion be regarded as attempts at salvation or as a form of harassment?

Consider this, particularly in the story of Coach Lee and his archery protégés in the Olympic training facility at Chula Vista. The athletes are teenaged kids, away from home, entirely under the care and the influence of their coaches, whose role by definition is to serve as mentors *in loco parentibus* for the duration of their training experience. As Richard Lapchick, director of the University of Central Florida's Institute for Diversity and Ethics in Sport, observed, "An athlete has a hard time resisting a coach. There is always a fear that you won't get picked. You won't have much support if a coach doesn't like you."[55]

Does such a role encompass concern and a will to mold the spiritual condition of the athlete, and not just his or her physical development? Can we understand—or excuse or even embrace—the actions of a Coach Lee as being derived from the sort of love and concern that we associate with parent-child relations? Can we accept such actions as focused not only on the physical success of the young athletes and on their mental stability but on their spiritual salvation? That is, can we view his behavior as legitimized by an intention that we consider positive, in his focus on souls that we might agree with him will be subject to immortality—and thus to long-term positive or negative experience in the world to come?

But what if we don't view reality in such terms? What, indeed, if we were to understand reality in the same terms as does Coach Lee, and the proselytic shoe were on other foot: that the coach in question were preaching a more secular gospel—an atheistic perspective not only in disagreement with our particular mode of God-centered spirituality, but devoid of God altogether, a perspective that considers absurd the very idea that there *is* a God? Would we then be inclined to view the aggressive bearer of such a message as harassing young athletes to abandon their faith in God and participate in ceremonies directed away from such a metaphysical superstructure?

Indeed, within the larger ambit of the relationship between sports and religion, we might wish to recall the United States' long-term post-World War II competitor for Olympic predominance, the former Soviet Union. If one end of the spectrum may be represented by the actions of someone such as Coach Lee, the opposite is represented by the athletic (and every other) program in the former USSR. The underlying ideology of the Communist state was, from the outset, to reject the reality of God and thus the validity of religious expression of any sort. By definition, then, any and all athletes competing in whatever form of sports enterprise were doing so not only without assumptions of divine patronage but with contempt for those who might think otherwise. Such a perspective is as fundamentalist in its convictions as is that of the most intense and emphatic of religious fundamentalists.

As we have discussed, the complex issue of religious thinking—and in particular the concept of God—is fraught with paradoxes. By definition, what God is (or even *if* God is), and what God would have us be so that we survive, is beyond our certain, everyday sort of *knowledge*: we understand these things through faith, not knowledge, and faith is typically formed within us in early childhood long before we develop the capacity to think about God in some rational manner. Accordingly, we must approach God with a certain humility—particularly in an age where we don't have individuals like Moses or Jesus or Muhammad walking among us, who are understood to be conduits through which God speaks to us. We are, instead, constantly caught in a matrix of interpretive possibilities with regard to the divinely revealed word.[56]

Indeed, the lead-in paragraphs of Joe Lapointe's above-noted article about New York Giants football player David Tyree focus on his humility derived from the setbacks within his life and the religious discovery that is said to have "saved his career and possibly his life."

Due to that discovery, a conversation with a football fan who diminished Tyree—without realizing that it was Tyree to whom he was speaking—produced a smile from the football star and the statement that the negative comment helped keep him humble. The article refers to his accepting "a certain level of surrender" to forces stronger than football or its players. The double question becomes:

does that surrender become and remain part of one's genuine humility in the world and/or does it lead—and *when* does it lead—to a point at which, in promoting that form of surrender, one achieves a form of egotism, rather than humility?

In Tyree's case, we may prefer to reserve judgment. His focus is, at least, on his peers. As for Coach Lee, however, every one of his comments—the context for which is imposition rather than mere promotion, and not upon peers but upon acolytes who look up to him for guidance—suggests an absence of humility. In its place is the absolute certainty regarding the belief system that he has found through whatever unspecified 1999 experience to which the *New York Times* article alludes. The coverage ends with his words, "...for me this [Christianity] is the best answer [as to how to clear the head and focus]... so that's why I'm encouraging people to be the same as me." This last phrase in particular—"same as me"—seems to me to sum up the egotism that can be as much an aspect of religion as humility. By "egotism" I mean the certainty not only that I know what God is and how best to gain access to God, but that the beliefs that I possess will serve *all* people, however diverse in other ways, more perfectly than any other beliefs that they may possess.

Humility causes us to recognize that, where God is concerned, since we humans are dealing *by definition* with something *other* than ourselves, we can access only by analogy from our own experience and understanding. When we call God "great" or "all-knowing" or "merciful" or "all-good," we do so using terms that we can only understand from our human perspective. And thus, we cannot *know* what the best path to God *is*. We can believe with all of our being, and we can know that our belief is perfect—for ourselves—but we cannot know that this belief is perfect for other. This is the great paradox among the many paradoxes offered by religion, whether its context is the prayer chapel, the sports arena, or the battlefield.

Instances in which religion has embedded itself in diverse and increasingly overt ways within varied aspects of sports continue as we follow forward in time, and the outward expression of this is reflected in an array of journalistic media, evident even in a small sample of sources. One sees it in an article regarding how Minnesota Vikings defensive back, Husain Abdullah, was fasting from sun-up to sundown during the heat of the month of Ramadan that coincided with that NFL team's training camp;[57] and in several articles regarding Saudi Arabia's decision to allow women to compete in the 2012 London Olympics.[58] One observes this in an article focused on the Florida Marlin's manager, Jack McKeon, who "Steps Into a Pew Before Stepping Onto the Field.... In each major league city, McKeon has a favorite, or at least a convenient, Roman Catholic church" that he attends, so that when "I go to the ballpark, I have no worries. God's looking after me."[59]

One finds the interconnection in the story of how Yuri Foreman, an undefeated boxer, (29-0, at that time), was balancing his physical training in the gym with the sort of mental and spiritual training that he needed to become a rabbi.[60] One encounters it in the reportage regarding Aly Raisman's choice of the Hebrew folk song, *Hava Nagila* ("Let Us Rejoice") as music for the floor routine with which she won gold at the London Olympics, declaring afterwards that this was intended, in part, as a tribute to the Israeli athletes murdered by terrorists, 40 years earlier, in the 1972 Munich Olympics.[61] One finds it in the article on the Jewish roots of former Boston Red Sox first-baseman, Kevin Youkilis, and a second article on the Jewish roots of New York Knicks basketball star, Amar'e Stoudemire.[61]

More recently, we find this in the observation that the Oklahoma Thunder NBA basketball team is the only one that, "preceding each game [offers] a stadium-wide prayer of invocation that on most nights briefly turns a raucous sports event into something resembling a mega-church gathering."[62] Interestingly, the Thunder offer another twist to an earlier issue raised in this narrative. One of their recently added players, Enes Kanter, is an observant Turkish Muslim.[63] Aside from his significance for our discussion in updating the issue of praying five times daily, maintaining hallal gastronomy on the road and playing during Ramadan, Enes reminds us of the ongoing interweave of politics with religion and thus with sports. He is a member of the *hizmet* movement—inspired by the teachings of the Turkish religious leader, Fetullah Gülen, who is an outspoken advocate of interfaith and multi-cultural dialogue and of service (in Turkish: *hizmet*) to humanity—and is involved in an inordinate amount of service to the community. But all of Gülen's followers have been singled out by Turkey's demagogic leader, Recip Tayyip Erdoğan for the kind of scapegoating and attacks that recall Hitler vis-à-vis Jews as he was beginning to assert his political power. Indeed, it is largely Enes' stature as a recognized public figure that protects his family from Erdoğan's violence.

Interestingly enough, Enes has become increasingly outspoken and at the same time has broadened the angles of his outspokenness, using his renown as an athlete to extend beyond the specifics of Turkish politics and his place in the Erdoğan-Gülen conflict. In the January 23, 2020 issue of the English-language *Jerusalem Post*, in the context of Holocaust Memorial Week, he penned an *Op Ed* piece, entitled: "We are in this fight together: Jews and Muslims"— in which he subtly connected some of these same religious and political lines: Hitler and the Jews, the current raging Islamophobia in the United States (and elsewhere), which underscores the complicated way in which religion and politics can be and have been, right up to the present day, intertwined.

His piece both recognizes historical connections between events of 80 years ago in Germany and those in the United states today, and also considers a specific way in which the connection between religion and politics can resonate from that connection.[64] He comments that "[h]atred is like starting a fire. Once it begins you don't know where it will end." And he adds that "[w]hen we take a closer look at the discourse and rhetoric used against Jews in the 1920s and '30s in Europe, we see a striking resemblance to the language used by today's autocrats. It's not surprising, because hatred has only one language…"

Kanter continues: "there is a particular duty that falls on the shoulders of American Muslims, who have faced their own share of Islamophobia and anti-Muslim hostility, to spearhead efforts to battle antisemitism and reject this scourge... I believe that America's secret sauce is its ability to co-exist... Antisemitism, Islamophobia, and other types of ethnic and religious animosities will never go away. We can tame them or we can suffocate them, but we always will have to be vigilant... No one can do this alone. We are in this fight together."

It is of interest that Kanter refers to himself, in the line identifying the author, as a Human Rights advocate first, and then as an NBA player for the Boston Celtics. It is very clear that he has come to view human rights-related issues as more important than sports, even as sports have helped propel him to a position where his human rights advocacy can offer a louder voice and a more substantial potential impact. So, in a manner apposite to yet different from Colin Kaepernak, Enes Kanter has activated the potential for sports to be a vehicle for addressing politics and the interweave between politics and the social scene.

So, too, the religion-sports connection is significant in the reference, in the midst of an article on the Golden State Warriors in the 2016 NBA semi-finals and finals, that "reserve power forward James Michael McAdoo texted a devotional prayer to the team's group chat. Rev, as the 23-year old McAdoo is known, started a Bible study for the Dubs this season attended by more than half the roster. On the road he gathers players for 10 minutes after lunch, but with only one day between Game 5 of the Western Conference finals in Oakland and Game 6 — away, against Oklahoma City — Rev had to *minister his congregants* another way [emphasis added]." Later in the article, in reference to the come from-behind victory over Oklahoma City in Game 6, McAdoo is quoted as saying, "I was praying a lot right then. It's not, 'God, let Klay [Thompson] make this shot.' That's not how the Lord wants me to come to him. It's praying for him to have the strength to remain positive and locked into the plan."[65] We might infer that Rev's belief is that the game plan is God's game plan.

No reference was made to team prayer or the idea of God's plan, although one might suppose that both were present, in the article covering the extraordinary—some might say miraculous— defeat of Golden State by the Cleveland Cavalier in the finals. The Cav's owner, Daniel Gilbert, asserted to ESPN reporter Doris Burke after the dramatic victory, "Thank God that God loves Cleveland, Ohio." Perhaps God switches sides from time to time, in this case deciding that Golden State win it all in 2015 and that it was not Cleveland's turn in 2016, after half a century of major-sports disasters during which God was apparently too often on the other side of the playing surface.

Notes

1. Alexis de Tocqueville, *Democracy in America* (Harper Perennial, 1988), 295. Tocqueville was not the only visitor of that era to find American religion interesting. Among others were Frances Trollope, (mother of the celebrated novelist, Anthony Trollope), whose *Domestic Manners of the Americans* was first published in 1832; Richard Gooch, whose *America and the Americans* was first published in 1833-4; and Harriet Martineau, whose *Society in America* was first published in 1837. The first edition of Tocqueville's book was published in 1835; a second edition followed in 1840.

2. I might add that in one of the inauguration ceremonies that I was privileged to attend—the 1993 inauguration of Bill Clinton to his first term—I was struck, particularly as I stood a few yards from several Sikhs who could be recognized by their distinctive turbans, by how the obvious and specifically Christological benediction "in the name of the Father, Son and Holy Ghost" (a phrase repeated more than once in the course of the preacher's remarks) was inappropriate to such an occasion, given the oath of a president to serve all of the people of the United States, and not only Christians. What of Sikhs and Hindus, Jews and Muslims? What of Buddhists and pagans and atheists? I have no quibble with inviting a preacher of any denomination to deliver an invocation or a benediction at such an event, however inherently contradictory that might seem for the inauguration of the head of a secular government, but it seems to me quite possible for such remarks to be crafted without the specifics that attach them to one rather than to all religious (or religious and secular) groups. Such crafting was masterfully accomplished with the benediction offered in 2009 at the inauguration of Barack

Obama. (On the other hand, such crafting was noticeably missing in the invocation offered at the same inauguration).

3. Even this is not entirely the case, since to a certain extent the matter of standing for election to public office was left to the individual states as part of the compromise between state and federal identity that the new republic worked out for itself. With that in mind, among the original 13 colonies, the State of Maryland did not eliminate Christian identity as a criterion for such public service until 1825, and New Hampshire did not do so until 1877.

4. The first was in an August, 2008 survey; the second, actually earlier, in a July, 2003 survey. I am not going to comment on this latter notion, which I find remarkable in a post-Kantian world in which countless numbers of people have been slaughtered in the name of God and in which any number of believers have shown themselves more than capable of immoral and amoral activity.

5. In Randall Balmer's *God in the White House: A History*: How Faith Shaped the Presidency from John F. Kennedy to George W. Bush,* (NYC: Harper Collins, 2008), Jimmy Carter's 1976 victory is ascribed in part to the reactivization of the Evangelical community after an absence of overt, organized evangelical political participation for several decades, to support him, and Balmer proposes that Carter's loss to Ronald Reagan in 1980 was due, in part, to that community's shifting its support away from him to his opponent.

6. Nancy Gibbs and Michael Duffy, *The Preacher and the Presidents: Billy Graham in the White House*, (NYC: Center Street, 2007).

7. Jacques Berlinerblau, *Thumpin' It: The Use and Abuse of the Bible in Today's Presidential Politics*. (Louisville: Westminster John Knox, 2008)

8. I am referring to the idea that a large part of the reason for the "roar" of the 1920s was the—desperate—need by the West to escape from the terrifying questions regarding what we are as a species in the aftermath of having used the results of the scientific revolutions begun in the 1760s to produce such destructive technologies. This development made possible the killing and both physical and psychological maiming of several million young men on the battlefield. Our hubristic sense of our ability to be gods through science was exposed by the Great War as an ability, rather, to be demons—and the 1920s offered the proof of a profound need to flee from that truth.

9. Bill Bradley helped lead the New York Knicks to two NBA championships in the early 1970s, and soon after retiring, he ran successfully for the U.S. Senate from New Jersey, serving for 18 years in that capacity. He became a fairly strong contender for the Democratic presidential nomination that eventually fell to Al Gore in 2000. Jack Kemp quarterbacked the Buffalo Bills to two AFC Conference championships in the mid-1960s, and soon after retiring, he ran successfully for

Congress—he served for nine terms—from western New York State. He became Bob Dole's running mate for the Republican ticket that ran against Bill Clinton in 1996. Jesse Ventura parlayed a successful wrestling career into an acting career and defeated an 18-year-long incumbent to become mayor of Brooklyn Park, Minnesota in 1990 and governor of the state in 1998 in an upset victory as an Independent. He served for one term and did not seek reelection. Arnold Schwarzenegger moved slowly and smoothly from a progression of seven Mr. Universe titles (1970-77) to a series of very successful movie roles, which he abruptly left behind to accept the Republican nomination for governor of California in a recall election against the Democratic incumbent in 2003; he won reelection in 2006. There are other athlete-politicians, but these four stand out.

10. Whether or not one understands anti-Zionism to be a disguised stand-in for anti-Semitism is a separate issue beyond this discussion. See fn 11.

11. This is not to *confuse* the religious with the political issue: the perpetrators may have been Muslim or Christian and the victims Jewish but the murders were not acts of Muslim Jew-hatred but of Palestinian Arab Israel-hatred. These two sentiments must be distinguished from each other—in theory, some of the Israeli victims could have been Muslim or Christian, given the multireligious nature of Israel and of the Israeli sports scene—although such sentiments can and often do overlap. See Soltes, *Untangling the Web.*

12. Quoted in an Internet article, http://www.jewishtoronto.com. A documentary film, *After the Cup,* followed the team for two years and took three years to secure distribution. It came out in 2010.

13. Ibid

14. The Rob Hughes article of March 9, 2011 is cited above, in my footnote for chapter 8, fn 13.

15. The sense of parallel derives from the fact that the Bnei Sakhnin team is largely made up of a minority, non-Jewish players, and was successful, just as the Jewish Austro-Hungarian soccer team was made up of a minority, Jewish players, and was successful, a century ago. See above, chapter 10, 179. Sports has interwoven religion as well as ethnicity and race in a broader worldwide sense when it has been used to bring youth from long-term, mutually hostile groups together by sharing the playing field instead of the battlefield. The article, "Sports Saves the World," by Alexander Wolff, in *Sports Illustrated* magazine (September 26, 2011; 62-74) reflected a year of travelling to study efforts—involving tens of thousands of individuals—to use the common ground of sports as a multivalent mechanism for peace, from Israel-Palestine and Ireland (where religion is an obvious central issue) to Rio de Janeiro and Caras; from Elizabethtown, South Africa to Nairobi; and from Chicago to Toronto and Vancouver.

16. Particularly since 1976; see above, 247 & fn 5.

17. She was also captain of the "Final Five" U.S. women's team that won gold in the 2016 Olympics in Rio de Janeiro—in which she also won silver in both the floor exercise and in the individual all-around competition. She and her teammate Gabby Douglas are the only Americans to win back-to-back gold medals in gymnastics.

18. This is a far from complete list. See the easily-located on-line article/chart, entitled "Key Dates in the History of Women in the Olympic Movement."

19. FINA is the *Federation internationale de natation* (International Swimming Federation), based in Lausanne, Switzerland, which is recognized by the IOC as the instrument that administers international competition in water sports of all sorts. FINA officially renamed the sport "artistic swimming" in2017 (a decision with which not everyone agreed).

20. See the 23 June 2014 *Time Magazine* article by Christina Hoff Sommers, "Title IX: How a Good Law Went Terribly Wrong."

21. Technically, she won the US Nationals, which was the precursor to the US Open. Aside from those five singles crowns, she won five doubles titles and one mixed doubles title—11 Grand Slam titles in all. In the 1960s she also became the first Black player to compete on the Women's Professional Golf Tour. An interesting parallel between the cordiality between Jackie Robinson and Hank Greenberg—although that context is far more intense—might be noted in that Gibson's doubles partner in her victories at the French Open and Wimbledon in 1956 was the British player, Angela Buxton, who was also Althea's one really close friend on the circuit—and a Jew, who has referred to the sense of isolation that both players felt; so "it was a good thing we found each other."

22. Ashe also won both the French Open (in 1971) and the Australian Open (in 1977) in doubles.

23. The woman was a Maryland high-school player, Je'Nan Hayes, who had worn her hijab during the previous 24 games of the season, so how did it suddenly become dangerous to one referee—or was this a symptom of that referee's ignorance or prejudice? See the article by Jesse Dougherty in The Washington Post, March 13, 2017.

24. Mariel Padilla, "'A Powerful Message': The Raptors Offer Hijabs," *The New York Times*, Monday, September, 2019, D4 (*SportsMonday*).

25. Ibid.

26. Ibid.

27. Curtish Rush, "Game Gear: Helmets, Hockey Sticks and Hijabs," The New York Times, Monday, July 30, 2018, D1 (*SportsMonday*)

28. Ibid.

29. Op Citum, D5.

30. Ibid.

31. Tariq Panja, "Iran Women Leverage World Cup," *The New York Times,* Tuesday, July 16, 2019, B8 (*SportsTuesday*).

32. See above, 279-80. Although not related to sports, an even more egregious mode of acquiescence was enacted, notoriously, by leaders of the International Red Cross, when they visited the concentration camp at Teresienstadt and permitted themselves to be deceived that the site was an ideal community provided for its Jewish residents by Jew-loving Hitler.

33. See Farnaz Fassihi, "Jailed for Sneaking Into a Soccer Game, She Died a Cause Celebre," *The New York Times,* September 11, 2019, A11.

34. See Tariq Panja, "Iranian Women Allowed to Attend Soccer Game for First Time Since 1981," *The New York Times,*" October 11, 2019, B7. 7

35. Lauren Messman, "New Report Reveals 20-Year Sex Abuse Scandal Across US Gymnastics Programs," *Vice,* December 15, 2016. An investigation by *The Indianapolis Star* over a period of nine months found that the abuses were widespread because "predatory coaches were allowed to move from gym to gym, undetected by a lax system of oversight, or dangerously passed on by USA Gymnastics-certified gyms" Besides Nassar, other coaches across the country were involved in the scandal, in localities such as Michigan, Pennsylvania, California, Rhode Island, and Indiana.

36. On July 11, 2017, Nassar pleaded guilty to federal child pornography charges, and was sentenced to 60 years in prison on December 7, 2017. On November 22, 2017, he pleaded guilty in state court to seven charges of first-degree sexual assault and entered another guilty plea a week later to three additional charges of sexual assault. On January 24, 2018, Nassar was sentenced to an additional 40 to 175 years in prison, set to run after he serves the 60-year federal prison sentence for child pornography. On February 5, 2018, he received another 40 to 125 years. As of 2019, he has been incarcerated at the Coleman United States Penitentiary.

37. See Juliet Macur and Ken Belson, "National Chief For Gymnastics Is Forced Out After Turmoil,," in *The New York Times,* Wednesday, September 5, 2018, B8 (*SportsWednesday*). The quote is from the statement made at the time of Perry's resignation by Senator Richard Blumenthal—Democrat of Connecticut and the ranking member of the Senate subcommittee that oversees the US Olympic Committee—and quoted in the article.

38. The three officials were the University president, Graham Spanier; vice-president, Gary Schultz; and athletic director, Tim Curley.

39. These were: a $60 million fine, a four-year postseason ban, scholarship reductions, and a vacation of all victories from 1998 to 2011. The sanctions were among the severest ever imposed on an NCAA member school. The Big Ten Conference subsequently imposed an additional $13 million fin on the university.

40. *Sports Illustrated* labelled Richards an "extraordinary spectacle," and described reactions to her as "varying from astonishment to suspicion, sympathy, resentment, and more often than not, utter confusion." The USOC stated that "there is competitive advantage for a male who has undergone a sex change surgery as a result of physical training and development as a male." Richards finally agreed to take the Barr body test that she had refused to take in order to compete in the US Open. The test results were ambiguous. She refused to take it again and was barred from play. There is more to her story of interest. See Renee Richards and Jon Ames, *The Second Half of My Notorious Life*, NYC: Simon & Schuster, 2007.

41. See the CNN on-line report by Christina Maxouris, Friday, February 14, 2020.

42. This entire gender-focused discussion was written prior to the emergence of the Corona Virus pandemic and its effect on sports, including the agreed-upon delay in holding the Tokyo Olympics.

43. See Greg Bishop, "In Tebow Debate, a Clash of Faith and Football," *The New York Times*, Tuesday, November 8, 2011, B13. The quotes offered in the next several paragraphs are from the same article.

44. Not only was this a crucial game coming down the home stretch in the pennant race, but in retrospect one might see this as the final turning point in a season with a number of twists and turns, that would eventually lead the Phillies to surge past the Mets for the Division Championship—and a step closer toward the pennant and World Series victories that Howard had proudly predicted toward the outset of the season, but which had not been anywhere in evidence up to that ninth-inning moment *during* the season.

45. An article by Karen Crouse—on the front page of the Thursday, January, 2011 *New York Times* sports section (B12)—focuses on Polamalu's faith, and offers an interesting contrast to the brief discussion of Tim Tebow. Polamalu is anything but a polarizing figure—he is admired even by his opponents and is the one his teammates turn to, as linebacker James Harrison puts it, "when we need a little guidance. Troy's a lot deeper than a lot of people who actually preach the word." Crouse's article, "A Defensive Anchor Walks a Spiritual Path," follows the Steelers' team MVP as he prepares for a play-off game against the Baltimore Ravens, quoting from *Counsels from the Holy Mountain*, a book of homilies and letters of a Greek Orthodox monk, Elder Ephraim, that "guides him in football and in life," for Polamalu describes Elder Ephraim "as his spiritual doctor." The visit to the elderly monk's monastery residence in southern Arizona and to Mount

Athos in Greece have led the football star to a mindset of selflessness, discipline, humility—and pacifism outside the context of his violent sport. These qualities complement—and in the last case contradict—his outstanding performances on the field in a perfect paradox. Polamalu retired in 2015.

46. See the January 22, 2009 article by Edward Paik in Syracuse University's *The Daily Orange*. The article was anticipating the upcoming match-up between Syracuse and Louisville, (won by Louisville. Louisville won their first Big East title and Tournament that year and were seeded #1 in the NCAA Division I championships, but were upset in the Midwest Regional final by #2 seed Michigan State, 64-52.).

47. Lapointe's article is on page D4, under the section entitled "Pro Football N.F. L. Week 6."

48. The full text of the Supreme Court decision may be found at http:supct. law.cornell.edu/supct/html/96-62.ZS.html.

49. Robin Shulman, "Case Tests Boundaries of Prayer in Sports," *The Washington Post*, October 7, 2007, A14.

50. Ibid.

51. Katie Thomas, "For Coach, God and Archery Are a Package Deal," *The New York Times*, August 19, 2008, A1.

52 Ibid.

53. Ibid.

54. In a follow-up *New York Times* article on November 18, 2008, also by Katie Thomas—"U.S. Archery Sticks With Its Coach"—the author noted that "in a recent telephone interview, Lee said he no longer held Bible-study classes, and executives for USA Archery said they had explained to Lee that such behavior was unacceptable." Lee remained the coach as the team prepared for the 2016 Rio Olympics, having completed the trials that began in September.

55. All three quotes in this paragraph come from Eric Lichtblau's article, "Questions Raised Anew About Religion in Military," *The New York Times*, March 1, 2009.

56. Ibid.

57. Ibid. About 18 months after the *Times* article, a September 20, 2010 *Truthout* report by Mike Ludwig, entitled "'Underground' Group of Cadets Say Air Force Academy Controlled by Evangelicals" asserted that an anonymous cadet at the Air Force Academy claimed that "some cadets must pretend to be evangelical Christians in order to maintain standing among their peers and superiors... [T] he whistleblower stated that he is a part of an 'underground group' of about 100

cadets who cannot rely on proper channels to confront evangelical pressure."
Included in the article is reference to "testimony from the parents of a [2010]
academy graduate who believe their... daughter was 'methodically brainwashed
into believing that she was unsaved in the Catholic religion' by a [Protestant]
fundamentalist group there, [and demanded] an investigation of the academy
and the evangelical academy ministry *Cadets for Christ.*" The results of a study of
the religious climate of the academy, according to the article, were suppressed,
but a leak to the press suggested that 353 cadets (almost 1 out of every 5 survey
participants) reported having been subjected to unwanted religious proselytizing,
and 23 cadets (13 of them Christians) reported living 'in fear of their physical
safety' because of their religious beliefs." Needless to say, the implications of the
two reports 18 months apart are both astounding and disturbing.

58. See, for example, the paper by Jack J. Porter, "Religion and the Military:
A Comparative Analysis (or to Serve God or Country or Both?)" presented at the
48th Annual Convention of the International Studies Association convention in
Chicago (February 28, 2007).

59. Some of these, of course, themselves became persecutors of those who
did not follow the form of faith that they prescribed. This was certainly true in
the Pilgrim-and-Puritan-developed Massachusetts Bay Colony. Roger Williams,
in effect a refugee from that colony, was the first founder—of the colony of Rhode
Island—to explicitly and unequivocally reject religious persecution, or religious
qualification for residing in or serving in the government of his colony.

60. Katie Thomas, *The New York Times* (August 19, 2008), *op citum.*

61. The issue of "interpretive possibilities" is a doubly complicated one. Not
only do we not necessarily agree on how to interpret given words that we agree
are divine, but we don't always agree on which words are divine revelation and
thus needful of our interpretive focus. On the one hand, Jews and Christians agree
that the book of Isaiah is the result of direct divine inspiration, but don't agree
on how to interpret certain passages that are key to Jewish and Christian beliefs
respectively—and on the other hand, Christians embrace the books of Matthew
and Mark as derived from divine inspiration, while Jews do not. Orthodox and
Catholic Christians consider the first two books of Maccabees to be part of the
divine writ, but Protestants (as well as Jews) do not. Muslims understand the
Torah (Pentateuch) and the Gospels as well as other works, such as the Psalms, to
have been divinely inspired but subject, over time, to corruption—necessitating
the shaping of the definitive divinely inspired text, the Qur'an, understood to have
come through Muhammad as the final conduit though which God has spoken to
humankind. Jews and Christians don't view the Qur'an that way.

62. Pat Borzi, "In the Heat Of Camp, The Hunger of Faith," *The New York
Times,* Monday, September 6, 2010, D1&D8.

63. Jere Longman and Mary Pilon, "Saudi Arabia May Include Women on Its Olympic Team," *The New York Times*, March 20, 2012; followed a few weeks later by tiny article by Pilon announcing "Two Saudi Women to Compete in London," and by a July 30 article by Longman, "A Giant Leap for Women, but Hurdles Remain" — both of these also in *The New York Times*.

64. Richard Sandomir, "A Career Sustained by Unwavering Faith," *The New York Times*, August 2, 2011.

65. See *The Jerusalem Post*, op ed page, 23 January, 2020.

66. Geoffrey Gray, "On Saturday, a Rabbi-to-Be Will Throw punches," *The New York Times*, November 11, 2009. The article anticipated Foreman's match with Daniel Santos, which Foreman won, making him the World Boxing Association champion at 154 pounds.

67. Allison Kaplan Sommer, "Gold Medal Jewish Gymnast Aly Raisman Pays Tribute to Munich 11," *Haaretz*, August 8, 2012. The article quotes heavily from a somewhat earlier article in the *New York Post*.

68. The Youkilis article is Richard Sandomir's "fascination with a New Yankee's Jewish Roots," *The New York Times*, December 13, 2012. After a stint with the Yankees in 2013, Youkilis retired from American major league baseball; he currently plays in Japan for the Tohoku Rahuten Golden Eagles. The Stoudemire article is Dick Friedman's "All-Star of David. As a Jew, Amar'e Stoudemire will have to learn a whole new rule book," *Sports Illustrated* Magazine, August 16, 2010. Stoudemire last played for the Miami Heat in 2015, and is currently a free agent.

69. Andrew Keh, "Praying for the Home Team," *The New York Times*, Friday, February 28, 2014.

70. By the time this volume reached its second printing, Kanter had been traded and had been faring very successfully as starting Center for the NY Knicks and subsequently as back-up center for the Boston Celtics..

71. Lee Jenkins, "The Game that Saved the Warriors," *Sports Illustrated* Magazine, June 20, 2016

EPILOGUES
Sports, Religion, and Politics—from Old Visual Art to New Stars of the Pulpit and Screen

*I*n a certain sense, one might say that we end where we began, for at the outset of this book we referred to a handful of works of art in order to introduce the idea of the idealized athlete as s/he is presented in visual terms, and how, in turn, the ideal athlete is cognate with the ideal warrior.

Thus, in observing the transformation in Greek statuary from its Archaic-period *kouros* figures to the Classic-period *Doryphoros* of Polykleitos, we noted both a transition from representing an eternal and unchanging, symmetrically perfect god to showing a god-like hero captured in a moment between two physical movements— and that one such figure may have represented Achilles both as an idealized warrior *and* as an idealized athlete. Conversely, we noted that, in the case of the Archaic-period images of Kleobis and Biton, the heroic perfection that they, and thus the statues representing them, are intended to convey is purely that of athletic prowess— strength of body and character in a religious, not a military con- text—spurred on by filial piety and respect for the gods.

The interest in depicting both hero-warrior athletes and *mere* athletes spills over into the realm of Greek painted-pottery. The im- agery captures figures in action and also in moments of repose.

Among the myriad vase-painting images of warrior-athlete-heroes, I would call attention to three in particular. The first of these is a scene painted on a black-figure *amphora* by Psiax around 520 BCE depicting Herakles wrestling with the Nemean lion—the destruction of which was one of his renowned 12 labors that rid the Hellenic world of dangerous wild beasts and other creatures [fig. 11].

What is most significant here is the typical Greek artistic interest in contrasting ideas—in this case, *ethos* (a calm, cool, collected Olympian god-like attitude that bespeaks being above the fray and recognizing the moment at issue as part of an extensive continuum) and *pathos* (an engaged, emotional, heated attitude that bespeaks an intense focus on the moment with the limited perspective that humans typically exhibit). If we examine the respective facial expressions of the hero and the wild beast that he grasps, we can note how calm his expression is—pure *ethos* is reflected in the non-emotive, no-sweat disposition of his features—and how, conversely, the lion is snarling ferociously, full of brute anger.

But the situation is more complex than this, and indicative of the Greek understanding of how paradox attends the divinely wrought world in which we dwell. For Herakles, although fathered by a god—Zeus himself, king of the Olympians—is a mortal on

Figure 11. Herakles and
the Nemean Lion (detail)

his mother's side, and so this means that he will ultimately die; his demise occasioned by his emotional, all-too-humanly *engaged* nature. The Nemean lion, being non-human, shares a certain common ground with the gods (i.e., that he *is*, like the gods, inherently outside the human realm)—and must be strangled by the hero because he cannot be harmed by ordinary weapons, proof of his god-like nature. So the lion might be expected to exhibit *ethos* and Herakles *pathos* if the world were simple, but it is not.[1]

A second work—a late fifth-century BCE white-ground *lekythos*—portrays a completely anonymous warrior, seated before a gravestone that is shaped, as such markers were at that time, like a small temple or a large altar. The warrior is attended by a youth and a girl who holds his shield and helmet. The point of the composition is that even though it suggests that the young warrior is dead, he is nonetheless immortalized by the "portrait" that represents him seated uninjured and glorious in his youthful mien before what we may take to be his own grave marker. Thanks to his athletic prowess, he is gathered to a realm ruled by certain gods of similar noble character and he therefore achieves a distinct visual form of *kleos aphthiton*—"undying glory"—that both belies and compensates him for his early death.[2]

The heroic warrior-athlete quintessentially associated with the phrase, *kleos aphthiton*, is, of course, Achilles. He is, after all, not only the son of a sea-goddess (Thetis) and a human (Peleus)—an immortal and a mortal—whose wedding on Olympus ultimately leads to the Trojan War, with its intense divine involvements and expansive human destruction. He is also informed by a prophecy that if he stays home, away from the battlefield before Troy, he will live to an obscure old age; if he engages in the war at Troy, he will die before the city falls, in the prime of his youth, but achieve the immortality of "undying glory" as a consequence.

Achilles is the emphatic exemplar of the ultimate question posed by the ancient Greeks: can we, and if so *how* can we, achieve immortality—we, who share mortality with the other spe-

Figure 12. Penthesilea Painter:
Achilles and Penthesilea (detail)

cies around us but possess a consciousness of the *idea* of immortality, thus somehow connecting us to the immortal gods? Although Achilles's preeminent skills on the battlefield and his foreknowledge of his own doom are attributable to his divine connection, ultimately his mortality cannot be avoided. Since all humans confront the matter of mortality and immortality (achieved in different ways through children, or artistic and scientific works, or great deeds that echo through the memory of others), then it is no surprise that Achilles is such a popular subject in Greek vase-painting.

Among the myriad images of Achilles, none is more poignant than that painted around 460 BCE on the interior of a red-figure *kylix* by the so-called Penthesilea painter (for this is the name-vase of this otherwise anonymous artist), which shows Achilles in the act of killing the Amazonian princess of that name [fig 12].[3] The poignant irony is twofold. First, this work apparently offers the first instance in a vase painting where there is eye contact between two figures—and in this case one is engaged in the act of slaying the other. There is a Greek tradition that asserts that Achilles fell in love with Penthesilea at the moment that he killed her—as he drove his sword into her—because of his admiration for her great courage and fighting skill.

Aside from the Freud-based notions yielded by this depiction of the relationship between death and sex—the apogee of which idea is surely expressed verbally in the French phrase referring to an orgasm as *"une petite mort"* ("a little death")—for the Greeks, such intense eye-to-eye contact between the hero and his victim represents another kind of paradox: that of the relationship between *eris* (strife) and *eros* (love). The entire Trojan War cycle is built around the paradoxic coexistence of these concepts commonly understood to be opposed to each other by definition, as it is built around the paradox of coexistent mortality and immortality.[4] In both cases, Achilles offers an intense conceptual centerpiece for the paradox.

The second poignant aspect of this story is that, as every Greek viewer of the image would know, Achilles is himself doomed to die before the Trojan War will—or *can*—end.[5] Thus, not only does he fall in love with a woman as he slays her, but if for some odd miraculous reason she were to have survived her Achilles-administered wound, their love relationship would be doomed to ephemerality, since he is destined to die soon. And of course, the centerpiece of the literary exploration of the Trojan War cycle, the *Iliad*, has as its starting point the argument between Achilles and Agamemnon over a woman, and the insult to Achilles regarding a woman is set within the context of everybody's awareness of Achilles's inevitable and tragic fate.

The depictions of such warrior-athlete-heroes invoke extensive and interlocking chains of issues and ideas that connect them and their narratives to the gods. But Greek vase painting also often directs itself to the representation of anonymous athletes. The intent of such works is either to show how the sport is being played, as in vases that depict footraces [fig 13]; or perhaps to show off the ability of the artist to render complex compositions, as in vases that portray chariot races; or, as in a fourth-century BCE black-figure Panathenaic prize *amphora* that represents a boxing contest, both to show the action of the sport and to show off the muscled bodies of the athletes represented [fig 14].[6]

The contexts invoked by this last image offer a threefold is-

Figure 13. Greek Vase with footrace (detail)

sue for our purposes—beyond the matter of the Greek aesthetic sense of the idealized human body. First of all, most of the vases with scenes of athletes competing were intended, as this one was, as *prizes* delivered to those who were victorious in various athletic competitions—in this last case, in the Panathenaic games. As such, not only are such vases inherently connected to sports and religion—an entire series of competitions that were organized specifically to celebrate the goddess regarded as the primary patron of the city of Athens—but they are inevitably decorated with an image of the goddess on one side and of the specific athletic competition at which the vase will have been won on the other.

Secondly, we must keep in mind that the artist (or artists, since one may have thrown the vase and another decorated it) are doing on a small scale—artists are *always* doing on a small scale—what the gods do on the grand scale: creating. Like the poet who sings of divine and human actions, the visual artist who depicts gods and humans is not only acting *in imitatio dei* (in imitation of God) but is deemed to be inspired—in-spirited—by the gods and thus functions in a manner analogous to a priest or prophet through whom (the) god(s) speak to us. This would of course be true under any

Figure 14. Greek Panathenaic vase with boxing (detail)

circumstances, but where heroes and athletes are being portrayed one might say that the artist and the artwork intermediate between the one depicted and the eventual owner of the vase and between *both* of these and the gods.

Thirdly, vases such as Panathenaic *amphorae*, which in part were devoted to glorifying the physicality of the athletes who compete for them, point us forward in a particular direction. If Roman art largely emulates Greek art, and therefore the same essential principles regarding the adulation of the athletic body remain operative, then the turn in early Christian and Byzantine art *away* from the body may be understood as more than a function of some degeneration of skill needed to depict the human body in action.

On the contrary, one might argue that the frontal and very ephemeral manner in which figures are represented in early medieval art reflects a turn in a different direction that synthesizes athletic with divinely directed concerns.[7] Thus, everything about such art—from the nearly shapeless bodies covered in garments showing only gesturing hands and enlarged heads with still larger eyes—bespeaks a focus on spiritual matters. The garments inevitably bear colors offering symbolic meanings—red for the blood of sacrifice, blue for the truth suggested by the sky above us in which God dwells, green for rebirth and resurrection, white for purity, and so forth—just as the hand gestures do, all of which reflect a *spiritual athleticism* that looks to victory not in the here and now but in the hereafter.

We can see this, for example, in Byzantine images of the Virgin and Child: the bodies hardly exist beneath the garments that are symbolically colored and which, instead of possessing dark shadows along the irregular crease lines that reflect our everyday reality, have stylized, rhythmic, unnaturally regularized lines highlighted in gold—that most valuable and precious of materials, reflecting the valuable and precious divine truth represented by the Christ child—that reflect an otherworldly reality. The figures neither quite sit nor quite stand in/on a very architectural throne placed within and against a backdrop that is no natural landscape of earth and sky but a preternatural, *spaceless space* of gold—through which two angels peer as through a window further connecting the world from which they have come to our own world [fig 15].[8]

The figures gesture—she toward her Son, He toward us, His hand raised in benediction—with hands presenting attenuated, ethereal fingers; her neck is non-volumetric and preternaturally long and His head is both oversized (to suggest the excess of soul within it) and configured like that of a fully cognizant adult, not a small child. Like his head, his eyes—the windows to the soul—are unusually large, and behind his head glows a halo (a sun burst)[9] as behind hers, but his is uniquely imprinted with a cruciform both anticipating his future, culminating in an earthbound act of self-sacrifice on the cross and, because his head and neck block the lower vertical arm from our eyes, offering the symbolism of the triune God of which the Christ is only one aspect.

In other words, while European Christian history eventually includes jousting sports that have as their ultimate purpose the training of surrogates for warring events to be carried out in the

Figure 15. Byzantine Icon of Virgin and Child

name of and on behalf of God, the art utilized on behalf of those events turns from physical to spiritual athleticism in its portrayal of Christ on his Mother's lap, for example, or of saints in the act of blessing or otherwise miraculously saving people through the connection that they possess to God. It is such a connection that gives them spiritual abilities analogous to the physical abilities exhibited by a hero-athlete such as Herakles or Achilles that are made possible through *their* connection to this or that god or goddess.

The same sensibility—perhaps even more so—will attach itself to Jewish and Muslim art through the course of the same centuries. In fact, one might suppose that Jewish and Muslim art might prefer not to depict *human* figures at all lest they be mistaken for association with a God who in these two traditions is rigorously understood to be without physical form. Yet this reluctance proves not to be absolute in either tradition. In the Jewish tradition, in antiquity, even the early synagogues were overrun with visual décor that included human representation—although it is true that the figures were typically very schematic.

One may see this in the mid-third century CE wall paintings at Dura Europus on the Euphrates River, or in the early sixth-century CE mosaic floors at Bet Alpha in the Galilee. Most interesting in these works is the solution taken to the problem of how to represent God in action—raising the righteous dead (as described in Ezekiel 37 and depicted at Dura) or staying Abraham's hand from sacrificing Isaac (as described in Genesis 22 and depicted at Bet Alpha). The phrase "God's hand" becomes literalized, and so God is represented by synecdoche, as a hand reaching out of a sunburst—often, but not always, possessing precisely seven rays [fig 16].[10]

Nonetheless, whatever might have persisted of Jewish visual self-expression between about the seventh and the twelfth centuries is lost to us. And as synagogue buildings begin to reemerge to visibility at the end of this period, we find them indeed almost entirely devoid of figurative decoration. It is not really until the great era of the timber synagogues of Poland and Lithuania, from the eighteenth century forward, that we begin to find extensive painted décor in evidence once again—often figurative, but rarely with *human* figures, or at least not in substantial number.

However, an illuminated manuscript tradition that is in evidence at least from the fourteenth century onward, does include

Figure 16. Bet Alpha synagogue floor mosaic: The Binding of Isaac (detail)

human figures, sometimes in abundance—but in parts of Europe, such as the Rhineland, such figures would be adorned with the heads of birds, rather than human heads, as if to undercut the representation of fully human beings, for "creating" humans is only God's prerogative. This circumspection would begin to change in the aftermath of Emancipation, in the nineteenth century. With the emergence of genre painting in Europe in general, there appears specifically Jewish genre imagery—scenes in the Jewish home or synagogue—but certainly no representations of sports events or figures.

Across most of the Muslim world, by contrast, there is a more extreme and continuous discomfort with human representation and a preference for abstract symbolic language, especially in obviously sacred contexts. Thus, for example, an edifice such as the Dome of the Rock in Jerusalem, built by Abd'al-Malak in 691 offers a spherical form surmounting a octagonal form surmounting a square: the sphere, without beginning or end, symbolizes the eternal God, the square represents our four-directional world of stops and starts; the octagonal form intermediates between the two.

The dome is a monumental singularity, undifferentiated by decorative elements. The octagon is overrun with endlessly minute elements, its multiple sections "finitized" by frames and offering contrastive colors, (sky blue and earth-plant green), and geometric versus vegetal forms. Writing—extensive quotes from the Qur'an—intermediates between the gold roof and the multicolored walls that support it. Thus the divine-human relationship is expressed: God is monumental and singular, we are minute and multifarious, God is infinite and we are finite.

A second, very different direction taken by Islamic art—that, with a number of important exceptions,[11] prefers abstraction to figuration—is found in the realm of illuminated manuscripts. Aside from their general beauty and figurative richness, such manuscripts are of particular interest to us because they often offer the visual testimony regarding sports activities, such as polo, archery, and wrestling that we have discussed as part of the Muslim world of the fifteenth through eighteenth centuries.

Any number of Persian and Turkish miniatures depicts these various sports being practiced. In an illumination from about 1500 we observe the Sultan Suleiman the Magnificent seated on a throne in a raised pavilion, observing a series of pairs of wrestlers practicing for the *kirkpinar*. And we are offered a direct, virtually bird's-eye view into the world of sixteenth-century Ottoman Turkish archery on horseback in the court of the sultans in a 1584 miniature from the *Huner-Nama* (*Book of Skills*), in which a rider—Sultan Murat II—practices the skill of shooting arrows while on horseback [fig 17].

I have begun this brief incursion into late-ancient through late-medieval Christian, Jewish, and Muslim art to underscore how such art diverges from earlier, pagan Greek and Roman works that gloried in the human body, and most particularly in the idealized

Figure 17 Ottoman Sultan Murat II
in archery competition

athlete's body as a surrogate for and, essentially, connecting them to, the perfect bodies of gods.

As the sports and war-related aspects of the life of a knight emerge and evolve, so, too, does the art in which such activity is depicted. Primarily in the form of book illumination, such imagery carries us from practice sessions in sword-fighting between young pages to the solemn ordination ceremony of a knight with his sword and spurs, as he gestures upward towards God [fig 18].[12] It also starts to move us from medieval to Renaissance visual thinking.

Indeed, one of the aspects of what we mean when we speak of European "Renaissance art"—emerging gradually in the fourteenth through sixteenth centuries (by the end of which time, Machiavelli was penning *Il Principe*)—is a return to the visual values and ideas that had flourished in antiquity, most obviously among the Greeks and Romans. The idea of Renaissance art—particularly in Italy—returns us to an interest in depicting the human body as a breathing entity, in both two- and three-dimensional media, but also to an interest in representing individuals whose claim to fame is not necessarily or simply spiritual.

The multiple portrayals of David confronting Goliath, from those by Donatello (1430s) and Verrocchio (1470s) to those by Michelangelo (1504) and Bernini (1623-4) all variously champion the human body with its childlike (Donatello, Verrocchio, Bernini) or adult (Michelangelo) musculature. Perhaps the most renowned of these is that by Michelangelo, in Florence, with is stylistic echoes

Figure 18. Consecration of a
medieval knight (detail)

of classical Greek statuary with regard to the dynamic stasis—
known as *symmetria* to the ancient Greeks, and as *contraposto* to
the Renaissance Italians—exhibited by the figure whose weight
shifts from one foot to the other, one leg slightly bent and the
other straight, one tensed and the other relaxed; one arm extended and the other bent back, one more tensed and the other more
relaxed. We might suppose that in the back (or front) of the mind
of each of these artists is the notion that David is a champion of
God going up against the godless Philistine warrior, and that their
depiction of him as physically beautiful is intended to reflect his
spiritual condition.[13]

Works like Antonio del Pollaiuolo's small bronze statue from
the 1470s of Hercules breaking the back of the giant Antaeus in a
wrestling match, or his famous engraving, *Battle of Ten Nudes* (1465),
showing naked men fighting with swords and knives, axes and
bow and arrow, and twisting and turning so that the viewer sees
them from diverse angles, exult in the human form for its own sake.
This is especially true of the masterful drawings by Leonardo da
Vinci of the human body—including scientific studies that indicate
internal bones and tendons. The most that one might suppose with
regard to a religious basis for these last-mentioned works is that
the artist and/or his audience recognized the beauty of the athletic
human body as a consequence of God's creative activity—but that
supposition is largely speculative.

In any case, we might follow this visual sports-and-God discussion in three more brief directions. One is toward the carrying of
the adulation of the athletic body forward into the twentieth century where it dominates the art of fascist states, particularly the Soviet
Union under Joseph Stalin or Germany under Adolf Hitler. With
the art of Soviet Socialist or National [German] Socialist Realism
we arrive, as it were, at the ultimate edge of an antireligious—at
least in the traditional Christian sense—marriage between art and
sports. Thus, the idealized figure who is young, muscular, smiling
and preeminent in whatever the endeavor—be it athletic competi-

Figure 19. Soviet Socialist Realist image: Javelin thrower
(" Young people – to the stadiums!")

tion or electrical cable installation high above the city—is simultaneously god-like (the cable-installer soars fearlessly far above the ground upon which you and I walk) and godless: his faith is directed to himself and to the state that has nurtured, educated, employed, and now visually adulates him. If his body is that of an Achilles, it is neither because he or she is connected to Apollo or Athena nor because he or she is blessed by the Christian God, but because he or she is linked to that idealized, god-like State [fig 19].

Another direction of note is that while in turning to the earliest of American sports enterprises—the Mayan game of *pitz*—one key source of information, the *Popul Vuh,* is literary, (as we have noted).[14] Myriad images from various Mayan sites are another source. The richly carved temples, altars, and ball-court walls corroborate the verbal description of the game—and its consequences for the loser. Thus, for example, in the relief carvings of the Great Ballcourt at Chichen Itza we find a depiction of the decapitation of the defeated team captain, as we have previously noted, with snakes spurting from his neck like blood; nearby, his severed head is held in the hand of the sacrificer, who holds a stone knife in the

314 God and the Goalposts

other. Other works portray players in action, most often diving and twisting to prevent the ball from hitting the ground.

Finally, if one fast-forwards to the late-twentieth century United States, one finds a number of interesting Jewish artists who have produced works that reflect on the national pastime from different, albeit all specifically "Jewish" angles.[15] The initial "angle" is that of the Jewish immigrant arriving in the late-nineteenth or early-twentieth century from the pogrom-ridden world of Eastern Europe to a country that declares itself free of such oppression and religious prejudice—moving forward socially, economically, and politically. As with most immigrant groups, especially in that massive immigration era, one of the answers to the question of how to become American,[16] was involvement in sports—and ultimately in baseball in particular as the American sport par excellence. For a Jew wishing to be religiously observant, this might pose small problems, such as that of participating in games played on Saturday, the Jewish Sabbath.

This is what is expressed in the central image in Marilyn Cohen's (1938-2006) extraordinary series of collage paintings, *Where Did They Go When They Came to America?* Cohen focused in the early 1990s on a Jewish family in each of the 50 states, sifting through old shoeboxes of photographs and attics-full of forgotten toys and furniture to extract a layered summary of each family's transition from Old World to New. Her medium of torn paper, dipped in colors and painstakingly attached to the backing of each work, literalizes the metaphor of torn, reconstituted, and layered memory. Again and again in her images, the stars and stripes of the American flag are somehow worked into the background, together with faces and figures from the family past.

And none of these is more intensely *American* than "Star of Local Kids: Memphis, Tennessee, 1923" [fig 20]. For the entire image is an American flag, but peering like ghosts out of the misty blue-starred section of the flag is a couple from the Old Country. The foreground is marked by a team photograph of kids in their

Figure 20. Marilyn Cohen: Star of Local Kids

baseball uniforms. Apart from them, in significance perspective, so that he is three times their size, is another kid in uniform, bat and catcher's mitt in hand.

The gigantic kid—the star of local kids—is Benny Kaplan, age 11, who in 1923 was the Most Valuable Player of his Memphis, Tennessee Junior Baseball Team—for which he was awarded a new catcher's mitt. His father, Shlomo Zalman Kalmonovsky (the old-fashioned-looking, bearded male in that sky-blue upper-left flag corner) arrived in the United States in 1902, and was followed five years later by his wife Rieva (also in the sky-blue section of the flag) and their five young children. Three more kids were born in Memphis, and Bennie was the youngest of these.[17]

Family lore tells how Bennie used to wear his baseball uniform under his Sabbath clothes during Saturday morning services. In artist Marilyn Cohen's collage, the gold fringe at the bottom of the image is a visual pun: it is both the fringe on the American flag and the symbolic fringe of the traditional *tzitzit*[18] on the *tallit* (prayer shawl) poking out from behind the flag as it would have peaked out from under Benny's uniform. (His clothes hid the uniform, which hid the *tzitzit*: they make up the layers that define Benny as an American

11-year-old and as a Jewish 11-year-old starting to think toward his
bar mitzvah less than two years away.) The Old World seeps into
the new; the Jewish world peaks out from the American uniform
hidden by the Sabbath clothes; layers of past and present bring cer-
tainties and questions into focus in equal measure.

By the time Benny was an adult and engaged in other endeav-
ors, another Jewish contemporary had become what 11-year-old
Benny had no doubt dreamed of becoming: a Major League Baseball star. The star, of course, was Hank Greenberg, the Jew who excelled at America's game, moreover playing for a team, the Detroit
Tigers, at a time (the 1930s) when the city was marked by a preeminent anti-Semite with a loud radio voice and a large following, as
we have noted.[19] And this was the time when Adolph Hitler was
consolidating his power and beginning to direct his destructive
attention to Jews and Judaism. In that context, Hammerin' Hank
became a figure of gigantic, messianic proportions for American
Jewry—especially the Jews of Detroit.

This is literalized in works such as the 1991 acrylic on board,
Hank Greenberg, by Detroit-born Jewish painter, Malcah Zeldis (b.
1931). The artist depicts her family huddled around the radio in
their carefully kept house on a street of carefully kept houses. The
stadium seems to grow directly out of the house as, in her folk-
style there is no sense of perspectival depth and the amphitheatre
of baseball action rises directly above and thus out of the Zeldis'
dwelling. But Greenberg's messianic grandeur is almost bigger
than the stadium itself, extending in true significance perspective
from home plate to scoreboard. He is the messianic *One* who would
lead Detroit's beleaguered team and its beleaguered Jews through
the green grass of baseball success to the paradise of World Series
victory [fig 21].[20]

A third American Jewish artist, the painter, R.B. Kitaj (1932-
2007), was born and raised in Ohio, but eventually immigrated to
England, where most of his early and middle career as an artist was
lived (he returned to the United States in 1997). As I mentioned in

Figure 21. Malcah Zeldis: Hank Greenberg

my book, *Fixing the World*, "[Kitaj's]work, diversely built on met-
aphors and allegories, is a labyrinth of dreams, intertwisted with
reminiscences" of a range of artists "and reflections on his abandoned home, America."[21]

Early on—but then even more so later, in his long, almost
exilic years away from the United States—Kitaj used baseball as
an idealizing self-reflective metaphor, seeing the national pastime
as a reflection of his own boyhood. That boyhood was immersed
in the American Midwest, and unconscious of the details of recent
Jewish history—he grew up unaware of either Jewish traditions or
the Holocaust—the baseball diamond offered a double symbol of
innocence.[22] Baseball represented eternal and unchanging youth to
him—the United States as a youthful actor on the world stage, but
also his own youthful ignorance about who he was.

The American pastime also shows up recently in an altogether different mode—the graphic novel, a genre that extends the
idea of the comic book into the realm of serious subjects. Among the
growing library of such works, James Strum's *The Golem's Mighty
Swing* plays with several ideas simultaneously.

Strum's graphic novel uses the all-American sport to address the matter of the American struggle to define itself, either as being open to diverse cultures, religions, and also *races* or as mired in prejudice and closed-mindedness—and places these issues in the setting of the 1920s and developing German Expressionist cinema, in which one of the most popular films, directed by Paul Wegener, played on the old Bohemian Jewish story of Rabbi Judah Loew and his creation: *The Golem and How He Came into the World*. Meanwhile, the rise of fascism was becoming embodied in a real-life Golem, Hitler—a shapeless destroyer presenting himself to Germany as a secular messiah.

Strum weaves these and other issues into his tale, in simple straightforward prose, narrated in the first-person and in an understated and effective drawing style that emphasizes rectilinearity (like the baseball diamond and its bases). His barnstorming Jewish baseball team makes itself *stereotypically* Jewish (in order to appear more exotic), by giving everyone a beard, even (with boot-polish) the sixteen-year-old younger brother of the manager. The team endures a range of complications that are mostly traceable to the anti-Semitism that they encounter in various ways, offering echoes of the experience of African American players during the same era playing games in the Negro leagues. Thus, he encompasses not only the question of the place of Jews as outsiders in the Middle America of that era, but the issue of the relationship between Jewish Americans in their struggle and African Americans in theirs, and whether that relationship offers team-camaraderie or competition.

As the *Stars of David* struggle to survive financially, the manager and narrator, Noah Strauss, reluctantly agrees to allow a promoter to attire their biggest, most powerful player in the costume of the Golem from the Wegener movie. The idea is to stir up greater interest by playing even more profoundly on the fears of their small-town audiences than the mere fact that the team's members are Jewish. The biggest, most powerful player happens to be the one non-Jew on the team: Henry Bell, former Negro League star, who has an array of tales to tell about baseball and America and his own experience as a member of a feared and despised minority. Henry is thus a "feared Negro" playing a "feared Jewish batter" playing the "feared mythic Golem." Wegener's dark cinematic version of the Golem and its story was alive in movie theaters from Germany to the United States. The team is an entire team of Golems to an uneasy Middle America—or rather, a team of devils, with horns and cloven hooves. More ironically, its star player is and is *not* one of them; for the team, he can play the role of the messianic figure who will offer salvation on the baseball field and in the bank; while for the fans, he can be a particular manifestation of the "golem," like his teammates, a creature that does not possess a genuine, fully realized human *soul* and wreaks *havoc* among civilized, fully human folk.[23]

One can trace a long and diversely interesting historical association between visual art and sports, both in general and specifically with regard to the ways in which we perceive the relationship between sports and religion—and politics and art. So, it should not surprise us to find material from some of the more recent art forms as well. The new technologies that have yielded such new art forms over the past century or so also yield further possibilities for discussion. Certainly, the technology of the motion picture—as it has evolved from the beginning of the twentieth century to the beginning of the twenty-first—falls into this category.

One might take note of any number of films made in the last generation that fall within our rubric—but two in particular come to my mind. One is *Chariots of Fire*. The 1981 movie[24] may best be remembered for Vangelis's highly popular synthesizer-dominated musical score, but its storyline is all about sports and religion—and the politics of religious and class prejudice. The film is based on the true story of two British track athletes—the middleclass English Jew, Harold Abrahams, and the upper-crust Christian "Flying Scotsman," Eric Liddell[25]—preparing for and then competing in the 1924 summer Olympics. While there are many historical inaccuracies in the film, there is also much that is factual in it. What strikes me as important for our discussion, however, is the manner in which the two protagonists are portrayed: the strong emphasis on apparent differences of personality and response to adversity that is offered, which presents the Jew in a negative light and the Christian in a positive light.

Abrahams is shown encountering both anti-Semitism and class prejudice when he arrives at Cambridge in 1919 and he exhibits a sense of anger that never leaves him. His desire is to win and he is willing to do so at virtually any cost—including hiring a professional coach (Sam Mussabini,[26] who shares the condition of being a looked-down-upon, dark-haired outsider in this blondish world of Roaring Twenties' Britain),[27] which at the time was considered illegal or at least unsportsmanlike for an amateur athlete.

Even with Abrahams' understandable antipathy toward the college authorities regarding their prejudices and outmoded manner of thinking, the viewer is more likely to walk away with a negative sense of his ethics—and an inevitable sense of a stereotype being confirmed regarding Jews and business (in this equation, running is a business)—than a negative view of the crotchety committee that criticizes him. Put another way, Jews who defy the stereotype of being physically weak do so by being morally weak.

By contrast, Liddell is a believing Christian for whom running is a means of glorifying God prior to journeying to China in order to serve there as a missionary. He explains this to his sister, who expresses concern that he is expending too much energy on running to be properly focused on their Christian mission. While Abrahams is shown succeeding at the Trinity Great Court run (running around the court between the time the clock in the clock tower begins and completes its 12 chimes at noon), Liddell is shown running in a race for Scotland against Ireland—and preaching a sermon on "Life as a Race" afterwards. In their first meeting, Liddell is shown defeating Abrahams (which is what sends Abrahams to a trainer to improve his technique—the film does not reveal that it was actually Liddell who introduced Abrahams to Mussabini).

Liddell is represented all along the way as God-serving and noble (he was) and Abrahams is shown as undignified, at best (he was not). Abrahams will do anything to win; Liddell won't even run a necessary heat of the 100 meters (in which he would have competed against Abrahams) at the Olympics because the heat falls on a Sunday. This, incidentally, offers us a rare instance of a member of the Christian majority finding himself in a quandary with regard to an essential aspect of his faith—analogous to the sort of quandaries we have earlier noted for Jewish or Muslim athletes in the modern Olympic and professional sports era—due to the essentially secular thinking that underlies the modern Olympics from its outset.

In any case, Liddell's fellow Christian teammate—a secular, socially gracious Christian, Lord Andrew Lindsay—is shown proposing a trade of places so that Liddell will run instead in the 400 meters while Lindsay takes his spot in the 100 meters—all at the last minute, in theory disadvantaging both runners, since they will not have trained at each other's distances.[28] Of course, this also helps enable Abrahams' victory in the 100, since he won't be competing against Liddell. Liddell is shown in church on Sunday praying and quoting from the Bible.[29] He wins his 400, as Abrahams wins his 100, but where the first is shown buoyed by his faith and, as it were, pushed to the finish line by God, the second is shown winning through the questionable legality and, more to the point, morality, of having utilized a trainer. Where Liddell's gold medal sparkles, Abrahams' is tarnished both by this issue and by the question of whether he would have won it had Liddell been racing against him.

In sum, the angry attitude of Abrahams—he offers snarly *pathos*, like the Nemean Lion wrestling with Herakles—is contrasted with the calm *ethos* of Liddell. While the astute viewer may recognize that the world has, from the outset, treated Abrahams differently from how it has handled Liddell—even prior to Abra-

ham's gold medal run, the Prince of Wales, Abrahams' own coun-
tryman, is shown supporting his American Christian competitors,
as if to suggest that Abrahams' Jewishness makes him more of an
athletic-performance enemy, even though he is English, than the
Americans who are Christian. There seems to be a valid historical
basis for this. In any case, most viewers of the film will simply see
the two as dark and bright figures whose respective dark or bright
hue is tied to their respective faiths (and not just to their different
depths of embracing faith).

Several years later, the 1989 film, *Triumph of the Spirit*, carries the issue of Jews and Judaism in a sports context in a different
direction altogether. It tells the story of a Greek Jewish stevedore
from Thessaloniki, Salamo Arouch, whose avocation and passion
is boxing. Sent with his fiancée and family to Auschwitz, Arouch
is placed in the unhappy position of boxing against fellow prisoners as a kind of entertainment for the Nazi overseers of the camp,
knowing that if he wins, his opponents will be sent to the gas cham-
bers while he will be given extra food rations for his family and
himself—a key to survival in the camp—and that if he loses, the
consequences will be dire and death-dealing for them all.[30]

The film is based on a true story, although it takes certain liberties (as in both the name of his fiancée and the timing of their
meeting, which was after, not before the war). The point for our
purposes is that it reveals how sports and religion are intertwined
in two simultaneous and ultimately very different ways. Most obvious is the strangeness of having a character engaged in a sport
specifically because of his religion. Arouch is where he is because
he is a Jew and the Nazis are involved in an attempt to diminish
and ultimately destroy the Jews and Judaism itself. His story becomes more than an anonymous one because he also happens to be
a talented boxer.

The second is that as a protagonist, Arouch symbolizes an issue that has existed since the beginning of human history, one that
bears particular resonance in context of the Holocaust. The issue

is free will—the matter of whether, in a world created by a God deemed not only all-powerful but all-knowing, we humans actually ever exercise true choice: if the all-knowing God by definition *knows* what choices I will make—even, arguably, years before I am confronted with them and obviously before I myself know—then am I making them freely? Or is it the case (as for example St. Augustine argued in the early fifth century) that although God knows what I will do—as God *knew* that Adam and Eve would abrogate the divine commandment not to eat from the tree of knowledge before *they* did—God does not influence much less dictate my choice (or the choice made by Adam and Eve).

One of the characteristic features of the Nazi regime was that it consistently offered its victims apparent choices, but they were invariably false ones, governed by illusion and deception. Even the "real" ones—do I go to the gas chamber today, or do I live today, but in any case end up in the gas chamber a week or a month from now?—were marked by an essential falseness.[31] In the case of Arouch, his choices are always choiceless choices. The culminating moment that encapsulates this truth is presented when Arouch is asked to fight Jacko, his best friend, and knows that, if he wins, his friend will be sent to the gas chamber, and if he loses, he and/or members of his family will perish—and when he hesitates, Jacko is simply executed on the spot.

While the first of these modes of interweaving sports and religion has a specific direction, connected to the specific religion of the protagonist and those around him, the second is broad, encompassing all religions and the questions that they address with regard to what we humans are and what our place is in the world—whether the world is construed as shaped by a single, all-powerful God or by a multiplicity of gods in contention with each other and themselves subject to fate. In what is perhaps a third aspect of the relationship between sports and religion, there is an echo of the world of the Roman gladiators, not only, of course in the obvious sense of two protagonists who fight until the defeated one is consigned to

324 God and the Goalposts

death, but in the sense that the audience being entertained is made up of the consigners. And thus, the Nazis encircling the boxing ring, like the spectators encircling the gladiatorial arena, are god-like in dictating who shall live and who shall die, a perverse echo of the audience decisions or imperial decrees of the Roman world of two millennia ago, where a collective or individual vote could allow a defeated protagonist to live to fight another day.

There is an inherent paradox in the very title of the film. It clearly echoes the infamous 1935 film created in the service of Hitler by Leni Riefenstahl, *Triumph of the Will*. Hitler's political triumphs at that time—and that was the year when the Nuremberg Laws began to formalize the disenfranchisement of Jews from German society, with their deluded articulation of "Aryan" superiority over against "non-Aryan" groups such as Jews, Gypsies (Roma), and Slavs—would ultimately arrive at a disastrous defeat on every level a decade later.

Arouch was among those who survived—and therefore may be said to have ultimately triumphed. The mood of the film, however, if on the one hand it offers that victory, on the other hand raises untenable moral quandaries, such as how one must sometimes endure moral defeat in order to survive, in the "choiceless choice" condition imposed upon the Nazis' victims that is the film's focus.

Moreover, as we, the audience, inevitably root for Arouch, we are drawn into the same horrific circle, for it means that we are rooting for someone else to lose and thus to perish, and aligning ourselves with the Nazis who cheer and boo and are entertained by the struggles in that boxing ring. Of course, the ethical emptiness with which we are left may be seen as an eloquent statement of what the Nazis created—as well as what *humans* can create and have created throughout history. Thus, the larger question of what we are as a species, and how that relates to what God is or is not, stands out before us as a thinking audience in this painful film.

There is any number of more recent films that expand the horizon of our awareness of the interplay among religion, sports, politics, and war (and sometimes gender and race). Among the more interesting and effective ones is the 2011 documentary, *Fordson: Faith, Fasting, Football*. It covers in some detail the story that leads up to the situation referenced above, (235) regarding how a high school football team that is the centerpiece of a pious American Muslim community that is devoted to the game deals with the issue of fasting during the month of Ramadan when that month falls during the late summer and pre-season football practice is at its peak of intensity.

In fact, the film is about larger issues, such as the prejudice and stereotyping that directs itself toward Muslims and to Arabs in the America of particularly the post-9/11 era. Well-shot, well-scripted, well-paced, the film wraps the issue of those prejudices and stereotypes around the interwoven American, Arab, and Muslim identities of the students, the players, the coaches, the teachers, the parents, the alumni, the principal—everyone associated with Fordson's team: the "Tractors"—named (consider the irony of this!) for the tractor built by Henry Ford, as the school is named (quite literally) for Henry Ford's son. It was established by Ford in Dearborn, Michigan, in 1922.

What emerges as a centerpiece of the narrative is the story is the intense competition with cross-town rival Dearborn High School, (also with many but many fewer Muslim students)—which in turn also resonates from the ongoing American story of immigrants who have embraced this country and its most basic values, including those associated with sports and in particular sports as they are shaped at the high school level when American boys and girls are in the process of becoming men and women. The families of these athletes come from a culture that, as in most of the world outside the United States, worships soccer and not American-style football, but as in so many other instances that this narrative has referenced for diverse immigrant groups generations earlier, the Dearborn Arab Muslim community, in embracing America, has embraced the most iconic of American high school sports.

So the film—which arrives at one of its several culminating moments with the issue of Ramadan and its fasts, in the context of team practice and the upcoming contest with Dearborn High School—offers an interplay between religion and sports at its most obvious and most profound, by way of an art form that transcends the possibilities from antiquity to modernity, and continues, from angles both parallel and oblique, the story of the religion-sports relationship that played out in the earlier films discussed in the previous paragraphs.

Virtually as I write these last paragraphs yet another twist to the various turns our narrative has taken is being offered on the operatic stage in Belgium, where a production of Camille Saint-Saens' work, Samson and Delilah is being staged in Antwerp. The nineteenth-century French composer turned the story of the Israelite strong man—the hero-athlete whom we encountered in the first chapter of this discussion—and the Philistine woman who ultimately betrays him—into a pageant of sight and sound. The cur-rent production, co-directed by an Israeli and a Palestinian, offers a modern political context in which Samson and the Israelites are Palestinian and Delilah and the Philistines are Israelis. So politics interweaves the art forms that focus on an ancient sports figure whose career is described in the foundation text of two Abrahamic religious traditions, Judaism and Christianity.[32]

One might say that we have come quite some distance from where this narrative began with respect to identifying the relationship between sports and religion—and politics, war, and art. But that is how perhaps it should be, since that relationship is almost inevitably broad in terms of the many perspectives from which it has been viewed throughout human history. Nor is such breadth diminishing as we move through our own time. On the contrary, consider the following: if one seeks out the Washington Speakers' Bureau on its Internet site, it's not surprising that one can go to "religion" among the many topics offered to potential customers.

One might expect to see there a list of individuals who are noted as theologians and philosophers, thinkers and writers on the matter of religion. Some individuals of that sort *will* be found there—but so will speakers such as Joe Gibbs, NFL Hall of Fame coach and NAS-CAR owner. That Joe Gibbs would be presumed or could presume to have an expertise in the field of religion might strike one as odd, had we not just made our way through this long narrative.

For clearly it is understood that Gibbs can and will (for a substantial fee) deliver an inspiring, *God-based* talk that is also unequivocally *sports-based*. Not a theologian or philosopher, not a man of the cloth or a religious scholar, but a man with a career in sports is deemed preeminently qualified to do this. And perhaps that is as it should be, not only if God is up there in the heavenly bleachers watching our performances on the many ball courts and playing fields of our lives, but also if that God occasionally intervenes to help us achieve success—or failure. Do I indeed owe my crucial double—or home run—to God? Is it Jesus whom I need to thank for scoring that acrobatic winning touchdown or the buzzer-beating three-point shot from 40 feet away?

Does God visit the locker room before the game and choose sides? Is God influenced in that choice by the greater or lesser fervency of prayers offered up by the coaches and team on this side versus that side of the playing field? Does God assure that nobody gets hurt in the game—and what is God's role when somebody *is* hurt, or even *killed*? Is God as involved with sports as with war and tsunamis? Does God only listen to prayers invoking assistance and care if they are uttered by a Christian? A Catholic? A Presbyterian? A Jew? A Muslim? A Hindu? A well-meaning atheist who hopes and virtually prays, but not actually to God, since she or he doesn't believe that God exists?

So, too, we think full circle back to the Greek warriors, and Achilles in particular, who was promised undying glory—*kleos aphthiton*—if he came to the war in Troy, where he would excel, and sacrificed a long life to one could short in its prime. We ask: don't successful athletes achieve that sort of *kleos*? Won't Babe Ruth and

Jim Brown and Michael Jordan and Hank Greenberg and Akeem Olajuwon and Rod Laver and Michael Phelps live on as long there are sports fans who read and talk about and revel in the endless array of statistical accomplishments associated with these, our heroes? Would Usain Bolt have won his record-breaking third Olympic gold medal in a row, in 2016 Rio de Janeiro, had he not crossed himself—twice—before he ran in the final (and again, once, afterwards)? His *kleos* will survive, certainly, even if we will have forgotten that the time of the 2016 victory was slower than those in 2012 and 2008. Will we remember the comment from Briana Rollins before the cameras—after she led Nia Ali and Kristi Castlin to an unprecedented American sweep of the women's 100 m hurdles in Rio—that "God did it"?

As the West moved   forward with increasing speed into modernity in the late nineteenth century, the philosopher Friedrich Nietzsche (1844-1900), a generation after Alexis de Tocqueville, reveled in what he saw as a gradual abandonment of religion. He saw Judaism and Christianity as having once conspired to destroy the greatness of the Roman Empire by *transvaluing* its values: by elevating the humble and the meek and mild over the virile, heroic and manly and by substituting a morality governed by conscience and therefore guilt rather than by natural law, in which the physically strong automatically enslave or destroy the physically weak. Where the barbarians remained tied to natural law, Rome, Nietzsche insisted, became mired in the hesitations provoked by moral guilt and was thus eventually overcome by its enemies. He hoped that, in the "new" era of which he was part, this was changing and Europe and particularly Germany could and would rise to new, natural heights.[33]

Nietzsche, it turns out, was both right and wrong. Two generations after his writing, Germany would fulfill his dream—but in a terrifying manner that he might well have rejected, under the Nazis—and, as someone who was physically weak and losing his mind, in his last years, he might well have been among those the

Nazis destroyed as unfit for their new society. Religion and its concerns, in any case, never fully seeped out of the West—and in recent decades seem to have re-asserted themselves in various ways, in politics, art and sports, among other disciplines.

The importance of humility and meekness and the victory of the physically weak over the physically strong through conscience and guilt is not, and never has been, a desideratum in sports even when and as religion is embedded within it. However much a thinker like Nietzsche would see religion and sports as contradictions of each other, they have been continuously intertwined in diverse ways across history.

The Houston Astros have forced this narrative to return to its beginning: the references in the preface of the first edition of this volume, which describe athletes who gesture or speak of God as if the Deity is personally focused on their athletic performances. The recent scandal that has emerged, regarding how the Astros stole signs from opposing teams throughout their championship 2017 season, leading up to and including the World Series games—certainly might cause us to ask how many of those players, coaches, and managers would have fallen into the category introduced in the preface? If so, do they somehow imagine that the God that they presume follows the action on the field and favors them when they are favored with victorious moments, is not sorely offended by their cheating? Do they suppose that God will forgive their cheating, no matter how angry the rest of the baseball world is at them?[34] Does God turn Its metaphorical back from time to time—perhaps distracted by non-sporting events like earthquakes?

One might also note that the uproar over the Astros' sign-stealing may be seen to reflect the role of baseball, as opposed to other sports, in the American imagination. As the "National Pastime" it has perhaps acquired the status of a kind of religion, with its obsession with sacrosanct statistics and analytics. So to abrogate a particular code of honesty in this particular sport induces that kind of reaction that one might expect toward a thief who steals the collection plate from his church during Sunday services.[35] This is the point made by broadcast legend, Bob Costas in the call-in program, the "Michael Kay Show," on February 20, 2020. While this may be an oversimplified explanation of the unprecedented response by various players—far more intense than, for instance, that toward steroid-using players several years ago—it is significant that the May/Costas analysis offers that sports-and-religion observation.

As we move into the third decade of the twenty-first century, it turns out that we have simply returned to—or perhaps continued without interruption—the sort of conviction that has defined the human engagement with divinity across time and space, and holds that the divine continues to be interested in and involved in our affairs; that it can help us or harm us, further us or hinder us, bless us or curse us, create us or destroy us. That God is believed in differently by diverse groups—and not at all by some groups—and is fervently sought out by athletes and their coaches, by soldiers and their officers, by politicians and their constituents, by artists and the viewers of their artworks is evidenced by how tightly religion interweaves sports, politics, war, and art in various modes.

By the third month of 2020 the world began to spin in new directions, thanks to a succession of unprecedented events, beginning with the Covid-19 pandemic and, in the United States in particular, continuing with economic complications not seen since the Great Depression and violence in the streets echoing that of the late 1960s. The world of sports has clearly been affected, from the cancellation to the delay of major and minor events to play taking place without live fans. The particulars, from one sport to another and from one level to another—high school versus college vs professional—has varied but in all cases have been profoundly altered. Whether this is temporary and if not, what permanent shape our diverse games may take, remains to be seen. It is clear, however, that aspects of race, gender, politics, and perhaps also religion have been and are likely to continue to be part of the continuously evolving process.

Some of us engage those around and against us with God as our presumed partner, whether on the playing field or the battlefield, or whether we limit ourselves to private belief or articulate that belief in public expression. Some of us engage those around and with us, whether in the locker room or the training camp, by applying pressure to feel God's presence as a partner in a defined and particular manner. Some of us, whether out of the courage of our convictions or the cowardice of our doubts, articulate the specific parameters in which to assert God's presence and interest—in the here and now *and* the hereafter. Thus God, or the sense of God's presence, is all around us, in the house of worship and the home, in the boardroom and the dining room—off the playing field and on: from pitcher's mound to batter's box, baseline to baseline, backboard to backboard, tensed bow to target, starting line to finish line, goalpost to goalpost.

Notes

1. There is a number of renditions of this scene, either done in black-figure or red-figure styles and attributed to various artists. The particular copy that I have in mind is found in the Museo Romano, in Bresica, Italy.

2. This work, from Eretria, is found in the National Museum in Athens.

3 This work, from Vulci, is found in the *Staatliche Antikensammlungen* (State Antiquities Collections) in the Munich Museum. By "name-vase" I mean that, in the absence of the actual name of the potter/painter, we refer to him/her by the vase for which s/he is best-known. Hence, the Penthesilea painter is so-called because s/he is anonymous but renowned for the vase with Penthesilea as its main subject.

4. Not only does the cycle begin with the wedding between a mortal and an immortal and continue to and through the possession of both those attributes by the offspring of that marriage, but at that wedding that celebrates love (as all weddings theoretically do) the goddess Eris (Strife) is not invited (of course not!) but shows up and tosses the fruit onto the table with its famous accompanying inscription "to the fairest." Zeus, preferring not to choose among Aphrodite, Hera, and Athena, sends the three goddesses down to Mount Ida, outside Troy, where the Trojan prince Alexandros/Paris, serving as the shepherd of the royal flocks,

is asked to judge. He gives the prize to Aphrodite—who has promised him the most beautiful woman alive—thereby earning Aphrodite's love and support, and the enmity of the other two goddesses. The problem, of course, is that the most beautiful woman, Helen, is married—to Menelaus of Sparta—and the stealing of her from her husband, to be brief, leads to the ten-year-long war effort that is required to get her back. Throughout the descriptions in Greek literature of aspects of the Trojan War and its aftermath there are myriad instances of interface between *eros* and *eris* on both the divine and the human planes. For a fuller discussion of this subject both in Greek literature and in Western literature at large, see Soltes: *Eros and Eris: Love and Strife in Western Literature.*

5. The tension between "will"—as in "is prophesied to"—and "can" refers to another tension and paradox important to Greek thought: that between free will and fate. Troy is fated to fall if Achilles participates on the Achaean side, and he is fated to die if he does so—and the city is only distinctly fated to fall in the fate-articulated sequence of events after Achilles, having decided to participate, is eventually killed—but he is theoretically free to choose not to participate, in which case either none of the other fated outcomes will obtain, or they will be arrived at any way, but by some other route paved by free human action. But Achilles, free to choose, chooses to participate—even as the story line makes clear at several junctures that he would have preferred to stay away from Troy and live a long albeit obscure life. And so on...

6. This particular work is found in the British Museum.

7. One might recognize in this an analogy to the rabbinic contempt for physical athleticism in favor of spiritual and intellectual prowess, as briefly discussed above in chapter 9, 162-3.

8. This particular thirteenth-century Byzantine icon resides in the National Gallery of Art, Washington, DC.

9. A reminder that the word "halo" derives from the Greek word, *"halios,"* meaning "sun."

10. A reminder that seven is—in all three Abrahamic traditions and before them, in the Egyptian, Mesopotamian, Persian, Greek, and Roman traditions—the number of perfection and completion, for reasons that carry beyond this discussion. But see above, chapter 1, 28 and fn 7.

11. Among the most obvious among these exceptions—aside from illuminated manuscripts, briefly discussed just below—are late twelfth- and early thirteenth-century Seljuk-period pottery from Persia, damascene metalwork from thirteenth-century Ayyubid Syria, and Safavid Persian carpets of the sixteenth century, as well as Qajar Persian carpets with hunting scenes of the nineteenth century.

12. This illumination is taken from *Le Roman de Troie*, by Benoit de Sainte-Maure, 14th c, MS Francais 782, folio 161, Bibliotheque Nationale, Paris. Just such a heavenward gesture anticipates what I have twice noted (in the preface and in chapter 13) with regard to contemporary athletes—such as Ryan Howard, arriving at second base after hitting a double in a key baseball game—raising their arms heavenward in a God-directed gesture.

13. Such a notion would connect these artist-thinkers back to the ancient Greeks, specifically Plato's teacher, Socrates, who was drawn to physically and intellectually beautiful youths such as Alkibiades explicitly for the spiritual and intellectual beauty that he believed their outer beauty betokened.

14. See above, 187ff.

15. That there is a particularly noticeable number of Jewish artists focused this way is symptomatic of the larger American Jewish obsession with "who is Jewish?" among successful figures but particularly among athletes, no doubt reflecting that long-held supposition that Jews have never been athletic.

16. See above, 215-16.

17. See *Marilyn Cohen: Where Did They Go When They Came to America?* (catalogue of the exhibition curated by Ori Z. Soltes at the B'nai B'rith Klutznick National Jewish Museum, Washington, DC, April-June, 1994), 10. See also Soltes, *Fixing the World*, 115-16.

18. The *tzitzit* is the stylized, four-tassled, fringed shawl worn under the shirt at all times—as opposed to the four-fringed *tallit* that is worn outside the clothes, and only during prayer—by traditional Jewish males in interpretation of the commandment set forth in Numbers 15:38.

19. See above, chapter 12, 216-17.

20. See Soltes, *Symphonies in Color: The Paintings of Malcah Zeldis* (catalogue of the exhibition at the B'nai B'rith Klutznick National Jewish Museum, Washington, DC, Spring 1992), 8.

21. Soltes, *Fixing the World*, 82.

22. For example, Kitaj portrays Lou Gehrig in his 1969-70 print series *In Our Time* and later, his black-and-white drawing, *Self-Portrait as a Cleveland Indian* (1994) and also oil paintings such as *Amerika (Baseball)* (1983-84) and *The Cleveland Indian* (1995-98). (Note his choice of a German spelling of "America" as "Amerika.")

23. For a fuller discussion of Strum's graphic novel, see Ori Z. Soltes, "Sports and the Graphic Novel form Diaspora to Diaspora: James Strum's *The Golem's Mighty Swing* and JT Waldman's *Megillat Esther* in the Tree of Contexts," in Leonard J Greenspoon, ed., *Jews in the Gym: Judaism, Sports, and Athletics*, (West Lafayette, IN: Purdue University Press, 2012).

24. It was written by Colin Welland, directed by Hugh Hudson, and produced by David Puttnam, Kae Eberts, Dodi Fayed, and James Crawford. It was nominated for seven Academy awards and won four, including Best Picture.

25. Ben Cross played Harold Abrahams and Ian Charleston played Eric Liddell.

26. The role was played by Ian Holm.

27. The historical Mussabini (1867-1927), who may be regarded as the first modern sports coach—and trained a number of gold and silver medal runners in the 1908, 1912, 1920, 1924, and 1928 Olympic Games—was born in London of mixed Arab, Turkish, Italian, and French descent.

28. Historically, Liddell knew about the schedule long before he left Britain, and trained for several months for the 400—in which he had, in fact, previously excelled—and no teammate had to give up his spot in the 400 meters in order for Liddell to have the chance to run.

29. Isaiah 40:31: "But they that wait upon the Lord shall renew their strength; they shall mount up with wings as eagles; they shall run, and not be weary..."

30. The film was written by Shimon Arama and directed by Robert M. Young. It starred Willem Dafoe as Arouch and was largely filmed at Auschwitz—the first feature film to be shot on location at that site.

31. A moving and concise presentation of this condition—including the "choice" of whether still to believe in God—is found in the first five chapters of Elie Wiesel's renowned memoir, *Night*.

32. The directors are Omri Nitzan and Amir Nizar Zuabi. See the review by George Loomis on Wednesday, May 6, 2009 and the discussion by Michael Kimmelmann, in Thursday, May 7, 2009, issues of *The New York Times*, section C.

33. See Friedrich Nietzsche, *The Genealogy of Morals*, 1887. There are several good translations into English, among them that by Walter Kauffmann and a more recent one by Douglas Smith.

34. Among the most recent of the myriad articles on this subject is that on the front page of the *SportsWednesday* section of the February 19, 2020 issue of *The New York Times*, B9, in which Yankee slugger Aaron Judge is interviewed at length.

35. Not all sign-theft is considered dishonest: for a player who has gotten to second base and tries from his vantage point to steal the signs between catcher and pitcher and transmit them to the batter on his team is considered to be playing "part of the game."

Selected Bibliography

In addition to the books and journal articles sampled below there are several dozen relevant newspaper articles, particularly with respect to the last four chapters of this volume; these are indicated in the chapter endnotes.

Ballard, Chris, "Dewayne Dedmon's Leap of Faith," *Sports Illustrated Magazine*, Nov 14, 2011, 98-110

Balmer, Randall, *God in the White House: A History: How Faith Shaped the Presidency from John F. Kennedy to George W. Bush* (NYC: Harper Collins, 2008)

Brenner, J.N., "The Golden Bough: Orphic, Eleusinian, and Hellenistic-Jewish Sources of Virgil's Underworld in *Aeneid* VI," *Kernos* 22, (2009), 183-208

Cleaves, Frances Woodman, transl & ed., *Secret History of the Mongols* (Cambridge MA: Harvard University Press, 1982)

Darrach, Brad: "A Different Kind of Superstar" (*Life Magazine*, December, 1995)

Fleischer, Nat, *Leonard the Magnificent: Life Story of the Man Who Made Himself King of the Lightweights* (Norwalk, Conn.: the O'Brien Suburban Press, 1945)

Friedlaender, Ludwig, *Roman Life and Manners*, Vol 2 (New York: Arno Press, 1979)

Gibbs, Nancy & Michael Duffy, *The Preacher and the Presidents: Billy Graham in the White House*, (NYC: Center Street, 2007)

Gleason, William, *The Spiritual Foundations of Aikido* (Rochester, VT: Destiny Books, 1995)

Grant, Michael, *Gladiators* (London: Weidenfeld & Nicholson, 1976)

Hindley, Geoffrey, *The Crusades: Islam and Christianity in the Struggle for World Supremacy*. (Carrol & Graf: 2004)

Homer, *Iliad*, esp. books xvi and xxiii, Richmond Lattimore, transl. (London: University of Chicago Press, 1951)

Hopkins, Keith, *Death and Renewal: Studies in Roman History*, Vol 2 (Cambridge: Cambridge University Press, 1983)

Jackson, Phil, *Sacred Hoops* (Logan IA: Perfection Learning Corp, 2010 [reprint])

Leavy, Jane, *Sandy Koufax: A Lefty's Legacy* (New York: Harper-Collins, 2002)

Levine, Peter, *From Ellis Island to Ebbets Field* (Oxford: Oxford University Press, 1992)

Popul Vuh, Dennis Tedlock, Transl. (New York: Simon and Schuster, 1985)

Rapinoe, Megan, *One Life*. (London: Penguin Press, 2020)

Reid, Howard & Michael Croucher, *The Way of the Warrior: the Paradox of the Martial Arts* (Woodstock, NY: The Overlook Press, 1966)

Rock, Tom, "More Than a Game: Lacrosse and the Onondaga Nation," *Lacrosse* Magazine, Nov/Dec 2002

Rosen, Charley, *The House of Moses All-Stars* (San Diego: Harcourt Brace & Co., 1996)

Ross, James, transl., *Gulistan* (*The Rose Garden*) (Ames, Iowa: Omphaloskepsis, 2000)

Ryan, Joan, *Little Girls in Pretty Boxes: The Making and Breaking of Elite Gymnasts and Figure Skaters* (New York: Grand Central Publishing, 1996)

Scarborough, Vernon L. & David R. Wilcox, eds, *The MesoAmerican Ballgame* (Tucson: University of Arizona Press, 1993)

Schiele, Linda & David Freidel, *A Forest of Kings: The Untold Story of the Maya* (New York: William Morrow & Co, 1990)

Sharnoff, Lora, *Grand Sumo* (Weatherhill Press, 1993)

Shenk, David, *The Immortal Game: A History of Chess* (New York: Doubleday, 2006)

Slater, Robert, *Great Jews in Sports* (Middle Village, NY: Jonathan David, 2010)

Soltes, Ori Z., "Centerfield of Dreams and Questions: Baseball and Judaism," in Raphael and Abrams, eds., *What is Jewish About "America's Favorite Pastime"*? (Williamsburg, VA: The College of William and Mary Press, 2006)

_____, *Fixing the World: Jewish American Painters in the Twentieth Century* (University Press of New England, 2002)

_____, "From Benny Leonard to Abi Olajuwon: Jews, Muslims, Evangelicals, and the Evolving Religious Challenges of Being an American Athlete," in Leonard J Greenspoon ed., *Jews in the Gym* (West Lafayette, IN: Purdue University Press, 2012)

_____, *Jews on Trial: From the Time of Jesus to Our Own Time*, Chapter Three, section IV (Savage, MD: Eshel Books, 2013)

_____, *Our Sacred Signs: How Jewish Christian and Muslim Art Draw from the Same Source* (Westfield Press, 2007).

_____, "Sports and the Graphic Novel from Diaspora to Diaspora: James Strum's *The Golem's Mighty Swing* and JT Waldman's *Megillat Esther* in the Tree of Contexts," in Leonard J Greenspoon ed., *Jews in the Gym* (West Lafayette, IN: Purdue University Press, 2012)

Spielman, Loren L., "Playing Roman in Jerusalem: Jewish Attitudes Toward Sport and Spectacle During the Second Temple Period," in Leonard J Greenspoon ed., *Jews in the Gym* (West Lafayette, IN: Purdue University Press, 2012).

Telander, Rick, *Heaven is a Playground*, Fourth Edition. (New York: Sports Publishing, 2013)

Uzo, Carmelo, "The History of Basque Pelota in the Americas," *The Journal of the Society of Basque Studies in America*, Vol XV, 1995, 1-16

Virgil, *Aeneid*, Book V, Rolfe Humphries, transl. (NYC: Charles Scribner's Sons, 1951)

Voss, Stephen G., "Kendo and Fencing: A Comparative Study in Their Practice and Philosophy," in Minoru Kiyota, *Japanese Martial arts and American Sports: The History and Cultural Background on Teaching Methods* (Tokyo: Nihon University Press, 1998)

Weinberger, Ilan, *Japanese Budo: An East Asian Religious Paradigm for Self-Cultivation, Morality and Conflict Resolution* (Unpublished 2008 MA Thesis available in Lauinger Library, Georgetown University)

Zirin, Dave, A *People's History of Sports in the United States* (New York: The New Press, 2009)

Index

Egyptian(s), 2, 7-8, 14, 26-27, 32-33nn, 37, 73, 92, 149-150, 153n, 154n, 180, 332n
Eidolon, 58, 67n
Eigil, 105
Eishoji, 123
Elder Ephraim, 295n
Ellis Island, 213-14, 236, 239n
Ellison, Brady, 276
El Moutawakal, Nawal,152, 253
Emancipation, Jewish, 173, 176, 179, 190n-91n, 309
Emin, Kara, 139
Enkidu, 16-17, 43
Enoch, Book of, 5
Entellus, 59
Ephesians, 266
Erdogan, Recep, 230-31, 287
Eretz Yisrael, 178
eris, 35-36, 303, 331n
eros, 54, 303, 332n
Esau, 23-24, 31n
Eshmont, Len, 228
Essenes, 160
Esther, 161, 169n, 334n
    book of, 31, 160, 161
ethos, 300-01, 321
Etruscans, 81
Eumelos, 46, 47
Eupeithes, 52
Euphrates (River), 120, 308
Euripides/Euripidean, 27n, 75-76, 79n, 84
Euryalus, 59
Evenus, 75
Exodus, 5, 26, 29, 159, 163, 243n
Ezekiel, 162, 308

F

Famous Jewish Trials. See Soltes, Ori Z.
Fariman, Lida, 144
Farsi, 149, 153n
fate, 3, 14, 18-19, 37, 39-44, 49n, 53-54, 56-57, 75, 78n, 303, 323, 332n
Ferdinand of Aragon, 116
FIFA,258-259

Figg, James, 174
FINA, 254, 292n
Firdawsi, 131, 137
firearms, 116, 131
Firmicus Maternus, 92
First Punic War, 82
First Zionist Congress, 177
Fisher, Brenda, 274
Fixing the World. See Soltes, Ori Z.,
Flanagan, Collette, 228
Flatow, Alfred, 182, 191n
Flatow, Gustav Felix, 182, 189n
Flood, Gavin, 133n
football, ix, x, 38, 213, 220, 226-27, 235-36, 240, 248, 261-62, 266-68, 271, 273, 75, 28-, 284-85, 293n, 295n, 325
    high school, 236, 255, 325
footrace(s), 59-60, 67, 71, 81, 303-04
Ford, Dr. Adam, 211
Ford, Henry, 216, 238, 325
Fordson High School, 235
Foreman, Yuri, 286, 297n
fortitudo, 85
Forum Boarium, 82
Franklin, Sidney, 184
Freidel, David, 197, 199, 207n
Friedlaender, Ludwig, 99n
Frumkin, Sidney. *See* Franklin, Sidney
Füehrer. *See* Hitler, Adolf
funeral games, 46, 56, 59-60, 67, 73, 81-82, 117n, 142, 204

G

gal ahs,(or *ga-lahs*), 203
galea, 91
Galli, 91
Gauthama Buddha, 120
Gaza, 28, 32n, 151, 192n
gendai budo, 124
Genesis, 23, 25, 32n, 120, 188, 308
Gershonides, 163
Geta, 93
Ghanim, Mazin, 249
Ghazi, Rashid, 235
Ghetto, 156, 168n, 232

334n
Longman, Jere, 152n, 153n, 235, 297n
   Lords of Death, 195-96, 200
Lorenzo II, 101
Louis IX, 106
Louis XIV, 171
Louis, Joe, 232
Louisville University, 270
Lucanians, 81
Luckman, Sid, 220
ludi (games), 84
Ludovico Ariosto, 108
Lycaon, 56
lyric poetry, 65, 68, 73, 78n

M

Maccabees, 4-5, 134n, 157, 158, 179, 296n
Maccabi club, 179
Maccabi Club (Berlin), The, 179
Maccabi World Union, 179, 181
Maccabiah Games, 179-181, 251
Machiavelli, Niccolo, 101-103, 110, 155
Madina, 128, 135-136n
Madonna of Provenanzo, 114
Madrid, 184
Mahabharata, 3
Maimonides, 163, 169n
Maitha Muhammad Rasheed Al-
   Maktoum, 146
Makka, 128, 135-136n
Manzikert, Battle of, 106
marathon, 77, 79n, 163
Marciano, Rocky, 231
Mark, Gospel according to, 4
Marpessa, 75
Marr, Wilhelm, 177
martial art, 116, 117n, 119-125, 133n,
   134n
martyrdom, 89
massacre, 185
Matamoro, 108
mawashi, 124-125
Maximinus Thrax, 88
Mayan Bible, 192
Mazzini, Giuseppe, 177
McAdoo, James Michael, 288

McGill University, 212
McGovern, George, 270-71
McLarnin, Jimmy, 234
mechanistic view, 172
Medea, 70
Medici, 101, 117n
medicine men, 203-04
mellah, 156
Mendoza, Daniel, 173-175, 178, 190n,
   232
Menelaus, 36-37 39-41, 46
Mentor, 52
Mercury, 33n, 87, 198
Meriones, 46
Mescalero Apache, 236
Mesoamerica, 201-02, 206n
Mesopotamia(n), 1, 16-17, 92, 120, 332n
messiah, 33n, 318
messianic, 166, 216, 316, 319
Michelangelo, 311
Middleworld, 195-96, 199
Midian(ite), 26-27
Minnesota, 248, 286, 291n
Minos, 11-12
mitte, 86
Mogollon, Jornada, 236
Mohawk, 203, 208n
Mongols, 130, 132 136n
Montreal, 205, 211, 219
morality, 120, 134n, 328
Mormon, 273-74
Morocco, 145,149, 150, 152n, 153n
Moses, 3, 4, 26-27, 29-30, 32n, 159-160
Mosier, Chris, 263
Mount Gilboa, 30
Mount Ida, 36
Mount Kurama, 123
Muhammad, 4, 23, 27, 126, 128, 130,
   133n, 135n, 136n(n), 224, 284,
   297n
Muhammad al-Bukhari, 127
Muhammad Ali, 175, 224-26, 230-32
Muhammad, Elijah, 224
mullah, 144-145
munera, 83
Munich Olympics (1972) 184-186, 252,

286
munus, 82-83
Musa al-Nasir, 107
muscular Jews, 178
muscular Judaism, 233
muscular Zionism, 178
Muslim Ibn al-Hallaj, 128
Muslims, xii, 23, 106-107, 111, 113, 116,
     128-129, 148,150, 155, 167, 173,
     185, 223, 236, 240n, 248, 251,
     257, 271, 287-88, 289n, 296n, 325
Myers, Lon, 178
Mykenae, 37, 48n
Mykenaeans, 13, 32n

N

Nahmanides, 164-165, 169n
Naismith, Dr. James, 211-212
Nassar, Lawrence G., 260-61, 293n
Nation of Islam, 224
National Cathedral, 245-46
National Football League, 213
National Prayer Day, 246
National Socialist Realism, 312-13
Native American, xiv, 117, 191n, 203,
     205, 215, 218, 236, 238n
Nausikaa, 51
Nazarite, 29
NCAA, 261, 267, 294n-95n
Negro Leagues, 219, 318
Nemean games, 66, 81
Nemean lion, 62, 66, 93, 300-01, 321
Nereids, 59-60
Nero, 78n, 83, 89-90, 94
New covenant, 126
New Jersey, x, 211, 274, 291n
New Mexico, 267
New Testament, 126, 134n, 135n, 277
New World, 116, 193, 205
New York City, 21n, 184, 211
New York Giants, 270, 284
New York Knickerbockers, 211, 238n
New York Mets, xi, 268
New York Nine, 211
New York Post, 297n
New York State, 202, 205, 225, 291n
New York Times, The, xvn, 152n,

153n, 154n, 192n, 220, 235-36,
239n-40n, 242n-43n, 250, 256-57,
266, 270, 275, 280, 285, 292n-97n,
334n
New York Yankees. 216, 239n, 268,
297n
Nicaea, 103, 107
Nietzsche, Friedrich, 328-29, 334n
Nike, 229, 256-57
Nisus, 59
Nixon, Richard, 254
Nizami, 131
Nomi no Sukune, 123
Nordau, Max, 178
Norman, Peter, 241n
North Africa(n), 53, 89, 106, 145, 149
Northern Mexico, 194
Northwestern (University), 220-21
n'shama, 12
Nuremberg Laws, 180, 324

O

Obama, Barack, 246-48, 255, 262, 275,
290
Obama-McCain presidential campaign
275
odes, 70-72
Odysseus, 13, 36-37, 41, 48n, 51-55, 57,
65, 207n
Odyssey, 51, 55, 132, 143
Ohio, 289, 316
Oileos, 47
Ojibwe, 201
Okeanos, 43
Olajuwon, Hakeem, 146, 153n,220, 250-
51, 272, 328
Old Covenant, 126
Old Testament, 135n
Old World, 236, 314, 316
Olympia(n), 53, 65, 68-69, 74, 77, 78n,
87, 92, 182, 300
Olympic Games, xii, 66, 144, 150, 154n,
181-183, 191n, 252, 266, 275,
334n
Olympics, ancient, 13, 66 modern, xi,
xiv, 75, 77, 144-146, 149, 152n,
187, 189, 191n, 218, 225, 241n,